British and American Systems of Government

British and American Systems of Government

Malcolm Walles

University of Leeds

Philip Allan/Barnes & Noble Books

First published 1988 by

PHILIP ALLAN PUBLISHERS LIMITED
MARKET PLACE
DEDDINGTON
OXFORD OX5 4SE (UK)

First published in the USA 1988 by

BARNES & NOBLE BOOKS
81 ADAMS DRIVE
TOTOWA
NEW JERSEY 07512

© Malcolm Walles, 1988

British Library Cataloguing in Publication Data

Walles, Malcolm
    British and American systems of
    government.
    1. Great Britain. Politics 2. United
    States. Politics
    I. Title
    320.941

    ISBN 0-86003-404-6
    ISBN 0-86003-704-5 (pbk)

Library of Congress Cataloging in Publication Data

Walles, Malcolm.
    British and American systems of government/by Malcolm Walles.
    p.   cm.
    Includes index.
    1. Great Britain — Politics and government. 2. United States —
    Politics and government. I. Title.
    JN231.W325 1988
    320.941—dc19

    ISBN 0-389-20795-0

Typeset in 10/12 Palacio by MHL Typesetting Limited, Coventry.
Printed and bound in Great Britain by The Alden Press, Oxford.

To my parents and my wife

Contents

Introduction

The United Kingdom and the United States might at first seem incongruous subjects for a joint study. One is a collection of off-shore islands onto which are crammed some 56 million people, the other a continent-spanning country across which are scattered 230 million persons. Britain is now a country of the second rank in terms of international stature, America a superpower. And yet history provides compelling reasons for looking at these countries together.

The colonial link of the past is obvious, but what also makes them interesting is the continuity of government in the two countries. Ever since 1789, government in the United States has been carried out under the general authority of the constitution. The nature of government has obviously developed since the eighteenth century, but the institutions and procedures remain basically unaltered. In the middle of the nineteenth century the integrity of the nation as a united state was threatened by the Civil War but the victory of the North over the Southern seces-sionists preserved the union and the constitution. During the same period in Britain, government proceeded without any major political upheavals although considerable change took place. Representative government and political parties now dominate the scene although the development has been characterised by evolution not revolution. Furthermore, while both countries have been involved in a variety of wars and armed conflicts, neither has had its boundaries violated by invading armies (if we over-look the 1812 skirmish between the British and the Americans themselves). If we put that history alongside the history of some of the major European countries we note that the Declaration of Independence of 1776 antedated the unification of Italy or of Germany by about a century; that since the eighteenth century

1

France has had revolution, restoration, revolution, and five republics; and that the Iberian peninsula has moved from absolutist monarchy to fascist dictatorship to representative democracy. And of course we cannot overlook the fact that virtually the whole of mainland Europe has been ravaged by wars and by invading armies during the last two centuries.

Historic links, evolutionary rather than revolutionary development, a tradition of peaceful rather than violent transfer of power, a common language (*pace* Oscar Wilde and Bernard Shaw who both in their different ways suggested that the two countries were separated only by that common language), the 'special relationship' to which many Prime Ministers, if not Presidents, have alluded, all go to justify study of these two styles of representative democracy which have been widely emulated throughout the world.

Having suggested the common grounds which make a joint study feasible we should also note the divergent developments which make it desirable.

Casual observation of the British and American political scenes might suggest considerable similarity between the two systems. Certainly the forms of government would appear to lend weight to that view. Both have representative government and regular elections; both have bicameral legislatures, developed legal systems and institutions of local government. But reliance on these forms for an accurate picture of the nature of political and governmental activity in the two countries would seriously mislead, for form and substance differ greatly.

A few examples will serve to demonstrate points which will be explored at greater length in the text. Political parties in Britain are thus seen as (relatively) organised bodies seeking the power of government through an electoral appeal founded in a programmatic and philosophic commitment to which their members more or less subscribe. Parties in the United States on the other hand are more like the 'vast, gaudy, friendly umbrellas' of Clinton Rossiter's description, giving shelter to political aspirants but demanding little in the way of fealty either to a programme or to a philosophy.

Again, elections in Britain provide an opportunity for the electorate to pass judgement on the record of the parties as parties, either as government or as opposition. In the United States elections, although nominally party contests, are primarily opportunities to judge individual representatives according to how well they have served their constituents. The former are, in the main, national verdicts, the latter local (except when the President is chosen).

Perhaps the greatest opportunity for confusion between the two systems arises, however, from the term 'government'. We talk of the 'government of the United Kingdom', the 'government of the United States', but when we do so we talk of quite different things. In Britain, we generally mean by 'the government' the leadership of the majority party in the House of Commons, controlling the executive organs of government but also, as a consequence of its domination of the party machine, able to control the legislature and thereby to ensure the enactment of its policies. In the United States, 'the government' is seen to be embodied in the President who heads the executive branch, but as he is neither part of the legislature nor leader of a united majority party in the legislature he can never be sure that his programmes will be translated into law. He may be the government but he is often unable to govern.

As these few examples illustrate, the institutions of the two countries are of quite different hue, coloured by their own distinct histories and environments. A major purpose of this volume is to highlight these differences and thereby to demonstrate how custom, usage and expectation combine to modify the workings of institutions.

1

The societies

The United Kingdom is a relatively small country of some 94,000 square miles, and is smaller than ten of the American states. With its population of 56 million it is ten times more densely populated than the United States, although the density ranges from 929 per square mile for England, down to 170 for Scotland. The full title of the country is the United Kingdom of Great Britain (England, Wales, Scotland) and Northern Ireland, but I shall use the terms Britain, Great Britain, or the United Kingdom (UK) interchangeably to refer to the whole.

The British people are largely descendants of a variety of races which invaded the islands over a time span of several thousand years. Little is known of the very earliest cultures which inhabited Britain, and to which Stonehenge stands as a great monument, but after them the Celts, Romans, Angles, Saxons, Jutes, Vikings, and Normans, all came and left some mark upon the country, their blood and cultures intermingling in a complex manner to help fashion the building blocks of twentieth-century Britain. The last invasion of note was that of the Normans, led by William, Duke of Normandy, in 1066. The parcelling out of land by William to nobles in return for their support established a new social hierarchy, one which was sharply delineated from the rest of society because it spoke French and was to do so for the next three hundred years. Since that time nothing has had such a profound effect upon the nature of the whole society, although the arrivals of Huguenots and Jews fleeing religious persecution, and of many from the Caribbean and the Indian sub-continent, seeking better economic opportunities, have also made contributions to the nation's development.

The title 'United Kingdom' refers to the Union of England with Wales, in 1536, and with Scotland, in 1707, but it could also be taken to refer to the basic unity of the country as a whole — to the fact that in recent centuries the country has not been divided by the racial, linguistic, regional or religious conflicts that have so often characterised other societies.[1] There are those in Scotland and Wales who wish to see greater degrees of independence for their countries from Westminster, whether it be full independence or merely the establishment of regional governments for regional matters, but, as yet, the two parties which represent these strands of opinion, the Scottish Nationalist party and Plaid Cymru, have failed to secure sufficient electoral support to persuade the government to make significant moves in that direction. Referenda on the subject of devolution for Scotland and Wales were held on 1 March 1979. A narrow majority of those voting in Scotland supported the idea, but not 40 per cent of the eligible electorate as required in the enabling Act. The Welsh rejected it decisively.

Apart from the tragic situation in Northern Ireland, religion now plays little part in the politics of society, and religious differences are no longer the cause of conflict they once were in British history. England and Scotland have established churches (the Church of England and the Church of Scotland, which are both Protestant), but this does not imply any discrimination against other religious denominations. It is perhaps salutary to recall, however, that Catholics and dissenters were not accorded the same political rights as Anglicans until 1828 and 1829, that Jews were excluded from Parliament until 1858 and atheists until 1888.

Minority groups have generally been assimilated into British society and have been accorded full political and civil rights (if at times belatedly, as noted above) but the arrival of immigrants from the 'new Commonwealth' and Pakistan since the 1950s has subjected Britain's liberal image to some considerable strain. It is not that these immigrants have been denied political or civil rights but, rather, that their colour has evoked a number of racist reactions which reflect poorly on the tolerance level of many in the society. The degree of that hostility may be gauged by the need for a variety of Race Relations Acts. The Race Relations Act of 1976, which strengthened the earlier Acts of 1965 and 1968, made it an offence to discriminate on the grounds of colour, race or ethnic or national origin in the provision of goods, facilities and services, in employment, training and related matters, in education, housing and advertising. It also strengthened the criminal law on incitement to racial hatred. Nevertheless, despite the law, racial tensions in some areas still run very high, exacerbated by the fact that a disproportionate number from these ethnic minority groups[2] are unemployed and live in poorer housing in run-down urban areas. However, while these developments are clearly disturbing, they should not be allowed to disguise the general picture of a relatively harmonious society.

The size of the country undoubtedly helps to sustain the concept of a united nation, although we must not overlook the regional variations which exist. Accents, speech patterns, customs and diet do differ considerably from one part of the country to another, but good rail, road and airwave communications provide the infrastructure which, supported by national media, helps imbue a strong sense of national identity.

A number of good regional newspapers exist in Britain, but it is the dozen or so national papers, largely produced in or controlled from London, which dominate the news-stands and which are delivered regularly to something like 80 per cent of households. These range from the serious 'quality', broadsheet papers like *The Times*, *The Guardian*, the *Daily Telegraph* or the recently launched *Independent*, to the tabloids such as the *Daily Mirror*, *Daily Express*, *Daily Mail* or *Sun*, where coverage of the news will vary, some attempting a serious, broad-based approach while others seem more concerned to pander to the salacious. The Sunday papers offer an equally broad spectrum. More copies of newspapers are sold per capita in Britain than in any other country and on average nearly 75 per cent of the population over the age of 15 read a national morning newspaper and an even greater percentage one of the national Sunday papers.

Radio and television are, to all intents and purposes, national media, reaching into virtually every home in the land, reinforcing the nationalising tendencies of the printed medium. A fundamental distinction should be drawn between the British Broadcasting Corporation, which is a publicly-owned organisation deriving most of its income from radio and television licence fees payable by all households with receiving equipment, and the commercial radio and television companies which raise revenue by selling air-time to advertisers. (The rules of the Independent Broadcasting Authority, which oversees commercial radio and television, strictly limit the amount of advertising which may be broadcast — a maximum of nine minutes an hour for the local independent radio stations and a maximum of seven minutes an hour, and an average over the day of six minutes, for television.) While both the BBC and the commercial programmes introduce an element of local news into their presentations, and while the commercial TV companies are required by law to devote some of their time to matters of local interest, the bulk of what is broadcast has nationwide appeal. Thus most of the popular programmes, homemade or imported, will be transmitted across the United Kingdom on the same day at the same time.

The very fact that Britain has no land frontiers with other countries, apart from that which divides Northern Ireland from Eire, has also had an effect upon the development of a national character. Britain, in Shakespeare's words, set in a 'silver sea which serves it in the office of a wall, or as a moat', has rarely felt itself part of Europe. Although now members of the European Community, many British, to the dismay of many on the continent proper, still identify with that apocryphal *Times* headline: 'Fog in channel, Europe cut off'. A sense of belonging to the larger grouping has still to develop.

In discussing a relatively united country we cannot ignore the considerable division that is so bloodily evident in one part of the country, Northern Ireland. The present-day problems in Northern Ireland spring from the history of the often violent relationships between Great Britain and Ireland. Between King Henry II's invasion in 1169 until 1921, when most of the island became the Irish Free State (later the Irish Republic or Eire), periods of uneasy peace had been regularly broken by uprisings and riots. However, the most serious event, perhaps, for future developments was the settlement of the Northern province of Ulster by Scots and English after the collapse of the insurgency in 1607. These settlers, largely Protestant when the bulk of the Irish population was Roman Catholic, were the cause of the division of Ireland in 1921, because they wished to retain a union with the predominantly Protestant United Kingdom. Ulster,

Northern Ireland, was thus born of a religious division which has since spawned political, economic and social inequalities. The slightly less than two-thirds of the population of Northern Ireland which is Protestant has consistently excluded Roman Catholics from political office and discriminated against them in a variety of ways. The ultimate reaction to this discrimination was the outbreak of violence in the late 1960s which continues to this day. Limitations of space preclude any lengthy description of the conflict or any predictions. Two observations might, nevertheless, be in order. First, there is the general point to be made that if a minority is repressed for too long the ultimate response to the denial of adequate constitutional rights may well be unconstitutional violence. Secondly, in the strictly Irish context, one of the major difficulties in the way of a solution is the fact that 'both sides of the community have tended to see themselves as besieged minorities': the Catholics who are in a minority in Ulster are fighting for a union with Eire in which the Northern Ireland Protestants themselves would be an even smaller minority.[3]

Northern Ireland aside, modern British society has been fortunate in the degree to which it has been free of religious, linguistic, or even ethnic stress. But having said this, we must still recognise the one great divisive feature that is evident in British life — the class system.

It might at first appear to be a truism to talk of the British system as being divided by class. After all, the hereditary monarchy and a House of Lords still largely made up of peers with hereditary titles, are there for all to see, perfect examples of a great divide. And yet these hereditary aristocrats — the 'real' peers as someone once described them when comparing them with the life peers — whose titles were awarded to their forebears for great statesmanship, or for heroic deeds for the monarch in battle (or in bed), or for their judicious contributions to political party funds, form only a small part of the class structure. For most people the peerage is an anachronistic symbol of a past age, of more concern to tourists or the gossip columnists of the less salubrious newspapers than to the man in the street. The aristocracy is, as it were, the icing on top of a layer cake, rich and eye-catching but not a particularly useful guide to what lies beneath.

Economic status is likely to be an important factor contributing to the class differences that exist, but it is only one of various elements which perpetuate those divisions. More than in many other developed countries, education would appear to have played a major role in helping to maintain the divides across which people do not easily move.

Although since the 1960s there have been moves, inspired by the Labour party, to eliminate the most socially-divisive aspect of the state education system, the 11-plus examination, significant vestiges still linger on and are likely to persist. The 11-plus examination, taken, as its name implies, at about the age of 11 by all children in state schools was, in crude terms, a separation of the sheep from the goats — of those children deemed not to have the intellectual capacity for, possibly, a university education, from those considered capable of benefiting from academic training. The former were sent to secondary modern schools, which concentrated on things practical (cynics would say 'on child-minding'), until they were released into the world, largely unqualified, at the age of 15. The minimum school leaving age is now 16. The latter went to grammar schools for a more rigorous academic training geared to the acquisition of qualifications for entrance to the universities and to the professions or other white-collar occupations. Success or failure in that series of tests at the age of 11 was likely to have the most serious effect upon the future lifestyle of schoolchildren. Little opportunity existed for those whose intellectual capabilities developed after the age of 11 to transfer from the secondary modern to the grammar schools. The divide was almost complete and tended largely to reflect the working-class/middle-class divide in society as a whole, with working-class children to be found predominantly in the secondary schools and middle-class children in the grammar schools. Of course, every year some working-class children would manage to 'cross over' but their numbers were limited.

The Labour government reforms were aimed at breaking down this barrier to mobility by abolishing the secondary modern/grammar school distinction and by introducing a comprehensive system of education — something akin to an American High School system — which would take account of differing needs and abilities over a period of time. The plans were resisted hard and long by supporters of the grammar schools who, although such schools were bastions of the middle classes, included many from the working class, and by the 1980s nearly 20 per cent of state schoolchildren were still in selective systems. It is too early to say exactly how the plans of the Conservative government re-elected in 1987 will turn out, but it does appear that there may be some move back towards selection if some schools take advantage of the option that is apparently to be offered of leaving the local education authority and electing to be funded directly from the Department of Education and Science.

In addition to the state system of education there is a thriving and growing system of private schools which are themselves a symbol of the class divide in Britain. There are about 2,500 registered independent schools catering for pupils of all ages and attended by something like 6 per cent of the school-age population. Among that number are to be found about 500 institutions perversely known as 'public schools'.[4] Fees, substantial at times, are paid and consequently it is generally the children of middle- and upper-class backgrounds who provide the bulk of the pupils, although the Thatcher government did introduce a scheme whereby assistance is given with fees to enable some working-class children to secure the benefits of a public school education. The advantages accruing to this kind of education would appear to be proved by the fact that this small proportion of school-children accounts for about 25 per cent of all university entrants while students from working-class backgrounds make up only 20 per cent of the university population.

Education then has helped to perpetuate the stratification of British society. Not only does it pave the way for a certain style of employment, but it also reinforces the social 'markers' of speech pattern and accent which, more than in many countries, are used as 'ready reckoners' for assigning people to a particular class. The BBC was for many years a contributor in this respect through its insistence that its presenters should speak only 'BBC English' — English shorn of its regional accents. This policy did much to spread the notion that regional accents were a token of lower educational attainment or even of lower intellectual ability. It is only in recent years that the policy has been abandoned and regional accents have been allowed to escape from their confinement in the drama department.

Although the jobs available to graduates may offer better remuneration than those available to non-graduates, earned income in itself is not a major factor in class distinctions as the majority of such incomes fall within a fairly narrow band — a band made even narrower by the progressive income tax. Furthermore, the generalisation about relative incomes by no means always holds good. For instance, many teachers, graduates of the universities, may earn considerably less than a large number of 'blue-collar' workers. More significant is the distribution of wealth in society. While the Thatcher government has sought to widen home ownership by encouraging the sale of council houses to their tenants, and share ownership through the manner in which some nationalised industries were sold to the public, practically a quarter of all personal wealth in the country is still concentrated in the hands of just 1 per cent of the population, while the bottom 80 per cent own only 20 per cent.

Given the persistent class divide and the great maldistribution of the nation's wealth, it is perhaps surprising that the British have generally exhibited a rather conservative attitude towards political change. Politics has remained remarkably non-ideological (despite the existence of the Labour party) and non-revolutionary, being more concerned with the attainment of goals through existing institutions than with massive upheavals intent on the imposition of a totally new creed. Neither demagogues nor ideologues have prospered and mass enthusiasms (or hysteria) have been rare. Far from being the hotbed of socialism that many Americans perceive, many would argue that Britain has shown itself to be a largely conservative, even complacent, society.

In contrast to the United Kingdom, which is such a relatively small country, the United States is the fourth largest in the world, both in geographic size and in population. Its 3,617,204 square miles are exceeded only by those of the Soviet Union, Canada, and China. Only China, India and the Soviet Union have a greater population. Overall population density is a comfortable 56.2 per square mile which compares very favourably with many European countries, but the average figure disguises great variations, from Alaska's 0.5 or Wyoming's 3, up to New Jersey's 949 which nearly equals the highest European figure of 982 per square mile in the Netherlands.

The American nation is the result of a long history of migration. Its earliest inhabitants, the Indians, are believed to have crossed the Bering Straits from Asia many thousands of years ago. Modern developments are usually dated, more in sentiment than in fact, from 1492 when Columbus made his epic voyage which brought him to landfall in the Bahamas. Samuel Eliot Morrison's comment that 'not since the birth of Christ has there been a night so full of meaning for the human race' may be somewhat excessive, but the voyage of Columbus did herald the start of many transatlantic voyages of exploration and discovery which ultimately resulted in settlement. A variety of European nations was represented among the early settlers, but it was the dominant British stock in colonies based on charters granted by the British king which created the early forms of government and secured independence from Britain. During the nineteenth century the continent was opened up by waves of migration from most parts of Europe and some parts of Asia. The native Indians did not fare well in face of this onslaught. Murdered by those who subscribed to the dictum that 'the only good Indian is a dead Indian', killed in wars against those who expropriated their lands or broke their treaties, forced to live on reservations inappropriate for their needs (because the newcomers wanted the best land), the Indians paid a high price so that the continent might be developed.

The outcome of this massive migration that took place during the nineteenth century and in the early years of the twentieth,[5] plus the importation of black slaves before and during the early years of the Republic, is a nation that is 87.5 per cent white and 11.5 per cent black. (NB 'White', used here to cover all the non-black population, encompasses a wide range of ethnic backgrounds including, most notably, those of Hispanic origin who now make up about 8 per cent of the population.) The different origins of this polygenetic country are revealed in the range of minority languages to be found: English is the official language, Spanish is preferred by nearly two and a half million (largely those of Puerto Rican and Mexican descent), Italian by 400,000, French and Chinese by 300,000 each, and German, Greek, Japanese, Filipino and Korean are each favoured by about 100,000. In addition to these, Polish, Yiddish, Russian and a variety of American Indian tongues are to be found. In terms of religion, of those who declare an affiliation, 34 per cent are Protestant, 23 per cent are Roman Catholic, 3 per cent are Jewish.

The process whereby the nation developed out of this multinational, multilinguistic and multicultural background has been described as a 'melting pot', but it might with more accuracy be called a 'stew pot'. The former implies the melting down of ingredients to create a new substance in which old, individual characteristics are submerged. The latter, as with any good stew, suggests a process in which the ingredients combine to create a particular dish but in which, at the same time, they retain their own individuality. Thus, for many Americans their 'Americanism' is beyond doubt, but so too is their hyphenated status as Irish-Americans, Italo-Americans, Polish-Americans, etc. As the twentieth century progresses, links with the old countries tend to lessen and cultural ties to weaken, but it is still possible in many large cities to find newspapers catering to the linguistic variety, and many areas which are, for instance, recognisably Hungarian or Polish or Chinese. Columbus Day and St Patrick's Day parades remain occasions for those of Italian or Irish descent to demonstrate pride in their cultural backgrounds.

Modern forms of transport and telecommunications make it very easy to communicate across the continent, but in many ways the United States is a nation of localities. It is estimated, for instance, that there are nearly 1,800 daily newspapers in America, producing 300 copies per thousand population (as compared with just over 100 in the United Kingdom which produce 400 per thousand). While the bulk of British newspaper production is national in scope, virtually all American newspapers are strictly local, concentrating on local news augmented by wire service reports and syndicated columnists and cartoonists whose work is sold throughout the country. The *Wall Street Journal* and the *New York Times* have attempted to span the continent but their readership is small and in no way matches that of the British national press. The parochialism of the printed news means that while readers may be able to discover something of what is happening in Washington DC or in the rest of the world — thanks to the wire services — they may well be quite ignorant of events in neighbouring states.

Matching the newspapers in their localism — exceeding them perhaps — are the thousands of radio stations scattered around the country. Largely dedicated to popular music or religion, interspersed with advertising or appeals for donations, the news content of these programmes will rarely stretch beyond the immediate locality.

Television, on the other hand, dominated as it is by the three large conglomerates, ABC, NBC and CBS, does provide a nation-wide service of news and entertainment. Their newscasters have acquired national reputations and are often trusted more than the newsmakers. The entertainment programmes broadcast by the big three, and by the host of local stations, have in the past presented a sanitised view of a white, middle-class society that could have stepped straight from an advertisement for soap-powder. During the last twenty years or so, however, programme makers have been forced to recognise that America is not all-white, all-comfortable, all-middle-class, and the quality of the soap operas that are the staple of everyday viewing has become somewhat more realistic and more socially aware.

No other country in the world has managed to assimilate so many national and linguistic groups, but this assimilation has not always been without problems. American history has been characterised by periods of intolerance from the earliest days. Prior to independence, several of the early colonies adopted draconian laws against Catholics, dissenters or Jews. During the nineteenth century various anti-Catholic, anti-immigrant, anti-masonic groups sprang into being. In the twentieth century the target of intolerance changed and communism became the *bête noire*, with Attorney-General Mitchell Palmer's 'Red Fleet' of suspected communist sympathisers shipped back to Europe setting the tone for the House Un-American Activities Committee of the 1930s and 1940s in particular, and Senator Joseph McCarthy's infamous sub-committee in the 1950s. Today, various groups of what is known as the Radical Right expound ideas of a conspiracy in American life which exists to undermine the political and moral fibre of the nation, thus making it easier for takeover by alien creeds.

Nevertheless, despite these eruptions of hostility or intolerance, the bulk of immigrants were absorbed into their new nation in fairly peaceful fashion. It is a stain on America's history that blacks and Indians did not receive similar treatment. We have already mentioned how settlers behaved towards the earliest inhabitants of the continent: blacks were similarly disadvantaged.

The history of white/black relations in the United States is one which offers the lie to those who looked upon the sentiments of the Declaration of Independence as a measure of what the Founding Fathers believed. The 'self-evident truth', that Jefferson had proclaimed, that 'all men are created equal' did not even extend to all white men in the early days of the Republic, although it was not many years before they were accorded at least equality of political rights (long before full adult male suffrage was achieved in Britain). Blacks, however, were in a different category. The existence of what has been called 'the peculiar institution', slavery, until the ratification of the 13th Amendment to the constitution in 1865 stood as testament to the vast distinction between myth and reality so far as equality was concerned. The abolition of slavery did little to change the picture. A variety of laws aimed at keeping blacks away from the polls, legislation instituting segregation of the races in most areas of life (laws sustained by Supreme Court rulings), mob violence, including lynchings, all combined to keep blacks in a subservient role politically, economically and socially.

While the most concentrated *de jure* discrimination was to be found in the South, *de facto* segregation was common in the North where economic circumstance, often backed by restrictive covenants, conspired to keep neighbourhoods white. As children went to neighbourhood schools, schools were also segregated. When blacks did manage to secure the resources to move into a white area, unscrupulous real-estate agents would play upon white prejudices to scare out existing home-owners, thus securing business for themselves. Integrated housing came to be known as that period between the first black moving in and the last white moving out.

The climate of opinion in the country did gradually change. A series of Supreme Court decisions in the field of segregation in education helped create conditions favourable to the Civil Rights legislation of the late 1950s and 1960s. Following the legislation the last vestiges of formal segregation were removed in fairly quick order. Of course, racial prejudice still exists, but the opportunities to pander to those prejudices are largely gone. Blacks now have political equality and many have achieved middle-class status — many more, proportionately, than have achieved it in the UK. Nevertheless they are still among the most disadvantaged in the society. They are disproportionately to be found in the inner-city ghettos, among the ranks of the under-educated, the under-employed. One in three is living in poverty compared with one in ten whites, and the black median income is only 60 per cent of that of whites. Affirmative action policies, to enable blacks to catch up in the race in which they have been handicapped contenders for so long, have been introduced in a number of areas, but more needs to be done if the majority of blacks are to be allowed to compete on equal terms with whites.

In contrast to the fairly rigid class distinctions which have long dominated the British scene, products of a feudal history in which people 'knew their place' and, as we have mentioned, of a maldistribution of wealth and of an education system apparently geared to their perpetuation, American society has been much more fluid. As long ago as 1835 Alexis de Tocqueville, that renowned French commentator on the young American nation, noted a fundamental distinction between society in the New World and society in the old. Americans, he suggested, were 'born free' — free of the feudal traditions that held people to certain roles and obligations within the community. In the absence of formal rank or status, mere wealth was the major distinction, and with so much land to the West to be settled, those unhappy with their lot in one place could and did move, more or less as equals, to establish new communities across the continent. If, as one commentator has put it, 'poverty of expectation' was a characteristic of the mass of people in Europe, 'wealth of expectation' would more closely characterise Americans over most of their history. Such optimism often meant that wealth in another inspired not so much negative envy as positive determination, and the novels of Horatio Alger, with their inspirational 'rags to riches' tales, captured the prevailing spirit of nineteenth-century America.

As industrialisation developed, as cheap or free land disappeared, as cities grew, so some of that optimism disappeared. Industrial conflicts similar to those in Europe became common, and the divide between owners and workers marked. Interestingly, although the battles were often bitter, and sometimes bloody, they did not spill over into the political arena in the sense of stimulating the creation of a significant working-class or socialist party as was common in Europe. Any aspirations of the workers were principally channelled through one of the two existing major parties, the Democrats, although it was Herbert Hoover, leader of the Republican party, who made the socialist-style pledge to abolish poverty in the United States.

Education in the United States, as in Britain, has had an important role in the socialisation process. Fawcett and Thomas[6] have suggested that 'Americans are screened for life in their schools', and while this may be a little strong it does contain a large kernel of truth. The basic principle of public education is that at the appropriate age all children go to their neighbourhood high school, with no separation of students having taken place as the result of an 11-plus test. (The neighbourhood school principle has been modified somewhat in recent years by the introduction of busing to integrate schools which would otherwise be all-white or all-black because of housing patterns.)

Equality of opportunity in education is a fundamental tenet of the public system, but the method of funding schools does have an impact on the quality of schooling available. Just as the neighbourhood principle plays a large part in determining where children go to school, so local taxes provide nearly 50 per cent of the money to run those schools. In recent years the state and Federal governments have been making greater contributions to this funding, but the strong local element has often meant considerable inequality of resource between one school district and another: affluent suburbs are better able to raise money than many run-down inner-city areas. It is also usually easier to attract teachers to leafy suburbs than to crime-ridden ghettos. Differences within states are matched, if not exceeded, by differences among states. Thus Massachusetts spends nearly twice as much on education per pupil as does Mississippi and its teachers' salaries are 50 per cent higher. So much does the quality of education vary around the country that some states will not recognise, for purposes of employment or entry into college, high school graduation certificates from certain other states. Poor whites, blacks, Indians and Hispanics, found disproportionately in less affluent neighbourhoods or regions are thus found disproportionately among those who do not proceed to college after high school.

Having pointed to the inequalities that exist within the American schooling system, we must still note the fact that the high schools, good or bad, do keep 95 per cent of their students until the age of 17, and that they do provide far more opportunities for social mix than did the élitist 11-plus divide of the British. Furthermore, each year some ten million Americans are enrolled in colleges — which range from the world-famous, like Harvard, Yale and the University of California at Berkeley, through a host of very competent state and private institutions, down to fundamentalist colleges of little academic status scattered throughout the United States. For British commentators, accustomed to the relatively small numbers who stay on at school beyond the age of 16, or to the even smaller numbers who proceed to degree courses, the American figures represent an unacceptable watering-down of the education process. And certainly it is true that for entry to the professions Americans require an advanced degree. However, to paraphrase Fawcett and Thomas, when measured against its own democratic standard, in which educating the many is more important than cramming the bright, American education is a success.[7] But Fawcett and Thomas also take note of the considerable disquiet being voiced about the declining standards in high schools compared with ten or twenty years ago and they quote Daniel Greenberg as asking: 'after the greening of America and along with the graying of America, are we witnessing the dimming of America?'[8] Nevertheless, education, reinforcing history, helps to explain one of the apparent paradoxes of American society, 'that in a country with large inequalities of wealth and income, most Americans will make an assumption of equality about each other'.[9]

The development of the particular ethos that is 'the American way of life' is perhaps best ascribed, as Richard Hofstadter has suggested, to the fact that 'almost the entire sum of American history under the present constitution has coincided with the rise and spread of modern industrial capitalism'. When this is allied with the absence of a prior social order of the feudal kind, and with the presence of so many opportunities for personal enrichment, it is little wonder that ideological creeds like Marxism have fallen on relatively deaf ears. There is a long history of utopian groups of one kind or another springing up in the United States, but their appeal has been limited and usually short-lived outside the main stream of American life and development. No major movement has emerged to challenge the cult of competition or what Hofstadter called the 'democracy of cupidity rather than a democracy of fraternity'.[10]

Notes

1. We must, unfortunately, enter a major exception to this general picture: the situation in Northern Ireland to which we refer later in this chapter.
2. Who now make up more than 4 per cent of the total population of Great Britain, and of whom over 40 per cent were born in Britain.
3. HMSO (1984) *Britain 1984*, p.14.
4. The distinction between the different types of independent school need not concern us here.
5. Since the early twentieth century, the number of immigrants has been sharply curtailed.
6. Fawcett, E. and Thomas, T. (1983) *America and the Americans*, Fontana, p.274.
7. *Ibid.* p.286. Although 'cramming the bright' does occur at the élite universities.
8. *Ibid.* p.283.
9. *Ibid.* p.8.
10. Hofstadter, R. (1958) *The American Political Tradition*, Vintage Books, New York. Both quotations from p.viii.

2

Constitutions

Constitutions are concerned with 'political authority and power',[1] with the distribution of powers between the institutions of government and between those institutions and the citizenry. These relationships may be spelled out more or less precisely in a written document or they may be discovered in a variety of sources in uncodified form. They may be a response to a national trauma, such as war, revolution or economic collapse — an attempt to restore order to a state of flux — or they may be the product of a gradual evolution in which relationships have changed more through consensus than through violent upheaval.

The two countries we are studying in this book give us prime examples of the two models just described. In the United States there is a written document known as the Constitution of the United States of America. Brief enough to be included as an appendix to any number of textbooks, this document provided the framework within which the 13 newly-independent states could develop as a unit and still provides today the yardstick against which the constitutionality of actions, private or public, may be measured. In the United Kingdom, on the other hand, the absence of such a document led Alexis de Tocqueville — who should have known better — to assert that Britain had no constitution. He was, of course, wrong, for, so long as there exist rules governing the relationships mentioned above, there exists a constitution. These rules do not have to be found in a specific document — some may not be found in documentary form at all — and this is the case with the British constitution, which is to be found scattered in statute law, common law and convention. It is a product of evolution not revolution.

In comparison with many other countries, British political development has been relatively painless. In the seventeenth century a Civil War led to the abolition of the monarchy and decapitation of the monarch, but in less than 20 years the monarchy was restored. A few years later, in a 'peaceful' revolution, the monarch fled, and was immediately replaced. Since then, there has been no national cataclysm requiring wholesale restatement of the principles relating to power within the state.

Neither the formality of the American document nor the absence of recent violent upheaval in the British system should, however, be taken to suggest that the two constitutions are static. Rather, it should become apparent as we study the two countries that over the last two centuries there have been considerable shifts in the power relationships within the societies, even though the outward forms have remained much the same. As Walter Bagehot wrote on page one of his *English Constitution:* 'An ancient and ever-altering constitution is like an old man who still wears with attached fondness clothes in the fashion of his youth; what you see of him is the same, what you do not see is wholly altered'.

It is in many respects easier to study the two constitutions by looking first at the American, for the existence of a formal document provides us with convenient reference points for comparison; it also allows those who might be inclined to agree with de Tocqueville to perceive similarities between the two systems that might otherwise be missed.

If the British constitution developed in the mists of time, the American emerged in the mists of gunpowder smoke, a creature of a revolution which threw off one form of government, but left 13 newly-independent states without leadership or direction. The heat of war had united the disparate colonists in a common effort but when the heat was removed unity disappeared. The Articles of Confederation, the first approach to a constitution for the region, drawn up in 1777 during the struggle, were more the product of suspicion than of any long-term desire to unite as a nation. It was not long, however, before this 'League of Friendship' was seen to be inadequate for the growth and expansion of 13 dis-united states. An ability to stand up to the possibility of external aggression demanded a strong economy and leadership.

Neither existed under the Articles. There were, rather, a number of obstacles to national growth: tariff barriers among the different states designed to raise income and to protect 'home' industries; the absence of a common currency or a common approach to the problems of inflation (in some states, debtor elements encouraged inflationary tendencies as a means of lessening their real-debt burdens); the absence of a common legal structure.

We need not rehearse here the range of problems that arose. Suffice it to say that ultimately there was a call for a meeting to discuss revision of the Articles and in 1787 representatives of the various states gathered in Philadelphia for that purpose. They did not, in fact, revise the Articles, they replaced them — with the Constitution of the United States.

When the Founding Fathers came together, they brought with them a range of fears and prejudices which derived from their past experiences and their present concerns. First and foremost, perhaps, having recently fought a war to get rid of a distant and centralised government, they were unwilling to hand over too much power to another distant and centralised authority, and they were particularly concerned that such power as was given should not be concentrated in too few hands. Checks and balances were written into the system so that no one part could become too strong in relation to the others. This separation of powers, or separation of institutions sharing power, to use Richard Neustadt's term, is thus central to the American constitution. A legislature, Congress, an executive, the Presidency, and a judiciary, the Supreme Court, were established. No person could serve in more than one office at the same time and the powers of the different bodies were shared in such a way as to require a significant degree of co-operation for policies to be put into effect. For instance, the constitution gives Congress the law-making authority of the nation but this is circumscribed by the requirement of presidential approval (through signature) or acquiescence (through allowing a bill to become law after a specified period without a signature). On occasions, the President may even use his power to veto a bill, in which case it can only become law if Congress can muster a two-thirds majority in both Houses. Furthermore, even if a measure should become law it may still be challenged in the courts of law and may be declared unconstitutional if the courts assert that Congress has exceeded its constitutional remit.

The Presidency is similarly limited. For instance, from the constitution the President has the power to make treaties, but such treaties require the approval of a two-thirds vote in the Senate. It is the President who is Commander-in-Chief of the armed forces of the nation but he is dependent upon Congress voting the funds to provide for the existence of such forces. And while he may be Commander-in-Chief, it is Congress, not he, which has the constitutional authority to declare war (a provision which, as we shall see later, has at times been circumvented).

The Supreme Court may not be so obviously subject to the balancing factors of the other institutions but nevertheless it does not act in a constitutional vacuum free from political constraints and pressures. For example, it may hand down a judgment but it has no power of enforcement. It is dependent upon the executive branch for such enforcement. As a consequence the Court may avoid delivering decisions which are so politically unpopular that they may be ignored. Apart from such inaction by the executive branch, which may damage the Court's credibility, action by Congress, which may constitutionally remove any area from the Court's appellate jurisdiction, could narrow the Court's range of activity considerably. Finally, in this series of interrelationships, while all justices hold office for life, subject to good behaviour (and none has ever been removed from office) they are appointed by the President, with senatorial approval, and Presidents, as we shall see, may be able to influence the direction of the decisions taken through the judicious appointment of 'right thinking' persons to fill vacancies as they arise.

The Founding Fathers, then, created a balance of sorts between the different arms of the Federal government, although, significantly, while they may have perceived the role of the Supreme Court as being what it is today, they did not spell it out in the document itself, and it was Chief Justice John Marshall's court in 1803 which arrogated to itself the power to declare acts of Congress unconstitutional. The balancing of the institutions at the Federal level was, however, only one of the tasks of the constitution-makers. The division of powers between a central, federal, government and the state governments was also a major component of the discussions. While those gathered in

Philadelphia were seeking answers to national problems, they were also representatives of their individual states and therefore many were anxious to give to the new government only such powers as would enable it to deal with those problems. As the 10th Amendment to the constitution states: 'the powers not delegated to the United States by the constitution, nor prohibited by it to the States, are reserved to the States respectively, or to the people'.[2] The Founding Fathers thus created a federal system in which constitutional authority was divided between a central government and constituent governments. Unlike a unitary system such as Britain, where ultimate authority rests with the national government which can constitutionally abolish all local governments, as they are subordinate to the national authority, a federal system preserves for its constituent parts rights and privileges which cannot be taken away without their consent.

The division of authority between Federal and state governments is, however, rarely clear-cut and unambiguous and many governmental powers are shared. For instance, while the national government has the sole responsibility and power to coin money, to establish a postal service, to defend the nation, or to admit new states, the powers to raise taxes, to regulate business and commerce, or to proscribe certain acts as criminal and to provide punishments for those who commit such acts are shared. Such an interaction denies the analogy of a 'layer-cake' federalism, with its distinctive planes, and lends more credence to the 'marble-cake' analogy with its inseparable mixtures. As Morton Grodzins has written: 'The federal system is not accurately symbolised by a neat layer cake of three distinct and separate planes. A far more realistic symbol is that of the marble cake. Wherever you slice through it you reveal an inseparable mixture of differently coloured ingredients ... Vertical and diagonal lines almost obliterate the horizontal ones, and in some places there are unexpected whirls and an imperceptible merging of colours, so that it is difficult to tell where one ends and the other begins. So it is with federal, state and local responsibilities in the chaotic marble cake of American government.'[3]

Perhaps one of the more striking features of the American constitution is its durability. It is remarkable that such a document, written in the eighteenth century, should continue to provide the guiding principles of government some two hundred years later.

Indeed, recently discovered letters of George Washington, the first President, suggest that even he did not believe the constitution would last more than 20 years. It has, of course, been amended (through a two-thirds vote in both Houses of Congress and with the ratification of three-quarters of the states' legislatures or conventions), but not often: only 16 times since the Bill of Rights was ratified, and some of those 16 are of little constitutional significance — in fact, two, those relating to prohibition, cancel each other out. But if formal amendments have been few, and their impact often slight, change has nevertheless occurred and the operational constitution of today bears only superficial resemblance to the original.

The development of the constitution has come about in a number of ways — through laws passed by Congress which have added flesh to the skeletal document; through interpretation of those laws and of the constitution itself by the courts of law, in particular the Supreme Court which has often changed the original balance established by the Founding Fathers; by usage (or convention) which, again, has modified the intentions of the constitution-makers. For example, Congress, through its power to regulate interstate commerce, has, with the aid of Supreme Court rulings, greatly extended its regulatory powers in relation to the individual states. The Supreme Court, through its adjudicative and interpretative functions in specific cases, has had a major role in adapting the constitution to the changing needs and circumstances of successive generations. Such has been the Court's influence that one can understand and perhaps forgive the hyperbole of Charles Evan Hughes' comment that 'America lives under a constitution, but the constitution is what the judges say it is'. Finally, convention or usage have managed to change the manner in which institutions have worked or relationships have developed. Thus the early growth of political parties quickly brought to an end the electoral college as an effective means of selecting a President; after George Washington rejected the idea of a third term as President, the convention developed that Presidents did not serve more than two terms (when Franklin Roosevelt ignored the convention it was enshrined in the constitution as the 22nd Amendment); modern-day Presidents are now expected to present to Congress a rounded policy-programme of much greater scope than envisaged in section 3 of Article 2 of the constitution which requires the President 'from time to time to give to the Congress information of the State of the Union, and recommend to their consideration such measures as he shall judge necessary and expedient'.

That the constitution has proven to be so adaptable over the last two hundred years, and still so central to the political process, has been ascribed by some to the foresight of the Founding Fathers. Others would suggest, however, that while foresight may have had some role to play, political pressures and circumstances dictated just what could be agreed. Certainly hard-won compromise among hard-nosed politicians who had sharply contrasting views as to the nature of the government they sought marked much of the proceedings at Philadelphia which were in ever-constant danger of premature termination.

The first major dispute to arise was between representatives of the large (more populous) states and those of the small states concerning the basis of representation in the new Congress. The latter feared that if representation were to be solely on the basis of population they would be constantly out-voted in the Congress. Ultimately, the Connecticut Compromise was accepted: that states should be represented according to population in the House of Representatives and as equal territorial units in the Senate. Conflict also arose over the issue of slavery, opposed by parts of the North, strongly supported in the South. It was eventually agreed that the importation of slaves should be permitted for a further 20 years and that for the purposes of apportioning representatives and taxes to a state, a slave should count as three-fifths of a white person. Slavery itself was not touched at all — a sad denial of the high-flown sentiments of the Declaration of Independence '...that all men are created equal, that they are endowed by their Creator with certain unalienable rights, that among these are life, liberty and the pursuit of happiness'.

The election of the President called for yet more compromise. Some argued for direct election by the people and were opposed by those who feared 'the mob'. Others sought election by Congress and were opposed by those who saw in this a breakdown of the principle of the separation of powers, and the possibility of domination of the executive branch by the legislative. Eventually the idea of an Electoral College was agreed upon. Each state would have as many members of the Electoral College as it had

Representatives and Senators. The electorate in each state (as determined by state law) would vote for the members of the Electoral College who would themselves cast their votes for the person they deemed worthy to be President. If no candidate received an absolute majority of the votes cast, election would then be given to the House of Representatives. The intentions of the Founding Fathers were soon thwarted, as we noted earlier, for the development of political groupings with Electoral College slates pledged to a particular candidate did largely turn presidential elections into direct as opposed to indirect contests. (The distrust of the masses was also demonstrated by the provision that Senators were to be elected by state legislatures and not by the people directly — a provision not repealed until the ratification of the 17th Amendment in 1913.)

Most of the document represents compromise but these three were fundamental: without them the constitution would probably not have emerged. But we should also note some of the omissions from the original document. First, it is remarkably quiet about the judiciary. It established the Supreme Court and gave Congress the authority to establish such inferior courts as it wished, but it says very little about the power of the Court and gives no hint of the role the Court would ultimately play in the political and constitutional development of the nation. Again, no mention is made of political parties although Washington, in his Farewell Address, was soon to be warning of their influence. Finally, the constitution ignored the question of how binding was the contract into which the states were entering — was it eternal or was secession possible? In the middle of the nineteenth century the Civil War provided the answer to this question: states could not leave the Union.

The constitution was a creature born out of compromise allied with much sophisticated thinking about the nature of political power. It was formed, we should not forget, in a culture of written constitutions. The individual states had their own written constitutions which were themselves often derived from the commercial charters granted to the companies that originally opened up North America. Many of the provisions of this new United States Constitution derived from those different state documents. It was a highly successful response to a crisis situation and although the Founding Fathers could not foresee the nature of the development that was to take place their document proved sufficiently elastic to permit the growth of a nation of 13 eastern seaboard states into a superpower of continental dimensions.

Not since the Norman Conquest of 1066 have the British undergone an upheaval comparable to that of the Americans. Even the English Civil War of the seventeenth century was different for, although it brought Charles I's reign and life to an early end and abolished the monarchy for a short time, it did not effect any massive or long-term changes in the nature of British society.

The 'Glorious Revolution' of the 1680s, when James II was driven from his throne and William and Mary were invited by Parliament to become joint monarchs, had greater significance as it marked a fundamental change in the relationship between Parliament and Crown. But although fundamental, and while accompanied by a Declaration, later a Bill, of Rights, denying monarchs the right to suspend the law of the land or to maintain a standing army in peacetime, it did not prove to be an occasion for a formal statement of all the various relationships which go to make up a constitution. Development was left to continue, as in the past, in a piecemeal, uncodified fashion.

As we have already noted, the development of a constitution may come from a combination of statute law, common or case law and conventions. In the United States they represent changes to an original, written constitution; in Britain they are the constitution.

The most readily recognisable part of the constitution is statute law, the product of the legislative process and possessing full force of law until superseded by subsequent statute. Of course, not all statute law is of constitutional importance: much is clearly of a subordinate nature. When we are discussing the constitution we are concerned with those statutes which relate to the powers of government, to the interrelationships of the different parts of government and to the rights and duties of the citizen — those acts which are concerned with 'society in its political aspect'.[4] We have, above, referred to one such Act, the Bill of Rights. Others we might mention include the various Representation of the People Acts which have extended the franchise; the Parliament Acts which have limited the powers of the House of Lords; the Habeas Corpus Act of 1679 relating to liberties of the subject; the Act of Union with Scotland; the European Communities Act of 1972. This list could be extended, although we would ultimately reach a point where general agreement would start to break down and controversy would arise as to whether a particular statute was of a 'constitutional' or of a merely 'administrative' nature. (One of the advantages of a written constitution is that it does establish parameters for discussion.)

The common law sources of the constitution relate to judicial interpretation in specific cases, many of which are concerned with the liberties of the subject, which have been largely defined by the courts rather than by the legislature. To one nineteenth-century commentator, Dicey, this function was so important he was led to write that 'the general principles of the constitution are the result of judicial decisions determining the rights of private persons in particular cases brought before the courts'. An exaggeration, of course, but a good example first, of how important the common law has been, and secondly, of how subjective interpretation of the constitution may be: to Dicey, private rights were paramount and he was therefore prepared to ignore all other political relationships in society. This heading also subsumes the royal prerogative — a dwindling authority but still the fiction under which many governmental powers are exercised. Thus the monarch still appoints ministers, dissolves Parliament, makes treaties, declares war, but does so on the advice of ministers — advice which may not be ignored. It may be 'Her Majesty's Government', but the decisions are taken by the government, not Her Majesty, and the government answers not to the Crown but to the electorate.

Conventions, the third source of the constitution, have developed over the centuries as an operational response to institutional difficulties or to changing power relationships. They are non-legal rules which are nevertheless accepted as binding by the participants in the political game. Conventions operate across the whole spectrum of political life. Thus, when out-voted on a vital issue the Cabinet has the right to dissolve Parliament and to hold a general election, but should the election go against the government it should resign. Or, when the House of Lords is acting as a Court of Appeal only the Law Lords sit. Again, the opposition in Parliament is assured of adequate rights in debate and the Speaker of the House of Commons acts impartially, avoiding political controversy (unlike his American counterpart). Most important, however, are those conventions which limit the royal prerogative. As indicated above, ministerial advice now limits the scope of royal action. The monarch appoints ministers but only those recommended by the Prime Minister. The right of the monarch to appoint the Prime Minister has been limited by the convention that the leader of the majority party in the House of Commons must be invited to form the government.[5] The monarch may still have some leeway if a coalition situation should develop, but so long as one or other of the major parties secures a majority, and so long as they continue to elect their leaders, the monarch's prerogative will be a formality. The monarch's signature is still required before a bill becomes law but no monarch since Queen Anne in the early eighteenth century has refused to give assent. Above all, the conventions insist that the monarch stay outside the realm of politics. The monarch is the ceremonial head of state while the Prime Minister takes the political responsibility.

We should re-iterate the point that conventions are not legally binding and that no court of law could take action if a convention were ignored, but Jennings' observation is well taken that conventions are obeyed 'because of the political difficulties which arise if they are not'. A good example of this occurred in the early years of the twentieth century when the House of Lords breached the convention that it did not interfere with House of Commons money bills. This ultimately led to the convention being enshrined in an Act of Parliament — passed with House of Lords assent after the King, responding to ministerial 'advice', had threatened to create a large enough body of new peers to ensure the bill was passed. Again, if the monarch became embroiled in the political arena many questions would be raised concerning the continued existence of the institution. However, in this particular case, we must recognise that many people regard the monarchy as the ultimate defender of the constitution and might actually welcome royal interference on a particularly controversial issue.

Dicey, the nineteenth-century constitutional lawyer to whom we have already alluded, wrote that the British constitution rested upon two major principles, the rule of law and the sovereignty of Parliament. However, the former, the rule of law, does not provide us with much help in understanding the British constitution as it is capable of many different definitions — indeed, any definition may tell us more about the prejudices of the person doing the defining than about the society to which it is supposed to relate. Thus, if we take S.A. de Smith's suggestion that 'the concept is usually intended to imply (1) that the powers exercised by politicians and officials must have a legitimate foundation; they must be based on authority conferred by law; and (2) that the law should conform to certain minimum standards of justice, both substantive and procedural', we have a definition that could apply to any society, democratic or totalitarian, that follows certain procedural guidelines. Indeed, in the specific case of the United Kingdom, when we introduce the principle of the sovereignty of Parliament, we can see how limited even de Smith's general statement is. '[T]he powers exercised by politicians ... must be based on authority conferred by law', but to paraphrase Charles Evans Hughes' comments from above, 'politicians may be bound by the law but the law is what politicians in Parliament say it is'.

We are left, then, with the concept of the sovereignty of Parliament being the major distinguishing feature or keystone of the British constitution. Briefly stated, Parliament, or more precisely the monarch in Parliament, may 'make or unmake any law whatsoever on any matter whatsoever',[6] and no person or body may override or question the validity of any parliamentary Act. No Supreme Court exists which can declare legislation unconstitutional. If a bill has gone through all the normal processes and become an Act it is constitutional. Furthermore, there are no entrenched provisions within the constitution, no areas which cannot be amended except through a special procedure or with a special majority. Thus an Act concerned with some fundamental right, extending the franchise for example, may be passed with as much technical ease as one requiring seat-belts to be worn in cars (although, even here, we should recognise that some regard the legal requirement to wear belts as a serious infringement of their personal liberties).

It has been suggested that Britain's relations with the European Community impose certain limitations upon Parliament's sovereignty. As a consequence of the signing of the Treaty of Accession in 1972 and the subsequent passage of the European Communities Act, Britain has undertaken to accept as legally binding the regulations and directives of the Community and the rulings of the European Court of Justice. These regulations and rulings do undoubtedly impose limitations or obligations upon British governments, but the point should not be forgotten that if Parliament decided to withdraw from the Treaty and repeal the Communities Act, nothing could legally stop it. Thus Parliament is limited only to the extent that it is prepared to be limited. Its ultimate sovereignty remains intact.

The British system, unlike the American, is unitary. That is, all political power and authority ultimately resides in one place, Parliament. There are no co-ordinate law-making bodies in the state. Local government units are therefore subordinate to Parliament; they derive their authority from it and may have that authority rescinded. There have, in recent years, been several examples of parliamentary omnipotence with regard to local authorities, with the wholesale change of boundaries and functions in the early 1970s and the breaking up of the metropolitan counties in the mid-1980s.

The emergence of Parliament as the dominant power in the land was the outcome of a long struggle with the monarchy, with Parliamentarians over the centuries nibbling away at royal prerogatives, principally by making demands in return for the voting of funds to the monarch. But it was the seventeenth-century clash between the Stuarts and Parliament that finally established Parliament as the dominant member of the governmental hierarchy: once it was recognised that the Crown was in the gift of Parliament the relationship had quite obviously changed. In 1867, Walter Bagehot expressed what is still the conventional wisdom concerning the political role of the monarchy today when he wrote that the monarch has 'the right to be consulted, the right to encourage, the right to warn'.[7]

Having stressed the dominance of Parliament, we must now introduce some qualifications to the general statement if the British system of government is to be understood. First, as the franchise has spread, the popularly elected body, the House of Commons, has become the major chamber, with the House of Lords, first by convention then by the provisions of the Parliament Acts of 1911 and 1949, now playing a secondary role. Secondly, along with the franchise have grown well-organised, hierarchical party systems. When one of those parties secures a majority in the House of Commons, its leaders form the government and they

normally receive the support of their back-benchers for the programmes they seek to enact. Therefore parliamentary sovereignty
has come to mean the sovereignty of the government for so long
as it retains the backing of its own supporters in the House of
Commons. Finally, it is important to remember that Parliament's
sovereignty is limited by its obligation to make regular appeals
to the electorate. In other words, Parliament may have legal
sovereignty, but the electorate has political sovereignty.

The two constitutions are, thus, creatures of the historical
circumstances in which they developed. In America, the overthrow of one central authority ultimately produced a different
kind of central authority. The 13 states could have attempted their
own separate survivals but they would probably have fallen prey
to one or another of the European powers who had interests in
North America. Just as earlier, at the signing of the Declaration
of Independence, Benjamin Franklin had remarked that they had
all better hang together or they would all hang separately, so,
when independence was attained, hanging together still appeared
to be the best recipe for survival. And having decided to unite,
the Americans then sought to avoid the evils, real or imagined,
that they associated with the newly-discarded regime. In Britain,
on the other hand, a transfer of power and authority took place
but it was largely peaceful and gradual and, more to the point,
it was from one central authority to another. Thus, when the
Americans created their new government they did so by a transfer
of power from the constituent parts to the centre, while retaining residual powers for themselves. The British experience involved no such transfer, indeed could not have done so, for there
were no constituent parts in which the power of the state rested.

Furthermore, when power was given to the centre in the
American context, assurances were sought that the powers would
not be abused and that rights would be preserved: hence the
separation of powers and the Bill of Rights. In Britain, in the
absence of such transfer, there is an absence of such safeguards.
Power, far from being separated and checked, is concentrated in
the hands of the government, and the rights and privileges of
citizens, far from being spelled out in a Bill of Rights, exist largely
as expectations which derive from tradition rather than
entrenchment.

What the Founding Fathers did in a hurry and what Parliament achieved gradually still prescribe the terms in which government is carried on and still help to set the tone of political debate. Some, on both sides of the Atlantic, argue, however, that the constitutions are now wearing out, that they no longer meet the needs of societies fast approaching the twenty-first century. Certainly the revelations at the 'Irangate' hearings suggest that all is not well in the American body politic, while injunctions curbing the freedom of the press over the Peter Wright book *Spycatcher* give weight to the arguments of those who maintain that the British need a Bill of Rights.

While it is not intended to evaluate the arguments over the modern-day relevance of the constitutions here, the rest of the book may provide material for readers to make their own evaluation. There is, however, one warning. Constitutions may provide the framework and may carry the guarantees that allow for peaceful and ordered government. But the guarantees are worth only as much as the society is prepared to accept. Thus a Bill of Rights is of little value if its protection is not extended to an unpopular minority. Conversely, the absence of a Bill of Rights may not mean the absence of rights if the society feels the rights should exist. Some tampering with institutions or constitutions may perhaps remedy a patent fault, but it cannot be relied upon to cure all the shortcomings of a society. At times, certainly, to paraphrase Cassius in *Julius Caesar*, the fault 'lies not in our institutions but in ourselves'.

Notes

1. De Smith, S.A. (1977) *Constitutional and Administrative Law,* 3rd edn, Penguin.
2. The first ten amendments, popularly known as the Bill of Rights, passed by Congress in its first session in 1789, and ratified in 1791, were basically agreed to before the ratification of the constitution and have claim therefore, in a sense, to be regarded as part of the original constitution.
3. Grodzins, M. (1963) in Goldwin, R.A. (ed.) *A Nation of States,* Rand McNally, pp. 3–4.
4. Greaves, H.R.G. (1955) *The British Constitution,* Allen & Unwin.
5. When Lord Home was invited to form a government in 1963, it was on the understanding that he would renounce his title and seat in the House of Lords and seek election to the House of Commons, for the convention has also developed that the Prime Minister must

sit in the popularly elected chamber. Lord Salisbury, in 1902, was
the last Prime Minister to sit in the House of Lords.

6.   De Smith, *op. cit.*
7.   Bagehot, W. (1963) *The English Constitution*, Fontana.

3

The spread of representation

The right to vote in the United States and the United Kingdom is in general accorded to all citizens over the age of 18 who are of sound mind and who have not been disqualified through conviction for certain crimes or, in the United Kingdom, through membership of the House of Lords. It is a right regarded as fundamental to both systems of government although its use is called for on many more occasions and for many more decisions in America than in Britain. However, before we consider those opportunities and the advantage taken of them, we will look briefly at the history of the franchise in the two countries.

Parliament in Britain has a long and chequered history dating back to the thirteenth century and owing its early existence to the monarch's needs, particularly for revenue to be raised through taxes. The counties and boroughs were each entitled to send two representatives to Parliament, regardless of size or population — a territorial rather than an individual representation, similar in principle to that in the United States where each state has two Senators. The entitlement to elect those representatives varied around the country but had as a general foundation property ownership or a degree of wealth that left most people without a vote. Furthermore, as population shifts took place over the centuries, as some areas declined and as industrial centres grew, traditional boundaries remained untouched, producing a situation in which many representatives came from constituencies with few or even no eligible voters — constituencies often in the gift of powerful landowners whose influence in Parliament remained secure while the burgeoning industrial interests were largely excluded. (It is interesting to note here that when the American colonists were calling for 'no taxation without representation' the developing centres of Birmingham, Leeds and Manchester were also without representation in Parliament.)

The illogicalities and the malrepresentation of interests that the system produced ultimately led to a clamour for reform that resulted in the Representation of the People Act of 1832, an Act more important for what it represented than for what it actually accomplished. The Great Reform Act, as it was popularly known, heralded a new approach to representation in Britain. The first steps were faltering but were harbingers of great strides that would eventually and inevitably follow later in the century. Changes were made in constituency boundaries to secure a better reflection of the interests in the country, although there was no attempt to secure equality of electorate within those boundaries. Greater rationalisation of the franchise was achieved but, rooted in property or wealth, it still left most citizens without the vote. However, 'the real importance of the [1832] Act was to make reform a respectable if not always an acceptable topic',[1] and it paved the way for the later Acts which both significantly extended the franchise and, equally importantly, reduced the corruption so long associated with British elections.

The second Reform Act, of 1867, by extending the vote in the boroughs to all householders, and all tenants paying more than £10 a year in rent, nearly doubled the electorate. At the same time, efforts were made to reduce the gross inequalities of size of the constituencies. The Reform Act of 1884 and the Redistribution Act of 1885 continued this work, but 40 per cent of the male population still remained without the vote until the Representation of the People Act of 1918 which finally accorded universal adult male suffrage and produced constituencies of roughly equal size.

If 1918 is significant for giving all men over the age of 21 the right to vote and for ensuring that the votes were of approximately equal value, it is even more notable for its provision of the right to vote to women for the first time, albeit not until they had reached the age of 30. Ten years later that age anomaly was abolished and women were accorded the same electoral rights as men, and Britain had firmly established, with one or two exceptions, the principle of 'one person, one vote, one value'.[2]

Slow though the expansion of the franchise may have been in Britain, its progress was relatively straightforward. The situation in the United States, and in the colonies before independence, was of a quite different order.

The relative insularity of the different colonies had produced a variety of approaches to the question 'who should have the vote?' 'Economic substantiality' was certainly a common factor — a requirement of ownership of land or of payment of taxes — as was the denial of the vote to women, but additional factors were introduced by the different colonies. Thus, many members of minority religious groups were denied the franchise — the Quakers in Massachusetts; the Jews in Maryland, New York, Rhode Island and South Carolina — while many states discriminated against blacks and other ethnic groups.

After the War for Independence, shifts in the property and tax requirements took place, with the emphasis gradually placed more on the payment of taxes than on the ownership of property: the impracticalities associated with land ownership in the rapidly-growing cities helped spur these changes, but the greatest impetus for liberalisation undoubtedly came from the influx of new states into the Union. Tennessee (1796) was the only new state to enter the Union with a property qualification, while Mississippi (1817) was the last state to enter requiring the payment of taxes for the privilege of voting. Vermont (1791), Kentucky (1792) and Indiana (1816) all 'became part of the United States . . . requiring neither property nor payment of taxes as prerequisites to vote'.[3]

The original states responded at different speeds to the impulses from the newer members of the Union. For instance, New Hampshire had abolished its property qualification by 1784 and its tax-paying requirements by 1792 while Georgia had abolished them by 1789 and 1798 respectively. Delaware, Massachusetts, Pennsylvania, Rhode Island and North Carolina, on the other hand, were still insisting on tax-paying for the vote as late as the Civil War: indeed, North Carolina even retained its property qualification until 1856. Nevertheless, despite the reservations of some concerning the apparent dangers of extending the suffrage

— that it 'jeopardise[s] the rights of property and the principles of liberty'[4] — the move towards a more liberal franchise was inexorable.

That political activity should have been so widespread so much earlier in the United States than in the United Kingdom should not be surprising in light of the particular circumstances of the two countries. We have already pointed to the influence of the newer, Western states in easing or removing the rigidities introduced by the disciples of Calvin or Mammon in the East. However, for some interpreters of American progress, de Tocqueville and Louis Hartz among them, far more significant was the fact that America was 'born free' — free of the feudal traditions that beset European liberal developments — and was therefore a happy breeding ground for political activity largely untrammelled by the reactionary forces of *'ancien régimes'*. In such an environment it is not to be wondered at that, in Lane's words, '. . . the extension of the franchise to free white males was relatively quick and even painless'.[5]

The emphasis, as in Britain, was on male franchise and, apart from New Jersey's brief and probably unintended grant of the vote to women taxpayers in its constitutions of 1776 and 1797 (a right withdrawn in 1807), women did not get the vote in the United States (except for school board elections) until 1869 when the territory of Wyoming started the piecemeal trend which culminated in 1920 with the ratification of the 19th Amendment which forbade the denial of the vote 'on account of sex'.[6]

In general, therefore, the right to vote advanced somewhat more rapidly in the United States than in the United Kingdom, but two problem areas existed in America which were largely absent in Britain — one of them representing a blight upon the American body politic until well into the second half of the twentieth century.

The first of these problems concerned the position of immigrants. One of the pillars of the development of the United States rested upon the influx of aliens, from Europe in particular. On arrival in North America, immigrants encountered a variety of reactions which ranged from the restrictions of Massachusetts, which insisted upon two years' residence after naturalisation before giving the vote, to Wisconsin or Indiana which allowed the vote to aliens if they simply declared an intention to become naturalised. This was not just another East–West divide however, for Pennsylvania had allowed the vote to foreigners after two years' residency while some far-Western states had excluded aliens, in particular orientals, from the polls. Nevertheless, this having been said, Croty's comment that 'in the West, immigrants were welcomed and afforded early entry into the political system' while 'in the East, the situation was quite different', does capture the general picture.[7] But even taking into account Eastern hostilities and the activities of the Native-American (Know-Nothing) party, founded in 1847, which opposed Catholics, foreigners and the Irish in particular, white immigrants fairly quickly became part of the political culture. Blacks would have to wait much longer before they received equal treatment.

While it is easy to associate oppression of blacks in the United States with the South, where slavery was entrenched until the Civil War, attitudes towards those free blacks who lived outside the South were generally far from liberal. By and large the New England states were content to treat blacks as other citizens so far as the franchise was concerned, but in the 1830s and 1840s 'half a dozen Northern states adopted measures prohibiting Negroes from voting, or imposed special tax and property restrictions on them'. The Border states generally prohibited Negro voting as did the 'newly admitted states in the Middle and Far West'.[8]

After the Civil War, the Northern states, 'somewhat reluctantly', extended their suffrage to include blacks. In the South, however, black suffrage was imposed by the Reconstruction Act of 1867, an imposition given added weight by the 15th Amendment, ratified in 1870, which forbade the denial or abridgement of the right to vote 'on account of race, colour, or previous condition of servitude'. For a time, blacks in the South voted in considerable numbers but once Reconstruction was over, and once Federal troops were withdrawn from the South, there began a series of manoeuvres — the 'grandfather clause', literacy tests, the white primary, the poll tax — backed up by intimidation and lynchings, which would effectively deny the right to vote to most blacks in the South for a large part of the next century. The 'grandfather' clause was held void by the Supreme Court in 1915 (in *Guinn* v. *United States*) and the white primary in 1944 (in *Smith* v. *Allwright*). Poll taxes lingered on, although in a dwindling number of states, until 1964 which the 24th Amendment to the constitution outlawed them in federal elections. Finally, the Voting Rights Acts of 1965 and 1970 brought to an end the various and shameful attempts to deny American blacks equality of suffrage with whites.

Accompanying the demand for the right to vote has been a concern that votes should be of equal value. The history of the spread of the franchise in the two countries has been marked by the existence of constituencies of vastly different size in terms of electorates. On occasions these discrepancies were the outcome of inadvertence, a failure to redraw boundaries to take account of population shifts. At other times, the search for political advantage was a positive force in the manner in which boundaries were redrawn. Whatever the reason for the different-sized constituencies, the outcome was a situation in which votes appeared to be of different value.

In the United Kingdom, the satisfaction of the landed classes with the constituency boundaries which heightened their influence, and minimised that of the developing industrialist classes, lay behind their reluctance to alter constituencies to reflect the shifts in population that had taken place. The clamour for reform produced moderate changes during the nineteenth century but it was not until the 1918 Representation of the People Act that it was accepted that constituencies should be approximately equal in size. In 1944, the House of Commons Act provided for the creation of Boundary Commissioners to make periodic revision of constituency boundaries and thus largely removed the subject of redistribution from the political agenda.[9] Today, the worst discrepancies have been abolished, although even as recently as 1983 there was a population difference of 48,850 between the largest and smallest English constituencies. (As a concession to nationalist feelings in Wales and Scotland, and as a recognition of the larger, less populous areas involved, those two areas of the United Kingdom have somewhat fewer electors per constituency than England. Northern Ireland, because for some time it had its own Parliament, is somewhat under-represented at Westminster.)

The history of malapportionment in the United Kingdom has, on the whole, been more a history of reluctance to change boundaries to reflect population shifts than of a readiness to redraw the political map to attain political advantage. In the United States the history is two-pronged, with some states failing to redistribute despite massive shifts in population and others only too ready to use the redistributing weapon for their own ends. 'Positive' malapportionment in America introduced a new word to the political vocabulary, the 'gerrymander'. Governor Elbridge Gerry of Massachusetts was such a manipulator of boundaries that when, in 1811, one of his more 'picturesque' districts was reputed to resemble a salamander he inadvertently bequeathed his name to the word in common use today to describe the unethical, but not necessarily illegal, activity of concentrating one's opponents' support in as few districts as possible while spreading one's own support as advantageously as possible to maximise political gains. The only legal requirements in the United States are that, following Supreme Court rulings in *Baker* v. *Carr* (1962) and *Westberry* v. *Sanders* (1964), electoral districts must have equal populations. This still leaves considerable room for imaginative map drawing.

It was not, however, the creative gerrymander that ultimately brought Supreme Court rulings on the matter, but the passive gerrymandering that allowed districts to continue unchanged over long periods of time, despite population movements. For example Keefe and Ogul wrote, in 1964, that in Vermont 'the lower house was apportioned for the first and last time in 1793. The town of Victory, Vermont, 46 inhabitants in all, elects one state representative as does Burlington with 35,531 people.'[10] The malapportionment in state legislatures was also reflected in Congress, for the congressional boundaries are drawn by the state legislatures. Thus, Keefe and Ogul could again write of Vermont that 'on the basis of the 1960 census, slightly more than one half of the 52 "suburban" districts were under-represented . . . Almost one half of the 102 rural districts were over-represented'.[11] Against this background, the Supreme Court in 1962 reversed a previous stand against becoming involved in apportionment cases and ruled, in *Baker* v. *Carr* (which concerned Tennessee's failure to re-apportion since the beginning of the century), that federal courts must consider suits alleging malapportionment of state legislatures, on the grounds that malapportionment violates the 'equal protection' clause of the 14th Amendment. The way was now open to consider congressional as opposed to state districts and in 1964, in *Westberry* v. *Sanders*, the Supreme Court ruled that 'while it may not be possible to draw congressional districts with mathematical precision ... [the constitution requires] as nearly as is practicable one man's vote in a congressional election is to be worth as much as another's'.

Disputes over the right to vote have, then, largely been resolved, as have arguments over the relative value of those votes.[12] We shall now look at the opportunities which exist to exercise those rights; the frequency with which those opportunities occur; the decisions to which they relate; and the extent to which citizens take advantage of those rights.

Ever since the 1911 Parliament Act, Members of Parliament in Britain have been elected for a maximum of five years, although the Parliament which was elected in 1935 sat until 1945 because of the emergency of the Second World War. Whereas in the United States the constitution specifies a finite term in office, and the laws state the specific day of the election (the first Tuesday after the first Monday in November), in the United Kingdom the legislature may be dissolved at any time within that five-year period. While the power to dissolve Parliament rests constitutionally with the monarch it is now only exercised upon the advice of the Prime Minister who will usually seek political advantage by requesting a dissolution at a time that appears electorally propitious.

A British general election is a fairly simple affair which, compared with the United States, makes relatively few demands upon politician and voter alike. After a campaign of only about three weeks' duration, the voter is asked to indicate a preference among those seeking to represent the constituency in the House of Commons. Furthermore, unless a very active member of a party, the voter will have had no part in the candidate-selection process which is done largely in the privacy of party meetings, although recent changes in Labour party selection methods do provide for greater rank and file participation. Thus, having made this one decision, by putting a cross on a piece of paper, the voter's national civic duty is done until the next general election. As for the contenders for office, an election is generally not very demanding either upon their time or their wallets. There are no real costs attendant upon securing nomination such as those associated with the primary process in the United States, while the law puts strict limits upon the amounts which may be spent in a constituency to promote a particular candidate's campaign.

In fact, most candidates do not even approach this fairly modest legal limit. For example, in the 1983 election, when the average legal limit for county constituencies was £4,700 and for borough constituencies £4,200,[13] Conservative candidates spent on average only £3,320, approximately 72 per cent of the legal maximum, Labour candidates £2,927, or 63 per cent of the limit, while the Liberals were the most frugal, spending £2,282 on average, a mere 50 per cent of what was legally permitted. The grand total for all candidates of the Conservative, Labour and Alliance parties was only £5.55 million. In the same election, the parties' central organisations spent a total of £7,034,000,[14] of which £904,000 went as grants to constituencies. A British general election is, then, fairly inexpensive and of brief duration. It may, at times, if the personalities of the leaders do not spark it into life, be very dull. As one American observer commented: 'watching the British general election in the fall of 1959 was, for me, like being at a very dull football game . . . An option of Gaitskell or Macmillan thrilled like the choice between blancmange and sultana roll on the menu of a British Railway hotel.'[15]

Elections in the United States, on the other hand, are quite a different matter. On that first Tuesday after the first Monday in November every second year, following a long drawn-out campaign, which has officially lasted many months, the citizen is presented with an array of decisions to be made. While the British voter elects one Member of Parliament, the American may be casting votes for the Presidency (contested every fourth year), the Senate (a third retire every two years), the House of Representatives (all of whom retire every two years), all at the national level, and for a group of state and local offices which may be contested at the same time.[16] In addition, in many states the ballot papers may contain a number of propositions arising from state constitutional requirements[17] or from citizen initiatives, which call for decisions.

A recent ballot sheet for a Californian congressional district gives some idea of the demands made upon the conscientious citizen. Apart from the national posts, the offices to be filled ran from the governorship and lieutenant governorship down to local school boards. A number of judicial posts were on the ballot and, although uncontested, required an indication of approval or disapproval. There were, in addition, 15 propositions put before the people that year, ranging from proposed constitutional amendments to fund-raising bills; from hand-gun control proposals to a call for the state to petition the Federal government to enter into an agreement with the Soviet Union to halt the testing, production and further deployment of all nuclear weapons. In order that the voter might understand the issues involved in the propositions, a booklet of some 76 close-printed pages was provided, outlining the proposals and the arguments advanced by proponents and opponents. In all, there were 44 decisions to be made by the electorate in that district that year. Across the country, more than half a million posts are regularly filled at election time, and the election is only the end product of a process which earlier in the summer afforded voters the right to participate in the candidate-selection process, the primary.

The task confronting the American voter is patently much greater than that which faces the British elector, even though it may be eased by technology which permits straight party-ticket voting through the pulling of a lever on a voting machine. And candidates for American electoral office must look wistfully across the Atlantic at the low-cost, short-lived campaigns which determine who shall enter the House of Commons.

As electoral campaigns for national office in the United States are at three levels — for the Presidency, the Senate and the House of Representatives — and include two processes — the primaries, concerned with candidate selection, and the election proper — it is difficult to make generalisations about them beyond noting that they are spread over a longer period than in Britain, that, where comparison is possible, they are costlier, and that the focus on party is much weaker.

The most publicised election in America, and one that has no counterpart in Britain, is the national election of a chief executive. The campaign for the highest office in the land has now become a long drawn-out affair, with potential candidates jockeying for position two or more years before the election, and formal declarations of candidacy being made well in advance of election year. Thus, six candidates had formally announced their candidacies for the 1988 presidential election by the spring of 1987, and one of them, Gary Hart, had apparently destroyed his hopes by the early summer of that same year through some indiscreet activity with a young lady to whom he was not married.

The initial objective of the campaign is the securing of the party nomination at the quadrennial national conventions held in the summer preceding the November election. To that end the contenders create their own organisations with which they will campaign to secure the support of a majority of delegates to those conventions. The emphasis is very much candidate oriented.

The costs of such a long drawn-out and geographically wide-ranging campaign have grown to the point where the total presidential election costs in 1980 were estimated to be in the region of $250 million. Fortunately for the candidates, they do not have to find all the money. Since the Federal Election Campaign Act of 1974, Federal money has been available on a matching basis for candidates in the primary elections, and in the election proper those who eschew the use of privately donated funds may finance their campaigns from the Presidential Election Campaign Fund.

Generalisations about election to the Senate are not easy. First, there are the vastly different constituencies, in both population and physical size, for which the candidates contend. As an extreme example, the largest state, Alaska, is nearly 500 times larger than the smallest, Rhode Island. The most populous, California, has approximately 50 times as many residents as the least populous, Alaska. Population density ranges from more than 900 per square mile in New Jersey to fewer than 1, again in Alaska. All of these factors contribute to the nature of the campaign. Secondly, there is the political make-up of the state. If it is one in which one party is dominant, the most important part of the process may be the primary of the incumbent party. If, on the other hand, it is a state in which neither major party predominates then the primaries of both parties and the November election may be hard fought, with the attendant increases in costs. An average expenditure figure for a senatorial race would be something in excess of $1 million, but averages of course disguise distribution and some Senators may spend as little as a quarter of a million dollars while others spend many millions.

Most Representatives have smaller districts than Senators — in those states entitled to only one Representative the district coincides with the state boundaries — and their costs per election are usually a lot smaller. On the other hand, as the House term is only two years compared with the Senate's six, Representatives may well face six electoral contests (primary and November) for every two for Senators. As with the Senate, it is the highly contested districts which are likely to occasion the greatest expenditure. The average figure for House elections is in the region of $300,000.

While those seeking to enter Parliament are subject to strict limitations on expenditure (and their election accounts are subject to strict scrutiny) there is no limit to the amount candidates for office in the United States may spend on their campaigns. Further, the attempts to limit the influence of big donors on campaigns through the imposition of restrictions on campaign contributions (no individual may give more than $1,000, no organisation more than $5,000 to any one candidate) have been largely circumvented by the proliferation of PACs, Political Action Committees, which have sprung up in their thousands to act as conduits for the transfer of funds from backers to favoured candidates.

Thus, every two years Americans are accorded opportunities to select and elect leaders which far exceed the opportunities available to British voters. But when we look at the voting figures for the two countries, we cannot fail to notice that the British are far more ready to go to the polls than the Americans. In the 12 general elections between 1945 and 1983 the turn-out in Britain has ranged from a high of 84 per cent in 1950 to a low of 72 per cent in 1970, with the average being 76.6 per cent. In the United States, on the other hand, over approximately the same period, in the ten presidential elections between 1944 and 1984 turn-out varied from a high of 63.5 per cent in 1960 to a low of 51.6 per cent in 1948, with an average of 57.3 per cent. The average turn-out in the two countries differs by more than 19 per cent, and if we confine ourselves to the more immediate past, to the period since the 1970 British general election and the 1972 American presidential election, we find the averages have dropped to 74.4 per cent and 54.1 per cent respectively, a gap of some 20 per cent. Furthermore, if we look at the mid-term elections in the United States, when the Presidency is not at stake but when all of the seats in the House of Representatives and a third of those in the Senate are being contested, we find that since 1946 on average only 40.6 per cent of eligible Americans have voted for their member of the House of Representatives, and since 1970 that average has dropped to a little over 38 per cent. (In 1978 the figure was 35.1 per cent, the lowest since 1942.)[18]

For those who take the degree of electoral participation as some kind of measure of the political health of a society, these voting figures, particularly those for the United States, do occasion concern. While few would argue for the compulsory voting system of, say, Australia, many would like to see somewhat more involvement by citizens in the decisions as to who should fill the elective posts of the nation. Their argument is that the legitimacy of office-holders may be brought into question when an MP can be elected with fewer than 40 per cent of the votes cast; when a Congressman may be sent to Congress on a plurality in a 35 per cent turn-out; or when a President may reach the White House with fewer than 50 per cent of the votes in a 55 per cent turn-out.

There is no easy or single answer to the question of why so many voters fail to take advantage of their rights to vote. Rather, there is a mix of reasons, both institutional and psychological, which contribute to the non-voting phenomenon.

Without seeking to rank these contributory factors overall, there is fairly widespread agreement among commentators that, so far as the United States is concerned, the registration requirements associated with voting are probably the single most important factor behind the low turn-out figures. In the United Kingdom, the government takes the responsibility for ensuring that potential voters are registered. Heads of households or owners of residential properties are sent pre-paid reply cards on which they are required to enter the names of all those eligible who are resident on a particular day. If the card is not returned, an official will call to collect it. Minimum effort is thus required to be registered to vote.

In the United States, it is up to the citizen to take the initiative to ensure that registration takes place, and procedures vary widely from state to state. In some a visit to an office during working hours is necessary, in others, postcard registration is possible. In some states, local officials seem bent on making it difficult to register by providing too few locations and only opening them at inconvenient hours, while in others positive attempts are made to increase registration through the provision of mobile registration centres. One or two states permit election-day registration and in those states one discovers a significant increase in voting — to a level approaching the British, although still staying well below the figures for other parts of Europe.

In mentioning Europe, we should also draw attention to another factor which might well have a significant effect upon turn-out, the day of the week on which elections are held. The British persist with Thursdays, the Americans with Tuesdays, but those European countries with regularly high turn-outs go to the polls on Sundays. Robert Lane has gone so far as to suggest that to move election day to Sunday would have more effect on turn-out than any other single reform.

The nature of the electoral system itself should not be overlooked here. Both countries operate on a single-member constituency basis: only one person is elected in each contest. The British vote for one MP per constituency, the Americans for one Representative in any one election or for one slate of electors in the presidential election. Neither country employs the techniques of proportional representation in an attempt to allocate seats in the legislature in some rough proportion to the votes cast. Thus in areas more or less permanently committed to one political persuasion or another — and we should recognise that the large majority of seats in the House of Commons and the House of Representatives (between two-thirds and three-quarters) are generally safe for one political party, rarely changing party hands — supporters of the minority party or parties have little likelihood of ever securing direct representation of their own views. Further, when more than two political parties enter the fray, as is common in the UK, the situation can arise, as it did in the 1983 general election, where more than half the seats in the House of Commons were won with less than 50 per cent of the votes cast. In other words, the majority of voters, in a majority of seats, failed to secure a representative in Parliament. Any system which apparently condemns significant sections of many constituencies to permanent minority status is likely to act as a disincentive to voting. A system of proportional representation which introduced multi-member constituencies and thereby increased opportunities for the minority groupings in regions to secure direct representation of their particular viewpoints might well increase electoral interest and turn-out.

While PR could be introduced quite easily into the United

Kingdom, it would have only limited application in the United States. The fact that the Presidency is a single office and that the individual states only elect one Senator at a time means that those two elections are beyond the reach of a proportional system. Furthermore, six states return only one member to the House of Representatives and could not, therefore, adopt PR. It would certainly be possible to introduce a proportional system for elections to the House in those states which are entitled to several Representatives, but a number of factors which do not apply to the United Kingdom argue against it. First, the size of any multi-member constituency would be a strong argument against its introduction. The present average size of a Congressional District is about 600,000. A five-member constituency would therefore have about three million residents: even a three-member constituency would have 1,800,000. In addition, except in the smallest states, geographically, or the largest cities, candidates would have vastly greater areas to cover. Such a growth in numbers of electors to be persuaded and in territory to be covered would undoubtedly increase the effort and expenditure of the candidates. Finally, members of Congress elected from a multi-member constituency might well lose that sense of connection with a district that is now such an important part of their electoral strategy.

In addition to the institutional factors, other circumstances have a bearing on the electoral involvement of citizens. Many of the countries of Europe have been rent by a variety of internal conflicts — religious, linguistic, historic, geographic — which have provided fertile ground for the growth of numerous political groupings and for the encouragement of political involvement. The United States and the United Kingdom have largely been spared such disruption and its consequent degree of political participation. Apart from Northern Ireland, it is virtually 300 years since religion was a major factor in British politics and it has not been a significant element of the political scene in America since Independence. Religious groupings in both countries have, from time to time in this period, played some role in political life but they have not, apart from in Northern Ireland, become dominant actors on the political scene. Similarly, while nationalist movements do exist in the Celtic parts of Britain, and some Welsh and a few Scots cling to their traditional language, regional and linguistic conflicts, Northern Ireland aside, have not been in the mainstream of modern British politics. In the United States, it is possible to perceive areas of different culture and traditions but, again, these differences have not generally caused division or conflict. This last statement may seem a little strange at first in light of the massive regional conflict which took place in the United States in the middle of the nineteenth century. However, while for a century after the Civil War the South did display its own particular characteristics, especially in relation to the race issue — it practised segregation — and to the Republican party — it abhorred it — it is important to note that politics in the South was nevertheless conducted in the name of one of the major national parties, the Democrats. The South did, in one sense then, stay within the mainstream of the country's political life, but whereas in Europe strong regional loyalties may well have contributed to increased voting, the one-party system which predominated in the states of the old Confederacy tended to keep electoral participation low, as the significant process was that of selection, in the primary, rather than election.

Political life in both countries has been characterised by a general acceptance of the constitutional framework and by the absence of any significant movements calling for a radical overhaul of the system itself. Politics may no longer be concerned solely with capturing the middle ground, and political groupings may now be more distinguishable in attitudes than in the recent past, but the offering of a choice rather than an echo does not seem to have induced any greater electoral turn-out.

If these are factors which have a negative impact upon voting, what are the positive elements involved in getting people to the polling booths?

It is interesting to note that in this both the Americans and the British display very similar characteristics. Education is the single most significant factor in determining whether or not a person will vote: the higher the level of education the more likely the citizen is to go to the polls. Again, turn-out tends to increase with age, with those of middle or old age much more likely to vote than those under 30. Increased affluence is also associated with increased turn-out, although the rate of voting does not continue to increase as people get richer — the very rich do not have a greater proportionate turn-out than do the middle-income groups.

There is therefore a pattern in which the participating electorate is made up disproportionately of the most secure, socially and financially, within the two societies. The converse of this does, of course, reveal the weakness of the arguments of those who suggest that low turn-out figures are a sign of contentment among the electorate, for the poor and the less well-educated are among the more disadvantaged of the societies and are hardly the most contented within the systems.

Notes

1. Hanson, A.H. and Walles M. (1984) *Governing Britain*, 4th edn, Fontana, p.23.
2. The business vote, whereby owners of businesses had a vote in their places of business as well as in their places of residence, and the university vote, whereby graduates of 12 universities had a right to vote for university seats in Parliament, lingered on until their abolition in the Representation of the People Act of 1948.
3. Croty, W.J. (1977) *Political Reform and the American Experiment*, Thomas Y. Crowell, p.11
4. Chancellor Kent at the 1821 New York Constitutional Convention, quoted by Key, V.O. Jr. (1958) *Politics, Parties and Pressure Groups*, Thomas Y. Crowell, p.647.
5. Lane, R.E. (1965) *Political Life*, Free Press, p.13.
6. Croty, *op. cit.* p.21.
7. *Ibid.* p. 16.
8. Lane, *op.cit.* p.14.
9. In 1969 the Labour government objected most strenuously to the Commissioners' proposals, fearing that they would reduce the number of Labour seats.
10. Keefe, W.J. and Ogul, M.S. (1964) *The American Legislative Process*, Prentice Hall, p.82.
11. *Ibid.* p.77 fn.29.
12. Bearing in mind the anomalies associated with the 'Celtic fringes' in Britain and those enshrined in the American constitution with regard to the election of the President and to the requirement that each state have two Senators regardless of population.
13. Because of their greater geographic size, permitted expenditure in the county constituencies was £2,700 plus 3.1 pence per elector, as opposed to £2,700 plus only 2.3 pence per elector in the boroughs.
14. Conservatives £3,558,000, Labour £2,057,000, SDP £1,054,000, Liberals £375,000.
15. Liebling, A.B. (1962) *The Earl of Louisiana*, W.H. Allen, p.143.

16. In Britain, the election of local government representatives does not usually coincide with parliamentary elections.
17. For example, that amendments to the state constitution or the raising of money through bond issues should be approved by the electorate.
18. The differences between the two countries are not quite as great as these percentages suggest as the British figures are based on the registered electorate, while the American figures relate to the eligible population — a figure that includes many who have not registered to vote.

4

Political parties

If an election represents the means whereby power is peacefully transferred within a state, political parties are the agencies which, in varying degrees, give coherence to that process. Parties simplify the task of decision making for the voter. By adopting a party label, a candidate enters into a context to which the electorate, consciously or subconsciously, may respond. The context is one of past performance, as enshrined in a party's history, and of future promise, as embodied in its current election programme.

Today, the situation in the United Kingdom and the United States is one where the bulk of the electorate vote for candidates of political parties and where all the national elective offices are held by party representatives. Furthermore, within these two countries there has long existed a dominant two-party system in which one or other of two major parties has generally held power. In Britain, during the nineteenth and early part of the twentieth centuries it was the Conservative and Liberal parties, and for the last 50 years or so it has been the Conservative and Labour parties. In America since the middle of the nineteenth century the Republicans and Democrats have held sway. However, this persistent two-partyism, which imposes a superficial similarity upon the two systems, should not be allowed to disguise the fundamental differences which, as we shall see, exist in the objectives, operation and organisation of the different parties.

Political parties in Britain exist to capture the reins of power within the state. By this we mean that they seek at a general election to win the majority of seats in the elective House of the legislature, the House of Commons. To the party which secures such a majority goes the right to form a government and to have its leader created Prime Minister. The constitutional power this bestows is enormous for, constitutionally, Parliament is supreme and the party that controls Parliament may therefore wield supreme power for the period until the next election. The political prize at issue in a general election is then so great as to induce the parties to act as much as possible as relatively united, homogeneous organisations so that they may appear to the electorate to be capable of using wisely the power that is at stake. Political divisions within a party are thought to carry with them electoral liabilities and efforts are generally made to play them down as much as possible. This having been said, we must recognise that in this regard the two major parties have different histories. The Conservative party has generally managed to keep much of its internal wrangling away from the public eye while the Labour party has almost seemed to revel in exposing its divisions to the nation. Ultimately, however, the apparent electoral liability of the Militant Tendency led the Labour party leaders to expel the more vocal Militants from the party in an effort to persuade voters that it had purged itself of what the media were describing as the 'loony left'.

Just as the power of the state is centralised in Britain, so too are the parties that contend for that power. Pyramidal structures exist, with a national leadership supported by a broad-based membership in the constituencies. There is, thus, a two-way flow of communication — of advice, of warning, and occasionally of discipline. Party activity is co-ordinated throughout the country in the sense that elections are conducted along party lines and the party will basically speak with one voice. Thus national manifestos for the parties will provide the backdrop for the debate which will take place, with the constituency candidates advocating, and defending, proposals which will have been determined nationally. Failure to support the national line can lead to local parties and candidates being censured or even expelled from the party.

Such is the pervasiveness of the party 'ethos' in elections that many voters tend to vote for a party almost regardless of the quality of the candidate. The apocryphal 'I'd vote for a pig if my party nominated one' may not quite hold true, but the general approach does seem to be one where the voters tend to support a candidate because of the support they expect him to give to the party leadership. Independence of action is not what is usually sought in a parliamentary candidate, and it is recognised that constituency matters may well have to take second place to national interests if the two fail to coincide. An MP will naturally be expected to argue his constituency's case where appropriate, and party whips may even accept a 'deviant' vote if a strong constituency interest is involved — but only if the life of the government is not thereby threatened or jeopardised.

The emphasis of party politics in the UK is then essentially national: in the US it is primarily parochial.

Political parties in America, as W.D. Burnham has suggested, are 'not instruments of collective purpose but of electoral success'. So far as elections to the legislature are concerned parties do not act in a co-ordinated, monolithic fashion in order to secure majorities in the House of Representatives or the Senate. Campaigns are essentially local[1] and personal, based on the projection of the individual, not the party. The promises made are not about supporting a national programme so much as about doing something for the district or the state, and those who get to Washington, particularly to the House of Representatives, do so more as delegates or ambassadors than as representatives in the Burkean model.

During those years when the Presidency is at stake, genuflections are made in the direction of a rather spurious national identity for the parties. A desire to partake of the spoils of office, and perhaps of any electoral 'coat-tail' effect that association with a popular presidential candidate might bring, may rally people behind a national banner-carrier. But in recent years, as we shall see later, even this centripetal influence has been waning as presidential candidates, with their personal electoral machines making use of the latest media developments, have tended to operate more and more outside the regular party machine and have been elected despite, rather than because of, party label.

The party label has come to be seen by candidates for Congress as a useful trigger mechanism for attracting support from those who have a natural affinity for a party: it does not entail programmatic or ideological commitment. Neither does it involve the acceptance of direction or discipline from above, from some national leadership. The pyramidal structure of the British parties is noticeably absent in the American. As E.E. Schattschneider has written, the system resembles more 'a truncated pyramid'. At state and local level the party machines do possess authority but on the national scene 'there are visible only the transparent filaments of the ghost of a party'.[2] The national leadership of a party, such as it is, could not seriously contemplate censoring or disciplining a state party because of its politics or candidates. The local parties are independent, jealous of their autonomy and resentful of any attempts which might be made by any national representative to encroach on that independence.

The simplicity of the British system, unitary and with one elective chamber in which, effectively, all constitutional power resides, is undoubtedly an important factor in helping to cement together the coalitions that make up the major parties. The complexity of the American system, diffusing power as it does between a Federal government and 50 state governments, between President and Congress, and between the Senate and House of Representatives, does little to aid the development of coherent parties able to hold their ranks together in a crisis. Even when all three national elective components — President, House, Senate — are of the same party, there is no guarantee of co-operation, for the three elements represent three types of constituency. The Presidency (the term includes the Vice-President) is the only nationally elected office and the imperatives associated with election to that post differ greatly from those associated with either of the congressional contests. Even within Congress, the differences between the two Houses are significant. Senators, representing a complete state, sitting for six years and therefore free from the ever-pressing need to secure re-election, are able to adopt a more statesmanlike approach to the problems they face than are members of the House. The members of the House of Representatives, elected every two years and generally representing smaller areas and fewer people,[3] are more concerned with parochial matters which may affect their political survival.

Having pointed to this tripartite division within the parties, it is probably more useful to think in terms of Burns' characterisation of the system as one of four-party politics. In this the major distinction that he draws is between the presidential parties — those groupings associated with the tasks of winning the White

House — and the congressional parties — those having their being
rooted in state organisations.

When one allies the simplicity of the British system with the
relative smallness and homogeneity of the United Kingdom, and
the complexity of the American with the size and diversity of the
United States, and when one takes into account the greatly different constitutional arrangements of the two countries, it is not
difficult to understand why the respective party systems
developed in their own particular ways.

The British system of government, once centralised under
monarchs, developed slowly into a system centralised under
Prime Ministers and Cabinets. As democracy, in the form of the
franchise, spread it became apparent to the contending factions
in Parliament, Conservatives and Liberals, that the fruits of office
would be won through organisation of the newly-enfranchised.
Registration societies were therefore established to encourage
eligible citizens to register and vote — in the 'right way' — and
in 1863 the first party headquarters was created, the Liberal
Registration Association. The next 15 years witnessed a flurry of
activity which provided the fundamental framework of the
present party system. The National Union of Conservative and
Constitutional Associations, forerunner of today's National Conservative Association, was formed in 1867. Its task was to encourage the spread of associations throughout the country and
to offer support and advice. Three years later, the Conservative
Central Office, the party headquarters, was established. Finally,
the National Liberal Federation, a national organisation of the local
Liberal parties, was set up in 1877. Both the Liberal Federation
and the National Union held annual conferences, as the major
parties still do today, with the emphasis in the Conservative party
on the pre-eminent role of the national, parliamentary leadership,
while in the Liberal party the role and functions of the extra-
parliamentary leadership were given greater weight. Thus, long
before the emergence of the Labour party in the early years of
the twentieth century, there existed in Britain a fully-fledged
national, hierarchical party system, reaching down from a
parliamentary leadership to local organisations in the
constituencies.

I use the term 'reaching down' advisedly, for these first two
modern political parties in Britain were created as a result of

impetus from the centre — from Parliament — rather than from the constituencies. Politicians at Westminster sought to bolster their support in the country. The Labour party, on the other hand, was created from below, a creature of the constituencies and socialist groups that were seeking to secure representation in the House of Commons. The élitist creation of, say, the Conservative party was now matched by the more democratic creation of the Labour party. While their institutions are similar, being hierarchical in structure, the formal distribution of power within those institutions reflects the different origins of the parties. Indeed, as Robert McKenzie pointed out in *British Political Parties*, the titles of the different organisations give a clue to the attitudes to be found in the two parties: 'The term "The Conservative Party" applies strictly only to the party in Parliament; it is supported outside Parliament by its creation "The National Union . . . ". The term "The Labour Party" is properly applied only to the mass organisation of the party outside Parliament; it supports in Parliament a distinct and separate organisation "The Parliamentary Labour Party"'.[4] In the former case, direction is seen as stemming from the parliamentary leadership, with the extra-parliamentary organisation having a right similar to that usually ascribed to the monarchy, namely the right to be informed, to encourage and to warn. The proceedings at the annual conference of the party, modified though they may have been in recent years, do serve to illustrate the élitist approach that the Conservatives adopt. By and large the conference serves as a mechanism for demonstrating party loyalty. It has rarely been an occasion for strong criticism of its leaders: indeed, until Mr Heath's leadership, the leader did not even attend Conference proper, but appeared, after the conference had formally adjourned, to give an *ex cathedra* address which could not be debated. Today, the leader does attend and becomes involved in debate, but the feeling still persists that in large part this is a rally of the party faithful rather than a working meeting.

Within the Labour party the situation is, in some respects, quite different. There, the annual conference lays claim to be the policy-making body of the party. It is not regarded as an occasion for rallying round the flag and demonstrating support for the parliamentary leadership. Rather, it is often taken as an opportunity for demonstrating the divergent views which exist within the party and for providing the extra-parliamentary wing with the chance to assert itself as the master of the parliamentary party. There is often a real clash between the two sides — a clash which, although usually resolved in favour of the parliamentary leader, particularly when the party is in power, does impose certain constraints from which the Conservative party leader is generally free.

Although the constitution contains no mention of them, political parties came into being very early in the life of the United States. Indeed, as mentioned elsewhere, by the time he left office George Washington was warning against them. As with the first parties in Britain, American political parties had their origin in the legislature and their goal was the capture of the elective posts of the nation. While the single most important target was the Presidency, as Scott and Hrebener have pointed out,[5] the parties also endorsed candidates for Congress, the state legislatures and other state posts. In a haphazard fashion, for party growth varied considerably from state to state, the parties developed 'techniques for nominating candidates and persuading the citizens to vote for them'.[6] From the end of the eighteenth century until the mid-1820s, the congressional caucus nominated presidential candidates, but when Andrew Jackson and his supporters perceived in 1824 that the caucus would be no friend to his presidential ambitions, their boycott of the proceedings sounded the death knell of congressional domination and in 1832 the first National Convention was held for the purpose of nominating a presidential candidate. 'King Caucus', as it had been characterised by its enemies, was dethroned and replaced by a mechanism apparently more in keeping with the democratic ethos of the age. The next two decades saw the parties actively mobilising mass participation and often securing voter turn-out of up to 80 per cent of the electorate. Finally, the creation of the Democratic National Committee in 1848 marked the last stage in the emergence of nationally organised mass parties in the United States, some 20 years or so before they were to appear in the United Kingdom.

Since that time there has been only one fundamental change in the nature of party organisation in the United States, the introduction of the direct primary for the selection of party candidates. The convention system which had replaced the caucus came to be dominated by local party bosses and 'thoroughly corrupted as an instrument of democratic expression'.[7] Disillusionment set in, but while a number of local party organisations used the primary system for candidate selection during the latter half of the nineteenth century, it was not until the Progressive movement took hold, around the turn of the century, that the primary became a widespread tool for curbing 'boss' power. Austin Ranney described the primary 'as the most radical party reform in American history'[8] and he may indeed be right, for this democratisation of the procedure for selecting candidates has important implications for the nature of party politics in the United States.

It has been suggested that those who control candidate selection control the party and there is some truth in this observation, particularly when most seats in the legislature are safe for one party or another and when, therefore, selection is essentially election. However, the suggestion does have limitations, for should the power to select be spread too widely, control may disappear altogether. The two-party systems we are considering offer interesting and revealing contrasts in this regard.

In the United Kingdom, candidate selection rests firmly in the hands of local party members, generally local party activists, subject to a control only occasionally exercised by the national headquarters of the parties. Until the 1980s the differences between the Conservative and Labour party practices were interesting but not fundamental. In the case of a Conservative selection process would-be candidates may nominate themselves for a vacancy, which means that in a safe Conservative area the local party may have to face the daunting task of creating a short-list out of several hundred applicants. In the Labour party self-nomination is not permitted. Those who would be candidates have to be nominated by local party groups or organisations affiliated to the local party. This requirement of a prior endorsement reduces the task of the local party's general management committee considerably, as there may be only a dozen or so names put forward. Both parties maintain national lists of approved candidates to which the local parties may turn if they so wish. In the case of the Labour party there are two lists, one of which contains the names of candidates sponsored by the trade unions affiliated to the party and who will generally bring with them generous contributions from the sponsoring union towards constituency party expenses. When the local party has drawn up its short-list the candidates are inter-viewed by a selection committee. In the Conservative case, the procedure may be to put one name forward to a general meeting of the constituency association, which any paid-up member of the association may attend, or several names may be recom-mended, in which case the meeting will hear short addresses and may ask questions before itself deciding who should be the candi-date. In the Labour party, once the short-list has been drawn up, the general management committee, which is the governing body of the local party, will make the decision, without the involve-ment of the rank and file membership of the constituency party. In both parties, candidates must receive national party approval, which is usually forthcoming.

One point particularly worthy of comment here concerns the re-selection of candidates, particularly when considering the relative safeness of seats. Until the beginning of the 1980s, when the Labour party changed its rules, sitting members of the major parties were generally automatically re-selected at subsequent general elections. So long as an MP did not offend his local party notables too much the constituency was his fiefdom. The headlines made on those rare occasions when an MP was rejected only served to illustrate the security that went with most consti-tuencies. The Conservative party still operates in this fashion but in 1980 the Labour party adopted the principle of mandatory re-selection. No longer was the seat automatically safe for the sitting MP. Instead, during the lifetime of the Parliament the local party was required to conduct a proper re-selection process and con-sider the claims of others. While, as yet, the procedure has not led to many MPs being denied re-selection, a number have had to face bitter fights within their constituency and a number have retired from Parliament in order to avoid such fights. It is interest-ing to note that while these changes made Labour MPs more ac-countable it was accountability to party activists, not to the rank and file membership of the local party, and it has been estimated that in the first 206 re-selection procedures the average number of people involved was a mere 37. In an effort to democratise the party (and to lessen the influence of the far left) Neil Kinnock, the Labour party leader, sought to introduce a policy of one member one vote in the selection and re-selection of Labour candi-dates, for the rank and file party supporters are generally more moderate than the party activists. However, the 1987 Labour Party Conference, while broadening the base, stopped short of giving Mr Kinnock what he wanted. (I have only dealt with the two major parties but I feel it is worth pointing to the practice adopted by that newcomer to the British political scene, the Social Democratic party. In the SDP all paid-up members are involved in the selection process through a postal ballot.)

Most of the responsibility for the selection process in the two major parties has rested, then, with party activists, subject to national party approval, with the paid-up membership involved, when at all, at a relatively late stage in the proceedings. The bulk of the electorate which has not joined a particular party has no voice at all at this stage, and, to re-iterate the point made above, as the majority of seats are safe the mass of the electorate has little effective voice in determining who shall represent it in Parliament.

The system in the United States offers sharp contrast with that in the United Kingdom, providing as it does opportunities for the electorate at large to become involved in the selection process. (I describe it as a 'system' although 'systems' might be more appropriate as practices do vary from state to state. However, I shall concentrate on the most general and widespread practices.)

When Americans register to vote they may also register as supporters of a major party, or as independents. According to the state in which they live, this provides them with the opportunity to participate in some way in the primary election which will be held a few months before the November general election. There are basically two types of primary used for the nomination of candidates for office, although there are variations to be found. They are the closed and the open primary. In the closed primaries, voters must have registered as supporters of a particular party some months before the date of the primary. Such registration bestows the right to vote in the primary of the chosen party and to indicate preferences among the contending candidates for that party's nomination. In an open primary, voters may decide on the day which primary ballot they will take, Democratic or Republican. In three states the blanket primary allows voters to help select candidates of more than one party, although not for the same post, for example they may choose to indicate a preference among the contenders for the Democratic party nomination for Governor, and among the contenders for the Republican party nomination for Senator. In no instance does registration as a Democrat or Republican commit a voter to vote for that party in the election proper.

Candidates for office, then, are creatures not of a party organisation or of a party clique but of a much wider group of the electorate. In those states where the closed primary is used, one might suggest that it is party members who make the choice, but for those accustomed to a European style of party membership — more formal and where fees are paid — the informality of the American system is striking. The simple declaration at the time of registration, carrying with it no obligation for the November election, hardly constitutes membership in the generally received sense of the term. Indeed, the fact that some people register to vote in the primary of the party other than that which they regularly support, in an attempt to weaken the opposition by hopefully selecting a weak candidate, or in an effort to ensure the selection of an acceptable candidate, does attest to the weakness of the concept of 'membership' in the American context.

The tasks which face an aspirant for office in America are, as a result of the primary system, considerably greater than those which face those who seek a seat in the House of Commons. Instead of persuading a relatively small handful of party workers of their worth, candidates in the United States must persuade a much larger section of the electorate of their merit. This, of course, entails something which is largely lacking in Britain — canvassing for support. The British candidate at the selection level does not seek, openly at least, to gather support for his nomination in the constituency. Such activity would, in fact, be frowned upon. But American candidates, confronted by a much larger selectorate, are likely to be involved in a campaign of full-blooded electioneering. Indeed, in light of the security of most congressional seats for a particular party, the primary campaign, particularly in the dominant party, may well be more intense and more significant than the inter-party confrontation which will eventually take place.

While the primary fight occurs under the umbrella of the party label, we should remember that it is essentially a personal fight. Individuals, seeking the right to bear that label, create their own personal machines. They hire their own staff and raise their own finances. Those who succeed do so largely by their own efforts and the party label they eventually bear they have taken: it has not been bestowed by a party clique which could then make demands in return for the accolade.

Once the selection processes are over, the parties in both countries rally round their candidates, but, again, differences persist. In the United Kingdom the election campaign is national, with dominant figures in the party appearing in rallies around the country in support of one candidate or another. Through advertising, the parties are presented as national entities. The free time given on radio and television[9] stresses the role of the parties as potential governments. The local campaign is largely limited to billboards, handshaking meetings on the streets and at front-doors, and short speech making. At all times, the major emphasis is on the national programmes of the parties.

In America the situation has generally been the opposite of the British experience. Until the Republican party at the end of the 1970s sought to re-vitalise itself, it was almost unknown for a political party to undertake institutional advertising on any significant scale. Local candidates stressed local problems and offered their personal solutions. Through the extensive use of radio and television advertising, available to all who could afford it, the cult of the individual was engendered, not the spirit of the party. It was Bill Brock, Republican party chairman who took major steps to rebuild the party as a national entity. He broadened the party's national fund-raising base and 'put a political party on television with a year-long programme of institutional advertising modelled on that of the British Conservative party in the year before the Thatcher government's victory in the spring election of 1979'.[10] The national party became the largest single contributor for almost all Republican candidates in 1980,[11] although it is important to note that candidates receive a large number of contributions and the party, through its donation, is competing with a number of other donors for the candidate's ear and, indeed, his or her loyalty. Finally, in this effort to create a 'national' party, presidential candidate Ronald Reagan was persuaded, as Lipset points out, to work 'for the election of others on the ticket' and undertook 'along with Republican members of Congress and GOP[12] candidates' to support a programme if returned to power — almost a party manifesto in the British sense. Such a tactic will only work, however, when the presidential candidate is perceived to be popular with the voters and therefore likely to have a 'coat-tail' effect. At other times, when the presidential candidate is seen as a liability, candidates for other posts will seek to avoid association with the party's national banner carrier.

The recent Republican efforts to establish a national party do help to highlight another glaring distinction between the party systems in the two countries — the nature of the party leaderships.

The hierarchical, unified system of Great Britain provides an ideal climate for the relatively ordered emergence of a recognised and accepted leadership role. Party leaders emerge after an apprenticeship in the party ranks in the House of Commons, generally moving from the back-benches to front-bench responsibility before becoming leader. The parties have different methods of selecting the leader but all now use some form of election. Until the 1960s, the leader of the Conservative party 'emerged' as a result of discussion, and intrigue, among party notables. However, the rather unseemly struggle of 1963, which elevated Lord Home to the leadership, led to the adoption of rules for election which were first used in 1965 when the electing body, Conservative Members of Parliament, chose Edward Heath. For a large part of its life, the Labour party elected its leader through a ballot of the Parliamentary Labour Party (PLP), but this method, which excluded the non-parliamentary wing of the party from a voice, was heavily criticised and in 1981 an electoral college was established in which a role was given to the constituent parts. Representatives of the unions, the constituency parties and the PLP now form the college in the ratio of 40:30:30. In 1983 Neil Kinnock became the first leader to be elected by the college. Finally, the Liberals and the Social Democrats, now the Social and Liberal Democrats, elect their leader through a postal ballot of all paid-up members of the party.

Thus the British parties, in their different ways, have formalised the election of their leaders — leaders who are accepted as the principal spokesmen for their parties and leaders who are, in a sense, perceived by the electorate as symbolising their parties. Psephologists tell us that these leaders are not in a position to cry 'le parti, c'est moi' but the media, by concentrating on their utterances, certainly help to give that impression.

The situation in the United States is quite different. The fractured party system and the diffusion of power militate against the emergence of a clearly recognised party leader behind whom the regulars or the faithful can rally, although, as history demonstrates, Presidents with forceful personalities, faced with pressing problems, may for a time, be able to transcend these difficulties and emerge as strong party leaders.

Popular mythology may have it that the President of the day is leader of his party but Presidents are constantly reminded that they lead a motley group of barons, each with his or her own power base and each ready to accept leadership only to the extent that it coincides with his or her own best interests or perception of the nation's best interests. Indeed, more often than not, the leadership that the President provides is one that transcends party lines for he may well need the support of members of the other party if his policies are to be accepted. Thus, although he carries a party label and although the policies he pursues may be more readily identifiable as the policies of one particular party rather than another, there is a real sense in which, having attained office as a Democrat or a Republican, he becomes a national rather than a party leader. But even this does not quite capture the tenuous character of the President's position with relation to his party. With the spread of primaries and the personalisation of the campaign, the person who wins the party nomination and ultimately the White House may well do so without the active support of party regulars and party bosses. Indeed, the National Convention, once a brokerage gathering at which presidential candidates were selected after hard-nosed bargaining among those who controlled delegations, has now been reduced largely to a ratifying body giving a formal imprimatur to a decision reached as a result of contests fought elsewhere. And if the President is not the party's man, the sense of loyalty towards him may not be the same.

To add to the distinction which may be drawn between the American President and the British party leaders, we must also recognise the different paths to the top that exist in the United States. We have noted the fairly orderly progression through the ranks of the legislative branch of the party which precedes the emergence of a leader in Britain. In America, there is no one basic source of candidates, no necessary apprenticeship which must be served. Presidential candidates, as we discuss in the chapter on the Executives, come from a wide range of backgrounds, some highly political, others barely so. Thus during the twentieth century we have seen Cabinet Officers, state governors, Senators, Vice-Presidents, and a general all move into the White House. For some, politics has been a career, for others a deviation from a career elsewhere: in this latter category we can particularly cite Dwight D. Eisenhower whose first elective office was the Presidency, or Ronald Reagan who, although he had been Governor of California, had spent most of his adult life as an actor. This variety of backgrounds, with vastly different political experiences, has not been conducive to strong party leadership, particularly when leadership has to be attempted in the context of the American division of powers and separation of institutions. Ranking members of the President's party in Congress may challenge the presidential conception of what is best for party/ country, as may governors of states. And given their different constituencies and their different terms of office, such challenges can prove decisive.

However, having said all this, it is still possible in some sense to talk about the leader of the 'in' party — the party which controls the White House. For the 'out' party, the situation is quite different. In the period between the National Convention and the November election, the party candidate for the Presidency is usually perceived as the party leader, and the party usually rallies behind him. But the role is short-lived. The election lost, the candidate's authority, such as it was, dwindles and the party becomes leaderless. A number of people may well lay claim to speak for the party — ranking members of the House and Senate, influential state governors, rivals for the next nomination — but they will speak with many voices and none will carry the authority carried by the leader of a British political party.

Party organisation may, then, differ between the two countries and leadership may be of a different order, but in both systems politicians have to appeal to electorates. The appeals, as we have already indicated, are made largely in party terms and we turn now to consider what images the parties project and to which groups of voters they appeal.

It is of some assistance when trying to put the two party systems into context to employ the simple idea of a political continuum from left to right, with the Labour and Democratic parties on the left, the Conservative and Republican parties on the right, although in general terms it is probably true to say that the American parties are to the right of their British counterparts. The use of the device does help to suggest the natural centres of gravity of the parties, their sources of support, the type of policy they pursue.

In Britain, for some, the Labour party, with its origins in the trade unions and socialist societies, is seen as the natural party of the working classes, striving for greater equality and justice for the 'have-nots' of society. For others it is the party of excessive union power trying to impose an alien socialist creed upon an essentially conservative (with a small 'c') middle-of-the-road electorate. Conversely, the Conservative party is seen by some, including many from the working class, as the natural party of government, rooted as it is in the monied, landowning and managerial sectors of society accustomed to leadership, and by others as a party of selfish interests seeking to maintain the socio-economic divide between the haves and the have-nots. Memories and mythology help to perpetuate these images and thus to provide the parties with their hard-core supporters.

Memory and mythology can, however, only go so far in providing parties with the bases of support they need to attain power. As society changes so memories fade and new responses are demanded. The recent changes that have taken place in Britain have left the Labour party with a shrinking traditional base and faced by an electorate displaying more and more middle-class characteristics. In the last decade, for instance, trade unionists have declined as a percentage of the electorate from 30 per cent to 23 per cent and now only 42 per cent of that diminished percentage give their support to the Labour party. Of the middle-class trade unionists, who represent 10 per cent of the voting population, 37 per cent voted Conservative in 1987, while the rest were evenly divided between Labour and the Alliance. The policy of selling council houses, adopted by Conservative governments and acquiesced in reluctantly by the Labour party, has had political rewards for the Conservatives. Thus, in 1987, among working-class home-owners, the Conservatives had a 12 per cent lead, while Labour had a massive 38 per cent lead among council house tenants — as 65 per cent of the electorate are now owner-occupiers this large percentage is of a dwindling base. The 'embourgeoisement' of the electorate has continued with the spread of share ownership by the Thatcher government through the politically astute manner in which many state industries were sold to the public at large.

The Labour party of mythology now faces an electorate in which more than half are in white-collar jobs; in which more and more are now share-owners and in which nearly two-thirds are owner-occupiers. Such an electorate does not appear to relate to the old-style party or to its newer 'Militant' connections. Neither does the prosperous 80 per cent seem to have much sympathy with the 20 per cent who have been losers in the affluence rat race. The party still has its strongholds in Wales, Scotland, the North-East and the Northern industrial cities, but when political maps are drawn displaying seats held by the different parties the Labour party is shown to have virtually disappeared in the South. Gradually, many in the party are coming to recognise that unless they are to be merely the party of the 'Celtic fringe', of the declining Northern regions, and of minority groups who cannot deliver the votes for electoral success, they must adapt to the new realities. The Conservative party, on the other hand, can of course afford to be complacent in electoral terms. Its success in creating a large part of the electorate in its own new image — an image less of the shires and of 'noblesse oblige' than of the City and of speculation — appears to be paying political dividends.

Parties in the United States have had similar traditional areas of support, although it is important to distinguish between support for members of Congress and support for the President: in the latter case personality factors have often led voters to abandon their 'natural' party. The 'have'–'have-not' dichotomy is again in evidence, perhaps best encapsulated in Adlai Stevenson's election cry, 'Vote Democrat so you can live like a Republican', but historical factors do impinge to modify the picture. For instance, Southern 'haves' long supported the Democratic party, reputedly the party of the 'have-nots', because it was the Republican party that led the fight against slavery in the middle of the nineteenth century. In the North, many 'haves', descended from late-nineteenth-century immigrant stock, have remained with the Democrats out of loyalty to the party which had assisted the assimilation of their forebears into American life. These two factors have, in the past, combined to give a rather odd look to the Democratic party, with its support coming from minority groups, including blacks, Jews and Catholics, and white, Southern racists, often of fundamentalist religious belief: from those at the bottom of the socio-economic scale and from some close to the top. When we add to this the presence of those with low levels of education and those who make up a 'liberal intelligentsia', we can see some basis for Will Rogers' comment that he didn't belong to an organised political party — he was a Democrat. The Republican party, on the other hand, has demonstrated a greater coherence in the socio-economic backgrounds of its supporters who are mostly to be found among rural, small town and suburban Protestants, the professional classes and businessmen.

These loose confederations are not, however, static. They do shift, for each coalition has contained within it stresses that ultimately produce some kind of re-alignment. Thus Southern whites could persist in their rejection of the Republican party for so long as blacks had little voice in democratic processes and for so long as the Democratic party did not pursue policies aimed at ending the inferior status of blacks in Southern society. Once the Democratic party began to adopt a stance which would enhance the position of blacks, Southern whites began to vote more in accordance with their socio-economic status. The South became a two-party region once more. A harbinger of the change was seen in 1948 when Strom Thurmond left the Democratic party over its 'liberal' ticket, stood as the 'Dixiecrat' candidate for the Presidency and then joined the Republicans. In a similar fashion, conservative Catholics and blue-collar workers who have objected to the social liberalism of the Democrats on issues like affirmative action, abortion, school prayers, pornography, have moved to support the Republicans, while socially liberal Republicans have rebelled against the reactionary tendencies of the 'Moral Majority' forces in their 'natural' party and have moved into the Democratic camp. The two parties have, thus, in recent years moved 'in the direction of ideological consistency, with the Republican party becoming socially as well as economically conservative' and 'the Democratic party moving towards social as well as economic liberalism'.[13]

While neither country has a major party committed to radical change of the basic framework of government (despite, for instance, the Labour party's long-standing pledge to abolish the House of Lords) the major parties in the two party systems demonstrate wide — and widening — differences in approach to the problems of the two societies.

Verba and Orren have written that the Democrats and Republicans are 'divided most unequivocally ... on economic equality',[14] a statement which also applies to the Labour and Conservative parties, and this division is reflected in the emphasis placed on the various welfare and social security programmes of the two countries. Neither party of the right has repudiated such programmes, but both exhibit little sympathy for governmental approaches which would significantly alleviate hardship or which would provide greater opportunities for the improvement of the lot of the less advantaged. Indeed, in recent years both Prime Minister Thatcher and President Reagan have demonstrated more concern with controlling inflation than with maintaining jobs, with the consequence that unemployment has risen and inequalities have grown. Again, both parties of the right seek to reduce the involvement of government in the state generally, either through the sale of assets in governmental control or through the reduction of taxes and of funding for programmes for which the government had in the past taken some responsibility.

In foreign matters, all four parties are committed to international involvement in varying degrees, to membership of NATO and to military preparedness. In Britain, the Labour party differs from the Conservative by its rejection of nuclear weapons and its commitment to require the removal of American nuclear weapons from British soil, while in America the Democrats, with the tragedy of Vietnam in mind, are less keen than many Republicans on the kind of involvement that President Reagan and his advisers have been pursuing in Central America.

Interestingly, while the four major parties are, as we have suggested, more ideologically consistent and while they have moved from the 'me-tooism' of earlier years and now give the 'choice' for which Goldwater campaigned in 1964, rather than the 'echo' of which he complained, support for them, as we noted in the chapter on Representation, has dropped.[15] In the United States this has largely been manifested in an increase in the number of abstentions, but in the United Kingdom a drop in turn-out has also been accompanied by a switch to the Liberal—SDP Alliance. Thus, the Conservative and Labour parties, which in 1951 had received almost 97 per cent of the votes cast, attracted the support of only 70 per cent of those voting in 1983, although to the chagrin of the Alliance the two major parties, through the working of the electoral system, retained more than 93 per cent of the seats in the House of Commons.

A number of explanations may be advanced for this decline, but few neatly fit the situation on both sides of the Atlantic. In both countries a disillusionment with the system has arisen from its failure to solve the ills of the economy and of society generally. Thus, in Britain since the 1960s the economy has staggered from mini-crisis to mini-crisis; social services have deteriorated; unemployment has grown; the gap between rich and poor has widened, and the divide between the flourishing Conservative South and the declining Labour North has become greater. A short-lived burst of national fervour over the Falklands campaign may have helped re-elect the Thatcher government with an increased majority in 1983 but, as mentioned above, this was with fewer votes in both percentage and actual terms than in 1979.

In the United States over the last 20 or so years a number of policy questions have had similar disruptive effects upon party support. Perhaps the most traumatic of those issues was America's involvement in Vietnam. From the near unanimity of support for America's actions as demonstrated by the vote in support of the Gulf of Tonkin resolution, there emerged, over time, a society deeply divided between those who saw America's withdrawal as a betrayal and those who saw it as a final recognition of the immorality of the conflict. Barely had the war ended and President Nixon been re-elected with a landslide than another blow was dealt to the country's self-esteem and to its faith in its institutions. The revelations of Watergate which ultimately occasioned the resignation of the President helped induce an even more cynical attitude towards politicians.

The increased cynicism in the United States occurred at roughly the same time as growing use of the mass media turned party campaigns into candidate campaigns, and this personification of the political battle has meant that for many voters the parties now simply lack relevance to the political process. In many campaigns the political action committees, which have grown in number and influence since the days of Watergate, have already supplanted local parties as major campaign fund-raisers, and 'some observers, such as Fred Wertheimer of Common Cause, have even speculated that soon PACs will virtually dominate congressional campaigns'.[16]

The picture in the UK is somewhat different from that in the United States. While disillusionment with the major parties has increased and the numbers abstaining grown, the British have had a third party, the Liberals, for a short time the SDP–Liberal Alliance, and now two centre parties (the Social and Liberal Democratic Party and the Social Democratic Party), to which they could turn if they wished. Americans have had little alternative to the two-party conflict. (Occasionally, a strong third party candidate has appeared in the presidential race — Theodore Roosevelt in 1912, Robert La Follette in 1924, Strom Thurmond in 1948, George Wallace in 1968 — and state legislatures have now and then fallen to a localised, state party, but the general history is one of a bifurcated system with abstention the only alternative to voting Democrat or Republican, although of course we should not overlook the additional opportunities Americans have to participate through the primary system.) Furthermore, the hierarchical organisation of the parties in Britain has made it difficult for individual campaigns to be personalised, particularly as time on radio and TV may not be bought for the promotion of a political campaign. Groups, as we shall see in a later chapter, are very active on the British scene, but they are not effectively in a position, as are the PACs, to replace a local party organisation.

The Americans now have a system which is 'capable of expressing a wide diversity of viewpoints but is rather poor at aggregating them',[17] while the British aggregate certain interests very well but make it difficult for all of them to be adequately expressed. In the United States the result is legislative anarchy or a legislative vacuum while in Britain it is legislative dictatorship. In 1950, the authors of 'Toward a More Responsible Two-Party System' wrote that the situation in America 'favours a President who exploits skilfully the arts of demagoguery, who uses the whole country as his political backyard and who does not mind turning into the embodiment of personal government',[18] while in Britain, in recent years, warnings have been uttered concerning the emergence of prime ministerial government through party domination. As will be discussed in the chapter on the Executives, these warnings or prophecies have not yet come fully to pass, but the conditions which might occasion their emergence do still exist.

Notes

1. 'Local' may seem to be strange work to use for, say, a senatorial campaign in California, a state some 57 per cent larger than the whole of the United Kingdom and with a population of 25 million.
2. Schattschneider, E.E. (1942) *Party Government*, Holt, Rinehart & Winston, p.163.
3. When the population of a state is so small that it qualifies for only one Representative, then House and Senate constituencies coincide, as in Alaska, Delaware, North Dakota, South Dakota, Vermont and Wyoming.
4. McKenzie, R.T. (1963) *British Political Parties*, Heinemann, p.12 fn.2.
5. Scott, R.K. and Hrebener, R.J. (1984) *Parties in Crisis*, John Wiley, p.30.
6. Goodman, P. (1967) in Chambers, W.N. and Burnham, W.D. (eds) *The American Party Systems*, OUP, pp.72–3.
7. Croty, W.J. (1977) *Political Reform and the American Experiment*, Thomas Y. Cromwell, p.201.
8. Quoted by Scott and Hrebener, *op. cit.* p.155.
9. Time may not be bought but is rather allocated among the leading parties after discussions between the parties and the broadcasting authorities.
10. Lipset, S. (ed.) (1981) *Party Coalitions in the 1980s*, San Francisco Institute for Contemporary Affairs, p.11.
11. *Ibid.*
12. Grand Old Party — nickname of the Republican party.
13. Schneider, W. (1984) in Bogdanor, V. (ed.) *Parties and Democracy in Britain and America*, Praeger, p.120.
14. Verba, S. and Orren, G.R. (1985) *Equality in America*, Harvard University Press, p.134.
15. The point about ideological consistency cannot be taken too far, particularly in the United States where electoral imperatives are always likely to occasion policy shifts.
16. Wattenberg, M.P. (1984) *The Decline of American Political Parties*, Harvard University Press, p.109.
17. *Ibid.* p.129.
18. American Political Science Association (1950) 'Toward a More Responsible Two-Party System', *APSR* 44, supplement 3 number 3 part 2, p.94.

5

Legislatures

Both the British and American systems are characterised by bicameral legislatures in which the formal law-making authority of the nation resides and in which white, middle-class, middle-aged males predominate. Having said this we have said nearly all there is to say about what is common to both countries, for study of the two systems reveals much more contrast than similarity.

In Britain, the Lower House, the House of Commons, is popularly elected and is answerable to the electorate via general elections at least once every five years. While able to trace its lineage back some seven centuries, to times well before popular election was ever considered, the House of Commons, with its 650 members, is now truly a creature of the democratic age. This cannot, however, be said of the Upper Chamber, the House of Lords, which still stands as an anachronistic representative of times past. The Lords still draws the bulk of its membership of about 1,100 from the hereditary peerage, although the introduction, since the 1958 Life Peerages Act, of something like 300 life peers (whose titles die with them) has given the House a slightly more 'relevant' appearance. But the Chamber is still not electorally responsible to any one, and only the fact that its powers have been drastically curtailed (formalised in the Parliament Acts of 1911 and 1949) provides any justification for its continued existence within a representative and responsible system of government.[1]

Both American Chambers are elected and regularly answerable

to the electorate, although, as we have noted elsewhere, direct election of Senators did not come until the ratification of the 17th Amendment in 1913. The 435 members of the House of Representatives have two-year terms and all seats are contested every second year. The one hundred members of the Senate, on the other hand, are elected for six years, with one third retiring every two years.

Whereas in the United Kingdom one house, the Commons, is dominant, this is not the case in the United States. The House of Representatives and the Senate are virtually co-equal, although some would argue that the Senate's responsibilities with regard to treaties (which require senatorial ratification by a two-thirds majority) and to Federal appointees (who must be approved by a majority of the Senators), allied with the longer term of its members, give that Chamber a greater authority. Even the restriction that all bills for raising revenue must originate in the House is hardly a limitation as the Senate has full power of amendment as with any other bills.

The greatest differences between the working of Parliament and of Congress derive from two factors: first, the integration of powers in the United Kingdom and their separation in the United States; secondly, and more importantly, the nature of the party systems in the two countries.

/ In Britain, the executive branch, the Prime Minister and Cabinet, is an integral part of the legislature. Apart from the few ministers who sit in the House of Lords and who, therefore, do not face elections, the rest of the government, including the Prime Minister, are elected to the Commons as individual MPs for specific constituencies in just the same way as all other MPs. The Prime Minister becomes Prime Minister not because of a special decision by the electorate but as a result of a party process which has elevated one person to its leadership, and of a general decision by the electorate which has given one party a majority in the House of Commons. The leader of the majority is invited by the monarch to form a government and this is done by offering posts to members of the party in Parliament. Occasionally a non-parliamentarian is given a governmental post but it is expected that such a person should enter Parliament at the earliest possibility and thereby become responsible to Parliament. Two examples of this occurred in the mid-1960s when Harold Wilson appointed Patrick Gordon Walker and Frank Cousins to his Cabinet. To enable them to enter the Commons, two sitting MPs were persuaded to accept life-peerages, thus causing two by-elections. In the event, only Cousins was successful and Gordon Walker had to resign.

Government and Parliament, executive and legislature, are thus inextricably intertwined and interdependent, with the nature of the relationship determined by the operation of the party system. The government continues in office and pursues its policies for so long as it retains the support of its back-benchers in the Commons or until the Prime Minister decides that the time is propitious for a general election.

- In America, the executive and the legislative branches are firmly separated by the constitution, and the President is elected as a national leader from a nationwide constituency while members of Congress and Senators represent more 'parochial' regions. The terms of office of the two branches are determined by the constitution and are not dependent upon the maintenance of a supportive relationship between legislature and executive. Indeed, American political history is characterised by numerous periods in which the President of one party has faced a Congress comprising a majority of the other. In recent years President Eisenhower had six such years; the full eight years of the Nixon–Ford Republican Presidencies saw Democratic majorities in both Houses; and Ronald Reagan, while having a Republican majority in the Senate for the first six years of his Presidency, was confronted by a House of Representatives which was firmly Democratic. When this situation is allied with the weakness of party bonds observed earlier, we shall see that Congress behaves as an independent agency which responds to a variety of pressures, of which party and President are but two.

While both legislatures are organised in party terms, with positions of authority going to the majority party, the strength of party organisation in Britain is such that the House of Commons should be seen more as a legitimiser than a legislature: as a body that gives constitutional authority to proposals that have originated elsewhere — in the executive branch. On the other hand, the American Congress undoubtedly remains a legislative body in the full sense of the term. It is true that in recent years most major legislative proposals have, as in Britain, originated in the executive branch, but whereas the British government is usually assured passage of its bills in an acceptable, recognisable form, the American President can rarely depend on Congress accepting his proposals in just the form he desires: the legislature is a major force in determining the ultimate content of legislation./

The legislative process in both countries begins with the first reading, the formal introduction of a bill. After that, practices diverge. In Britain, most controversial legislation is first introduced into the House of Commons. Following the first reading is the second reading which is a debate on the general principles of the bill. In this debate, the government will explain its proposals and offer a defence to the attacks which will normally be made by the opposition. This is a set-piece confrontation in which both sides are talking less to each other than to the nation, and in which the parties are publicising their positions rather than seeking to convert fellow parliamentarians. The vote at the end of the debate signals acceptance (very rarely rejection) of the major proposals contained in the bill. It is usually very tightly whipped — the party whips do all they can to ensure that their members are present, and voting the party line. Such a vote is normally recognised as a vote of confidence and, should it go against the government, convention (though not always practice) has it that the government should dissolve Parliament and hold a general election to determine whether or not it still retains the confidence of the electorate.

After a successful second reading a bill is sent to a standing committee[2] for detailed consideration. This is an important opportunity to ensure that the bill actually says what it was meant to say. It is also an occasion for the introduction of amendments as a consequence perhaps of points made during the second reading or of approaches made by interested parties. And, of course, the opposition will usually be seeking to hinder passage as much as possible. An important point to note here is that the committee cannot make substantive changes to the general principles of a bill: these have already been approved by the whole House at the second reading. As the government always has a majority on the committees it can usually ensure that amendments it wants are accepted and those that it opposes are rejected, although on occasion party lines break down in committee and the government is defeated on an amendment: such defeats are sufficiently rare for them to merit headlines when they occur.

Unless a bill has been considered by a committee of the Whole

House, a procedure only usually employed for bills of some considerable importance, the committee stage is followed by a report stage when the whole House is given the opportunity to look once more at the bill, amended or unamended, and to move amendments itself, should it so wish. This is followed by the third reading at which debate may take place but no amendments may be moved. The vote at the end of this process represents the final acceptance or rejection of the bill by the House.

After the Commons has finished with a bill it is sent to the House of Lords where similar procedures are followed, although in the Lords the committee stage is taken on the floor of the House rather than in a standing committee. The power of the House of Lords is now strictly limited by the terms of the Parliament Acts, and should it wish to defeat a government bill the most it can hope to achieve against a determined government with a solid majority in the Commons is a delay of approximately one year. In practice it has avoided even this degree of confrontation and by and large in recent years has acted as an amending chamber undertaking work of a collaborative kind for which the House of Commons had too little time, and as a forum for general debate, calling upon the expertise of some of its distinguished members. In general, the amendments moved by the Lords have been of a constructive nature, acceptable to the government of the day, and at times the work the Lords have put into a bill has been considerable. Thus in 1986 the Upper Chamber made 581 amendments to the Financial Services Act, Britain's first comprehensive scheme of investor protection.

Having said this, however, we must recognise that the House of Lords does not automatically jump through the House of Commons' hoop. The Conservative governments of the 1980s have discovered that while the Second Chamber is also dominated by Conservatives it has a mind and a dignity of its own and is jealous of its right to be treated with some respect. Thus the Lords have been antagonised by a government demanding speedy action on bills which had been little debated in the lower House because of the use of the guillotine motion to curtail debate. Furthermore, the government was accused of legislating 'on the hoof', producing badly drafted bills which the Lords had then to put into reasonable order. In all it was estimated that by November 1986 the Lords had inflicted more than 100 defeats on different parts of Thatcher government bills, and had also forced the government into a lot of negotiations to prevent further defeats. A few examples will serve to demonstrate the influence of the Second Chamber in recent years. The Lords insisted on adding wide consultation rights for workers in the Dockyard Services Bill; on giving local councils the right to decide if elderly tenants can buy council houses; on making all health service undertakings, not just hospital kitchens, subject to prosecution under health and safety laws in the NHS (Amendment) Bill; on the abolition of caning in the Education Act.

When both Houses have approved a bill (or just the Commons if the terms of the 1949 Parliament Act have been invoked — a procedure that has not yet been necessary) it goes to the monarch for the Royal Assent, which has not been denied since 1707.

So far then as major bills are concerned, the whole British legislative process is very ordered. The firm hand of party control is ever present and the legislation which emerges is very much the legislation that the government wants. Party loyalty, a readiness to toe a party line, are the hallmark of the Commons. This contrasts starkly with the procedures in the United States Congress.

In America, after a bill has been introduced into the House it will generally be assigned by the Speaker to an appropriate standing committee. It is quite common practice for a similarly worded bill to be introduced into the Senate at the same time, and it too will be assigned to a committee by the presiding officer — the Vice-President or the President *pro tempore*. These committees, unlike the British, are true standing committees and are also specialised in nature. In the House they are: Agriculture; Appropriations; Armed Services; Banking, Finance and Urban Affairs; Budget; District of Columbia; Education and Labor; Energy and Commerce; Foreign Affairs; Government Operations; House Administration; Interior and Insular Affairs; Judiciary; Merchant Marine and Fisheries; Post Office and Civil Service; Public Works and Transportation; Rules; Science and Technology; Small Business; Standards of Official Conduct; Veterans Affairs; Ways and Means. A similar, but slightly more limited, list exists in the Senate. The use of committees is central to the work of the legislature and they are vitally important to Congress in its attempts to deal effectively with the huge number of bills introduced in each session — an average of 13,000 or so in recent sessions.

Most bills when referred to committee simply die there. Committee chairmen decide whether or not a bill is worthy of consideration and, if it is, whether or not it will be considered by the full committee or by a sub-committee. If it is decided to proceed with a bill, hearings will usually be held to which interested persons will be invited to give evidence or to express opinions. At such meetings, representatives of pressure groups or government departments are likely to predominate, although private citizens may also be present. The committee may question witnesses and it may, further, call for the submission of written evidence concerning the bill. Following the hearings the committee will proceed to consider the bill in detail and probably make a number of amendments before agreeing on a final form. (If the bill was originally dealt with by a sub-committee, it is reported back to the full committee which may itself decide to hold further hearings and make other amendments.) If the bill is ultimately reported out of committee, in whatever form — and most die, unconsidered, in committee — it will usually go to the Rules Committee which stands 'as a strategic gateway between the legislative committees and the floor of the House'.[3] Ranking members of the committee which reported the bill will appear before the Rules Committee requesting that it issue a rule permitting the bill to be brought to the full House. Should the committee act favourably, and it may well hold a full set of hearings itself before so acting, it will issue a rule specifying the length of the debate which may be held and the type of amendment, if any, which may be moved. The rule itself must be accepted by the House and this is generally a fairly automatic procedure, although on occasions it may be challenged for strategic purposes, usually with the aim of killing the bill.

Debate on the bill will be controlled by floor managers, usually the chairman of the committee which reported the bill and the ranking member of the minority party or grouping on the committee. They control the time of the debate which is evenly divided between the proponents and opponents, and allot it to those who wish to speak. If the House votes to accept the bill, and most which reach the floor are accepted, it is sent to the Senate for similar consideration, although in actual practice the

Senate may well have been dealing with its own version of the bill at the same time as the House was deliberating.

Procedure in the Senate is similar in many respects to that in the House except that the relative smallness of the body has meant that the processes are generally more relaxed. No rules committee guards the 'gateway' to the Senate Chamber. The Senate timetable is set by agreement among the senior members of the two parties and debate is not strictly limited as in the House but continues until Senators have finished speaking. This freedom of speech does introduce a potential barrier to a bill's progress — the filibuster, whereby a group of Senators may endeavour to talk a bill to death by refusing to allow it to be brought to a vote. Debate may only be curtailed if 60 per cent of the membership vote in favour of closure. In the past the filibuster proved a particularly effective tool in the hands of Southern Senators seeking to prevent the passage of Civil Rights legislation aimed at improving the conditions of blacks in society.

House and Senate versions of a bill must be identical before they can be sent to the President, and it is rare for this to be the case in anything but minor, relatively non-controversial bills. Generally, discrepancies exist and when they are incapable of resolution through informal consultations and negotiations between the Houses, or through the acceptance by one House of the amendments made by the other, a bill must face another hurdle in the form of a conference committee. This committee, comprising members from the two Houses — usually ranking members of the committees which originally dealt with the bill — will endeavour to produce a version of the bill which will be acceptable to their respective Chambers. At times this can involve a considerable re-writing of the bill. When the Conference committee has produced its agreed version, the bill is returned to the two Houses for debate and vote. If the bill is not now acceptable to either House it is lost.[4]

The final step before a bill becomes a law involves the President. All bills must be sent to the President for signature. He has four options. He may sign, and they become law; he may veto — return them to Congress with his objections — and it then requires a two-thirds vote in both Houses if they are to become law; he may fail to sign and they become law after ten days, Sundays excepted; finally, he may fail to sign and if Congress should adjourn within that ten-day period they are lost. This last is known as the 'pocket veto'.[5] The reason a President may allow a bill to become a law without his signature is that he may object to it, or some of its provisions, but not wish to carry that objection to the point of a veto which might be politically unpopular. It is relatively uncommon for a presidential veto to be overridden (it being difficult for Congress to muster the necessary votes) and the threat of a veto can therefore be a potent weapon in the presidential armoury.

What is noticeably lacking in Congress in comparison with Parliament is the sense of direction given to a programme. In Parliament, the majority party leadership controls the timetable of the House of Commons and ensures that its proposals receive full consideration and then full support from its back-benchers. Party loyalty — some would argue party discipline — dominates most of the legislative activity of the Commons, arraying the supporters of the government against the supporters of the other parties in the House. While, from time to time, some members may ignore the party whips and abstain on a vote, it is rare indeed for dissent to be taken to the point of actually voting with the other side. Parliament operates in a confrontational fashion — a fashion emphasised by the seating arrangements with the government party facing opposition parties across a gangway, symbolically two sword-lengths wide (a reminder of more fiery times). The spirit of party is everywhere.

Whereas power in Parliament is centralised through the operations of a strong party system, power in Congress is dispersed. No party leadership in Congress is able to dominate its followers in such a way as to be able to command their support. While a sense of party loyalty may be the single most important factor in influencing the way in which a member of Congress votes, other factors often intrude and party leaders seeking to build a majority for a particular position on a bill have to resort to tact or persuasion (occasionally threats or promises) to win support. The power to command barely exists in institutionalised form. Those leaders who have been effective, like Johnson or Rayburn, have achieved their authority through their ability to put together bipartisan coalitions. We have already noted how rare it is for a British MP to break the party line: statistics demonstrate just how different is the situation in Congress. Party unity voting studies in Congressional Quarterly Almanacs, as reproduced by

Davidson and Oleszek[6] show that in the 20 years 1960–80 the percentage of time that the average member of Congress or Senator voted with his or her party majority in partisan votes varied from a high of 70 per cent down to a low of 59 per cent for Republicans, and from a high of 69 per cent down to 57 per cent for Democrats. To those brought up with the British system of party voting, this lack of party loyalty is at times bewildering. In fact, these percentages hide even greater deviations by some individuals from the party line. Thomas 'Tip' O'Neill, a House Speaker, is recorded as saying, 'We have ten fellows who haven't voted with us 10 per cent of the time.'[7]

In place of party government, the Americans have what Woodrow Wilson, as long ago as the 1880s, described as 'government by the chairmen of the standing committees of Congress'.[8] Were he writing today he would undoubtedly expand his comment to include the chairmen of the sub-committees, for they too are acquiring the kind of autonomy and freedom of action that has in the past characterised the actions of the committee chairmen. Chairmen generally emerge as the result of the operation of the seniority system, the post going to that member of the majority party with the longest uninterrupted service on the committee: it is not a reward for loyalty to party leaders. Reforms by House Democrats in the early and mid-1970s, providing for election of chairmen by party caucus, put an end to the automatic working of the seniority rule and in 1975 three chairmen who had used their power in an autocratic fashion were voted out. However, seniority is still largely recognised and few are denied the post they would have occupied had the old system been retained. Nevertheless, the reforms have had the effect of making chairmen more amenable to the wishes of their committees. Furthermore, a Democratic caucus decision that no member could chair more than one legislative sub-committee has opened up a large number of chairmanships to relatively junior members.[9] Thus, Charles O. Jones could write in 1982 that in the 96th Congress 55 per cent of House Democrats were chairmen of one or more of the 22 standing committees and their 148 sub-committees, while in the Senate all but one of the 59 Democrats was a chairman. In the next session, when Republicans had secured a majority in the Senate, all 53 Republicans chaired one or more of the 15 standing committees or their 90 sub-committees.[10]

This 'democratisation of decision making', producing, as it has, 'countless power centres', has made it much harder for party leaders to organise Congress for decision-making purposes. 'The "party principle" organises Congress. But the "committee principle" significantly shapes most issues ... These two principles are often in conflict. The first emphasises integration, the second fragmentation.'[11] For with so many generals, who can command the army? The brief answer to this question is 'no one'. Each of the chairmen — of committee or sub-committee — has his own little fiefdom where his authority is significant, although by no means absolute, and party leaders, as we suggested earlier, have to negotiate with these 'barons' to secure their objectives.

Such party leadership as does exist in the House of Representatives comes, for the majority party, from the Speaker, the majority leader and the majority whip. The Speaker, the presiding officer of the House, is elected by the majority party caucus or conference and then ratified in the post by a vote in the full House. Unlike the Speaker of the House of Commons who, once elected to the post by the House, acts as an impartial chairman and continues to serve even when the party complexion of the government changes, the Speaker of the House of Representatives will use his position at times to advance party ends and will lose the position if his party loses its majority. While he is no longer the force he was in the early years of the century, when he appointed all committee chairmen and controlled the timetable of the House through his domination of the Rules Committee, his role in assigning bills to committees and his influence with regard to committee assignments, when allied with the formal authority of presiding over the House and the natural advantages that brings, still make him a formidable figure. But, as Davidson and Oleszek have written, 'his success rests less on formal rules than on personal prestige, sensitivity to member needs, ability to persuade, and skill at mediating disputes'.[12]

The next most important figure in the hierarchy is the majority leader, a kind of second-in-command to the Speaker and, in the case of the Democratic party, his natural successor. The majority leader has the task of managing the legislative agenda, 'working closely with committee chairmen, paying close attention to the flow of business from the committees'.[13] He also works closely with the party whips who will keep him informed of opinion within the party on particular legislative measures and who will help him with the task of trying to create majorities for bills. Again in contrast to the United Kingdom, the whips carry no effective sanctions. In the past, members of Congress have on occasion been denied a committee assignment or been stripped of seniority for disloyalty, but by and large threats cannot be made and persuasion and argument are the only weapons that can be used.

The minority party has a similar hierarchical structure, except of course it does not have the Speaker as its head. This role goes to the minority leader who is seen as a spokesman for his party and who attempts to organise opposition to the majority programme.

In the Senate the presiding officer, from the constitution, is the Vice-President of the United States. In practice, for most of the time the president *pro tempore,* by custom the most senior majority party member in terms of years in the Senate, will preside. Unlike the Speaker of the House, however, the presiding officer of the Senate does not wield much political influence. The positions of power in the Senate are those of majority and minority leader, although as Davidson and Oleszek wrote of the Speaker, the extent of that power is much more dependent on personal ability and prestige than on formal rules.

With strong party leadership in one system and weak leadership in the other, the effective roles that individual legislators may play offer interesting contrasts.

We have already suggested that in Britain a primary role of Parliament is to sanction policies which have originated elsewhere, and for some commentators the toeing of a party line is the only useful function that an MP performs. Undoubtedly, giving support to the party provides for the stability of government and the placing of responsibility, which are major characteristics of the British system: a government assured of the majority necessary to enact its programme can ultimately be held responsible for the success or failure of that programme. But the suggestion that an MP's role is limited to a knee-jerk loyalty to party leaders is a blinkered 'lobby-fodder' analysis which ignores those functions of representation of constituency interests and of oversight of government activity that are also fundamental to government in the United Kingdom.

Two basic elements are subsumed under the heading of 'representation' in the House of Commons. There is, first, that which relates to party. Nominated by a party organisation, elected on a party ticket, pledged to a party line, the Member of Parliament represents his constituents in one sense by accepting the constraints of party membership and by supporting the leaders the voters expect him to support. Secondly, there is that which relates to individual constituent and constituency interests. MPs are the target for a wealth of correspondence asking for assistance with this, advice on that, support for something else. A recent estimate suggested that on average MPs receive more than 10,000 letters a year. Most concern housing and social security matters, but they may also include proposals of marriage and even death threats. For some MPs, handling constituency problems represents the bulk of their activity in the Commons and they acquire reputations as 'good' constituency MPs. But all, even those with ambitions to reach the front-benches or those already there, will be faced with such individual problems. These may be handled in a number of different ways. If the problem involves a particular ministry, the MP may refer the matter directly to the appropriate civil servants for comment and perhaps action. If this does not produce a satisfactory response, the minister may be approached personally on the matter and should this not have the desired effect a question may be asked in the House. Four days a week the activities of the House begin, apart from prayers, with a session of questions directed to the government. The questions are of two types, those for which an oral reply is requested, and those for which a written reply is all that is sought. Oral questions are now more geared to political point-scoring than to eliciting information and action, and it is in written replies that one may find the serious role of questions retained. Alternatively, the MP may seek to have a matter discussed as the subject of the half-hour adjournment debate which closes each day's session. Since 1967 an MP has also been able to refer any matter for which a government minister is responsible to the Parliamentary Commissioner for Administration, the Ombudsman, who is authorised to investigate any complaints of maladministration and to report the findings to the MP and to the agency involved.

Just as we may consider 'representation' in party/non-party terms, so oversight activities may be similarly divided. In the first instance, there are those occasions when, in debates either on bills or on motions brought before the House by the government or the opposition, the government is required to explain and defend its actions. Conducted in party terms, with the whips on if a vote is to be taken, these debates do not usually occasion any change in government thinking or activity, but they do help to publicise what the government proposes and what alternatives the opposition offers. Casting light in this manner is undoubtedly valuable, but that value is nevertheless limited by the rather general nature of the debate and by the demands of party loyalty. Fortunately, other opportunities exist for MPs to exercise their oversight functions in a more detailed and more apolitical fashion. The vehicles for this activity are the select committees.

Select committees, which may be concerned with the scrutiny of a particular government department or of a particular sector of government responsibility, have a long, if chequered, history in Parliament, but it was not until 1979 that a serious effort was made to systematise their work. Prior to that date, scrutiny of executive action was undertaken in a piecemeal fashion by a limited variety of committees.

The oldest of those committees, and still operating today, is the Public Accounts Committee which, stressing the bipartisan approach of its work, is always chaired by a member of the opposition. Dating back to the nineteenth century, this committee has been concerned with oversight of government expenditure, and reporting if money has or has not been spent as Parliament intended. In 1983 its remit was extended to permit it to 'consider the efficiency and effectiveness of the expenditure'.[14] Two other committees worthy of note, which were disbanded when the 1979 system came into effect, were the Select Committee on Estimates (after 1971 the Select Committee on Expenditure) and the Select Committee on Nationalised Industries. The former, which was concerned with economy and efficiency in the departments, was also 'an instrument of general administrative review and scrutiny, and a major source of information about how the departments operate'.[15] In 1971 it was given the power 'to examine projections on public expenditure and to consider the policies behind those projections'.[16] The latter, the Committee on Nationalised Industries, concerned itself with the reports and accounts of the separate industries and produced a number of in-depth studies of different aspects of policy and administration. Despite the fact that these committees were often involved with potentially contentious matters, both prided themselves on the fact that their work was carried out in a non-party-political fashion.

The major change in, and extension of, the select committee system which took place in 1979 had been preceeded by some half-hearted attempts in the 1960s to give the Commons greater scrutiny powers. Select committees on Agriculture, Science and Technology, Education, Overseas Development, Scottish Affairs, and Race Relations, were established as the result of impetus from Richard Crossman when he was Leader of the House. Hostility from civil servants and from some MPs effectively put a stop to the development for a decade or more. Eventually, in 1979, after a recommendation from the Select Committee on Procedure, 12 committees were established to scrutinise the work of government departments. These were: Agriculture; Defence; Education, Science and Arts; Employment; Energy; Environment; Foreign Affairs; Home Affairs; Industry and Trade; Social Services; Transport; Treasury and Civil Service. In addition, select committees were established on Scottish Affairs and Welsh Affairs. It was at this time that the functions of the Expenditure and Nationalised Industries Committees were transferred to the appropriate new committees.

With power to hold hearings, to question ministers and civil servants,[17] and to receive documents, these committees have greatly increased the potential for parliamentary scrutiny of the executive. Membership roughly reflects party strength in the full House but emphasis is very much on scrutiny, on oversight of the executive by the legislative branch rather than on the party political divide: this is perhaps attested to by the fact that half of the committees are chaired by members of the opposition. Indeed, most committee reports reflect a degree of cross-party consensus at times surprising in light of the controversial nature of some of the subjects investigated. (We should note, however, that not all committees have adopted the same approach and some, like Employment for instance, have achieved a high level of consensus by deliberately avoiding areas of potential conflict.)

This still relatively new select committee system represents the most significant move in recent years to improve the opportunities for the House to monitor the activities of the departments of state, but, while many MPs may clamour to be appointed to the limited number of places, the full potential of the committees has still to be realised. They suffer, first, from the same tight-fisted approach which keeps MPs poorly housed and under-staffed. A full-time clerk, a committee assistant and a secretary, plus some temporary advisers barely stand comparison with the army of personnel which services an American committee, although this comparison cannot be taken too far for, as we have seen, the American committees perform considerable legislative as well as oversight functions. Nevertheless, the fact that some 20 committees have to fight among themselves for a share of the mere £343,000 allotted for travel each year speaks for itself. Secondly, there is a niggardly approach to time, for, with only three days given for debate, few reports are ever fully discussed in the House. A major advance would be the automatic provision of sufficient time for debating, if not for all of the reports then at least a representative sample from each of the committees. After all, committees which attract so much attention from the media and from groups eager to testify before them have surely reached a point where they are worthy of a proper hearing in the House of which they are a part. However, a major obstacle arises from the fact that, while these committees have largely acted in a non-party-political fashion, they have not been averse to criticising aspects of policy, thereby embarrassing, although in no way threatening the existence of, the government. Governments so embarrassed are unlikely to look with favour on suggestions geared to strengthening committees or increasing their exposure.

While the pursuit of constituents' grievances or work on a select committee may well occupy a great deal of an MP's time, in the final analysis such activity is regarded as ancillary to the fundamental obligation to support the party. In the United States, while party membership provides a natural starting point for action, ultimately it may well take second place to activity related to committee and constituency pressures.

Parties, as we have seen, are the vehicles by which members of Congress and Senators reach Congress but, as David Mayhew has argued,[18] once elected it is the pressures for re-election which colour congressional activity. In pursuit of such re-election, Mayhew points to three basic kinds of activity in which members of Congress indulge. There is, first, advertising or self-promotion. By adroit use of the generous postal facilities available to them, or through assiduous attention to district or state activities, members can ensure that their names are ever before the voters. Recognition is important if challenges for re-nomination or re-election are to be fought off. Secondly, there is 'credit-claiming'. This is members of Congress pointing to what they have managed to get for the district (for example, in the form of Federal contracts, or jobs, or relief) and what they have managed to do for individuals in their case-work capacity — in their 'ombudsmanic' role. This case-work activity is regarded as vital by members of Congress for they believe it plays a large part in securing their links with the voters. For this reason Congress has consistently refused to act on the numerous proposals that have been made to introduce a Federal ombudsman into the United States. In terms of overall efficiency and of procuring better operating methods, the office would indeed be beneficial but, in severing essential links between members of Congress and their districts, it would weaken their claim to the support or gratitude of the electorate. Finally, there is position taking — 'the public enunciation of a judgmental statement on anything likely to be of interest to political actors'.[19] Position taking is unlikely to bring any direct benefit to constituents but it establishes in their minds an image, however hazy, of what the Representative stands for. The clever politician is able to do this so effectively that he or she manages to minimise hostility to that image.

Naturally, not all members of Congress indulge in all these activities to the same degree, but few can afford to ignore any one of them entirely. In the House, with its more frequent elections and generally more compact electorates, 'credit claiming' would appear to be of particular importance, and one of the most important channels towards achieving that end is committee membership. Members generally seek appointment to a committee which will enable them to help their constituents and hence themselves. Thus people from farming communities seek the Agriculture committee; from the cities, Banking, Finance and Urban Affairs; from the far West, Interior and Insular Affairs. Not all secure the committee position they most desire, but generally, from the position of authority they acquire with their membership of almost any committee, they can indulge in the kind of horse-trading — log-rolling — which will bring benefits to their community. As their seniority on a committee increases so does their opportunity to make better 'deals', and eventually their seniority will become a campaign issue in itself, as a demonstration of what can be achieved as compared with a freshman member. Senators, with their longer terms and more diverse electorates, while not eschewing credit-claiming are in a position to adopt more statesman-like approaches to problems. They may acquire a national reputation for an expertise not directly related to the state they represent but which nevertheless keeps the voters loyal. For many years Senator William Fulbright's chairmanship of the Senate Foreign Relations Committee kept him in the national and international limelight and as Senator from Arkansas. Even such renowned Senators, however, must be careful not to antagonise dominant opinion within their states.

With a total staff of more than 31,000, it might be thought that Congress was admirably suited to the twin tasks of investigation and oversight. In fact, its record in this regard is very chequered. At times, as with investigations into the munitions industry, monopolistic practices, crime, the Vietnam War or Watergate, creditable work has been accomplished. At others, as with the House Un-American Activities Committee or Senator Joseph McCarthy's infamous Government Operations Permanent Investigations sub-committee — with their head-line grabbing, red-baiting activity — considerable harm has been done to the image of Congress. As for oversight of the vast bureaucratic machine, while most members of Congress 'believe that systematic oversight ought to be conducted', 'systematic, all-inclusive oversight is simply impossible to perform'.[20] With the notable exception of the work done by the sub-committees of the House Appropriations Committee, much of what is done is performed in a largely haphazard, non-programmatic fashion. It does not have political sex-appeal, and offers little electoral reward to members of Congress in return for time-consuming, detailed and often tedious work. With their multiple priorities, members concentrate on those activities which more obviously relate to their constituents' interests and their own electoral hopes.

If Congress does not perform the investigative and oversight functions as well as it might, this is in no small measure a reflection of the fact that both Houses are better organised (if that is the word) for obstruction rather than promotion. The dozens of overlapping jurisdictions among the committees and sub-committees provide numerous opportunities for affected interests to delay or prevent action. Jurisdictional jealousies, fear of losing pieces of empire, contribute to the tardiness with which Congress acts on so many matters — a tardiness which led columnist David Buckley to comment: 'it is widely believed in Washington that it would take Congress 30 days to make instant coffee'.[21] In the absence of firm control and leadership, Congress is ill-equipped to establish priorities which can then be readily translated into action.

In operation and in expectation, then, the two legislative systems display great dissimilarity. A British commentator might describe Parliament as 'ordered', the Congress as 'anarchic', whereas an American might suggest that better terms would be 'autocratic' and 'responsive'. Cultural background undoubtedly colours our perceptions, but we should note that there are many in both societies who would like to see their respective legislatures develop in the direction of some kind of 'mid-Atlantic' system, where the rigidity of party domination is loosened and greater independence is given to individual MPs in the British system, and where stronger party leadership provides greater coherence and direction in the American.

Notes

1. For many the changes are still insufficient to provide that justification and the Labour party, for instance, has for many years pledged itself to the abolition of the Lords. Interestingly, when in power, the party has steered clear of this commitment, apart from Harold Wilson's abortive attempts at reform of the Chamber in his Parliament (No.2) Bill of the late 1960s.
2. The term 'standing committee' is somewhat misleading for once it has considered a bill it is dissolved.
3. *How Congress Works* (1983) Congressional Quarterly Press, p.96.
4. The foregoing is a general outline of the progress of a bill. Space precludes discussion of the details of parliamentary procedures and the exceptions to the general picture. For an excellent description of Congress and the legislative process see *How Congress Works*.
5. It has generally been accepted that the 'pocket veto' may only be used when Congress has adjourned *sine die* (for the rest of the session). President Nixon attempted a pocket veto in 1970 when Congress had adjourned for Christmas. The action was challenged in the courts by Senator Edward Kennedy and the Court of Appeal upheld Kennedy's complaint. Since then only *sine die* adjournments have been regarded as appropriate for pocket veto action.

6. Davidson, R.H. and Oleszek, W.J. (1981) *Congress and Its Members*, Congressional Quarterly Press, p.194.
7. Quoted in *How Congress Works*, p.16.
8. Wilson, W., (1956) *Congressional Government*, Meridien, p.19.
9. *How Congress Works*, pp. 109–12.
10. Jones, C.O. (1982) *The United States Congress*, Dorsey Press, pp.203 and 280.
11. Davidson and Oleszek, *op. cit.* p.197.
12. *Ibid.* p.170.
13. Jones, *op. cit.* p.230.
14. Hanson, A.H. and Walles, M. (1984) *Governing Britain*, 4th edn, Fontana, p.80.
15. Johnson, N. (1966) *Parliament and Administration*, Allen & Unwin, p.128.
16. Hanson and Walles, *op. cit.* p.81.
17. Although the committees do not have the power to compel a minister's attendance (or the right to receive Cabinet papers) ministers usually feel it politic to accept an invitation to appear before a committee.
18. Mayhew, D.R. (1974) *Congress, The Electoral Connection*, Yale University Press.
19. Mayhew, *op. cit.* p. 61. For a general discussion see pp.49–77.
20. See Ogul, M.S. (1981) in Dodd, L.C. and Oppenheimer, B.I. (eds), *Congress Reconsidered*, 2nd edn, Congressional Quarterly Press, p.318.
21. Quoted by Woll, P. and Binstock, R (1984) *America's Political System*, 4th edn, Random House, pp.294–5.

6

Executives

A study of the executive branches of government in the United Kingdom and the United States offers interesting contrasts in growth and potential. Thus, the Cabinet and the office of Prime Minister are largely the result of an unplanned, haphazard development, while the Presidency owes its existence to the work of the Founding Fathers in Philadelphia. The Cabinet and Prime Minister emerge within the context of party and Parliament while the President reaches the White House after a campaign which may play down party and which owes nothing to Congress. In Britain it is the party which selects the person who will ultimately become Prime Minister, while in America it is the people who, through the medium of a largely defunct Electoral College, elect the President.

The British Cabinet, like the constitution, has emerged gradually over the centuries, its origins to be found in the Curia Regis, the group of advisers who surrounded the Norman kings. The Curia Regis became the Privy Council and from this body, which became too cumbersome, Charles II selected a Cabinet Council. A major step towards modern practice came when William III, needing to keep parliamentary support, appointed as ministers members of the majority party grouping in Parliament. Thus, by the beginning of the eighteenth century the idea of a Cabinet selected for the support it could command in the legislature had taken shape. The monarchy still had considerable influence — over specific membership, discussions, and decisions — but the move towards replacing it by party influence was now under way. The development of the post of Prime Minister undoubtedly helped this shift.

The title, first Prime Minister, is generally accorded, post-humously, to Sir Robert Walpole who was First Lord of the Treasury and who presided over Cabinet meetings between 1721 and 1742. While he did not have the authority of a modern Prime Minister, his use of the nation's finances to secure victory for sup-porters of the King in parliamentary elections gave him influence at both Court and Parliament, and he became an essential link between the two institutions. The growth of the office, as we might expect, was not smooth and monarchs still intervened in sporadic fashion, but the shift of power to the Prime Minister and the Cabinet was ineluctable and by 1783 Britain had 'an undoubtedly dominant Prime Minister, dominant not only over his colleagues and the House of Commons but also, to a substan-tial extent, over the will of the King'.[1] But while the office may be traced back to the eighteenth century, this most important of posts has received very little statutory recognition. Indeed, first mention of the Prime Minister in an Act of Parliament did not come until the 1917 Chequers Estate Act which provided for a country house for the Prime Minister. Since that date, other statutory references have been few and equally inconsequential: the power and authority of the post derive largely from custom and usage rather than from specific authorisations. (We might mention here that the Cabinet itself did not receive mention in an Act until 1937.)

As we have already noted in the chapter on the Legislatures, the monarch still retains the constitutional authority to decide who should be invited to form a government (i.e. to be Prime Minister), but this authority has been greatly circumscribed by the develop-ment of close-knit parties which elect their own leader: political realities require that the monarch should invite the leader of the majority party in the House of Commons. In the event of no party having an absolute majority in the House, there may be some room for royal manoeuvre but even this is likely to be limited. The real choice of Prime Minister, as we have said, rests with the parties which elect someone to lead them and with the electorate which determines which party shall have a majority in the House of Commons. And just as the monarchy has little influence over the choice of Prime Minister so it has little or no role to play in the selection of people to fill governmental posts. Royal assent is still needed but, by virtue of the convention that the monarch should not be involved in the political processes of the state, that assent may no longer be withheld. The legal fiction remains that it is Her Majesty's Government: the reality is that it is party government.

The fact of party is central to government in the United Kingdom and the Prime Minister's freedom to select a Cabinet and government is undoubtedly limited by party considerations and expectations. Unlike the situation in the United States where a President may appoint to his Cabinet persons of different party persuasion, although not necessarily of different political philosophy, the British Prime Minister is constrained to select his or her team from among the parliamentary members of his or her own party.[2] Furthermore, there will be certain members of the party who, because of their status and experience will have a fairly automatic right to a place in the Cabinet, occasionally even to a particular post. A Prime Minister could not easily ignore such people and hope to retain a united party. (Recent changes in Labour party practice, as yet untested because Labour has not had a majority in the House of Commons since they were adopted, limit that party's leader even more severely for they require a Labour Prime Minister to appoint to his Cabinet those who were elected to the Shadow Cabinet.)

The size of the Cabinet may vary from administration to administration but it generally contains between 20 and 25 members. The heads of the important departments of state will be members as will a few 'ministers without portfolio' — those without any significant departmental responsibilities. Beyond the Cabinet there is the rest of the government, another 80 or so less senior positions. These will include ministers of state or under-secretaries of state attached to particular departments, as well as some 20 or so whips. A certain number of these posts are held in the House of Lords but as the government in the final analysis is answerable to the House of Commons the Prime Minister and most senior departmental heads are to be found in the Lower Chamber. When a senior minister is in the Lords a junior minister will answer for him or her in the Commons.

When creating a government, a Prime Minister is trying not only to keep the party in the Commons happy but also to form a team which will be able to work together in reasonable harmony. In seeking to achieve that harmony, which is seen as being an important electoral asset — it is believed that people do not vote for parties which appear divided — it is expected that all members of the government will accept the constraints of the convention of collective responsibility. This convention requires that all members should speak with one voice, that they should not publicise any grievances that might arise among themselves and that, once a decision has been taken, they should be prepared, if necessary, to defend it in public even though they might disagree with it. Lord Salisbury in 1878 spelt out the convention most succinctly when he stated that 'for all that passes in Cabinet, each member of it who does not resign is absolutely and irretrievably responsible, and has no right afterwards to say that he agreed in one case to a compromise, while in another he was persuaded by his colleagues'. The corollary of this is that it would be 'constitutionally improper for a minister to remain in office if he has overtly dissociated himself from Cabinet policy'.[3]

While both quotations appear to limit the convention to the Cabinet, modern-day practice has extended it to cover the entire government, and what was once seen as a useful means of maintaining harmony among a smallish group of people who had been party to the decision-making process is now more a means of enforcing discipline on a much larger body, most of whom were not actively, or even passively, involved at the formative stages of that process. Lest it should be thought that the convention limits the rights of members of the government to express their feelings on a subject, it must be pointed out that if disagreement is sufficiently intense a member may resign and express his or her views from the back-benches. A recent example of such a resignation was that of Michael Heseltine in 1986 over the Westland affair. The rule is not completely hard and fast and on occasion ministers of some standing have taken positions opposed to their colleagues and have survived as members of the Cabinet: for example Mr Callaghan in 1969 and Mr Benn in 1979. Three times Prime Ministers have actually announced the suspension of the doctrine: over the tariff question in 1932 and over Britain's membership of the Common Market in 1975 and 1977. Nevertheless, general expectations are that members of the government are bound to the formula as spelled out by Lord Salisbury.

Allied with the collective responsibility of the government is the individual responsibility of ministers. One of the central tenets of the British system of government is that ministers should be 'politically answerable in respect of matters lying within their statutory or conventional fields of authority'.[4] However, 'answerability' is an ambiguous term. At one time it was believed that evidence of maladministration in a department required the resignation of the appropriate minister, but the growth in size of departments, both in number of employees and in range of responsibilities, makes it unreasonable to expect resignation over a matter about which a minister could not normally be expected to be aware. Thus, for example, the Secretary of State for Health and Social Security would not resign because of errors of judgement by a social security clerk in, say, Bootle. He or she would be expected to answer questions in the House of Commons, should the matter be raised, and to promise improvements, but there the responsibility would rest. On the other hand, should the matter relate to something about which the minister could reasonably be expected to know, or, indeed, to a ministerial decision itself, the mere answering of questions or promising to do better may be insufficient: resignation may be the only answer.

At times culpability is not easy to affix, the line between collective and individual ministerial responsibility may become blurred. In such circumstances the government may decide to stick together and no resignation will be forthcoming. Alternatively a minister may resign in order to relieve the political pressures on the rest of the government: Leon Brittan's resignation in 1986, also over the Westland affair, eased pressures being brought to bear on the Prime Minister herself. Finally, 'personal misconduct by a minister calls for the clearest application of the rule. If misconduct is proved, resignation is expected'.[5] Thus, when a minister is shown to have been involved with a call-girl and to have lied to the House of Commons about it, or to have fathered a child by someone other than his wife, he is forced to depart the political scene. As these 'extra-curricular' activities generally have little or nothing to do with the manner in which a minister performs his or her political tasks, it is difficult to understand the self-righteous attitudes which demand resignation. (The departure of a minister in such circumstances may not be permanent, as was demonstrated by Cecil Parkinson's return to grace when recalled to the Thatcher government following the 1987 election.)

In general terms, then, individual ministerial responsibility provides the House of Commons with a departmental spokesman towards whom they can direct their questions and attacks and from whom they can demand answers and explanations, thereby giving the House some semblance of control over executive actions. This doctrine also provides, in some measure, anonymity for civil servants who, being permanent, must serve governments of any political persuasion and whose advice to ministers is expected, therefore, to remain confidential. Twenty or thirty years ago, this anonymity was largely preserved but the spread of select committees which call for evidence and are prepared to cross-examine civil servants, the spread of investigative journalism, and the increase in memoir-publishing have all contributed towards creating breaches in the walls of secrecy. The protection afforded by ministerial responsibility is obviously no longer what it was.

If individual ministerial responsibility has changed so too has collective responsibility. We have already indicated that its tentacles have been extended to all members of the government outside the Cabinet — even to parliamentary private secretaries who work for ministers but who are not officially part of the governmental machine. But the changes are greater than this. As government has grown in scope and complexity the full Cabinet is no longer seen as an appropriate forum for the discussion of most problems in any depth. Instead, the Cabinet now does most of its work through a series of committees and sub-committees. While these have been in existence for a number of years, Prime Ministers have been loth to discuss them, although Mrs Thatcher in 1979 did admit that four such committees existed to deal with economic strategy, defence and overseas policy, home and social affairs, and legislation. She did, however, refuse to acknowledge the existence of a much larger number of committees and sub-committees which, through leaks, were known to be operating. She argued that to do so would be to weaken the doctrine of collective responsibility. Officially acknowledged or not, these committees, as reports in the press confirm, are the means whereby most of the work of the Cabinet is now done. They are the places where decisions are reached by a handful of Cabinet members and, as *The Times* once wrote, full Cabinet meetings are now 'occasions for co-ordination and for keeping busy departmental ministers in touch'.[6] Thus, even for members of the

Cabinet, collective responsibility on many issues is really collective acceptance of decisions taken elsewhere.

For many, this development is taken as further evidence to support the thesis that the British now have a prime ministerial form of government. The Prime Minister, it is argued, is much more than a first among equals, a necessary chairman for the government. The powers to appoint and dismiss members of the government, to set the Cabinet agenda, to assign problems to Cabinet committees, which she may chair, thus by-passing the full body, all speak of primacy in relation to colleagues. The support given to the Prime Minister by the Cabinet Office — in addition to its role as secretary to the Cabinet — and by the PM's policy unit (a creation of Mr Wilson in 1974) help strengthen her hand by providing the kind of oversight and leadership that departmental ministers, burdened with the minutiae of departmental administration, cannot match. And, of course, attempts at personification of the party, by astute use of the media, limited in success though they may be, have helped to elevate the Prime Minister to a place in the eyes of the electorate which far outranks the status of other ministers. Press, radio and TV coverage concentrate on the Prime Minister, both in political and governmental roles, and a skilful Prime Minister will seek to ensure that this concentration will lead to an ascendancy over colleagues.

Naturally, the advantage taken by a Prime Minister of these opportunities is very much dependent on the will and personality of the occupant of the post, allied with political circumstance. Thus a strong-willed leader like Mrs Thatcher may be able to make the party over in her own image, discarding from positions of authority those who oppose her views. A weaker person may have to act as the conciliator. Again, events may conspire to help or hinder the image making: Mrs Thatcher, for instance, was rescued from the doldrums of her Prime Ministership by the Falklands crisis. An appeal for national unity, for cross-party support in meeting external aggression from Argentina, not only kept the Falkland islanders out of the hands of the Argentinian generals, but restored the Prime Minister's reputation as a strong and resolute leader and put her in a position from which she could proceed to implement the major and controversial programme of de-nationalisation — a programme which a former Conservative Prime Minister likened to 'selling off the family silver or Canalettos'.

In the final analysis, however, it must be remembered that prime ministerial authority is not founded upon any clause in the constitution or in any Act of Parliament. It does not derive from any direct decision by the electorate that one person rather than another should be Prime Minister — although some party leaders would have their party believe that a general election is really a clash between leaders. There is no specified period of time in the office: a Prime Ministership may be as short as Sir Alec Douglas Home's, from October 1963 until the general election in 1964, or as long as Mr Harold Wilson's, from 1964–70 and from 1974–77, or Mrs Thatcher's which has lasted since 1979. Continuance in office depends upon the interplay of a number of factors involving both the party and the electorate. If a leader loses the support of other party notables, or if sufficient back-benchers revolt, then change will come. If the government proves unpopular with the electorate it will be defeated at the next election and, again, the Prime Minister will go. Thus, although it may appear that the Prime Minister is all powerful and able to dominate the House of Commons, that power comes from the support given by the party and the majority given by the electorate. Remove either and the office and its power are lost. This contrasts sharply with the position of the President in the United States.

While the British need hindsight to give an approximate date to the emergence of their first Prime Minister, the Americans, as a new nation, are able to point quite specifically to the adoption of their constitution for the creation of the office of the Presidency. But while the one emerged as an unplanned response to political developments and the other as part of a deliberate attempt to remedy the shortcomings of the Articles of Confederation, both have grown in a manner which owes more to changing demands and political circumstances, to personality and to usage, than to formal processes for extending powers and responsibilities.

The Founding Fathers were a suspicious group of men who feared the concentration of power in the state, whether in the hands of the Congress, the President or the people. Those fears led to a dispersal of powers and responsibilities among the different organs of government and limitations on the involvement of the electorate. As we have noted, Senators were to be elected by state legislatures and Presidents by an Electoral College. Only in elections to the House of Representatives were the electorate to have a direct voice. While direct voting for Senators came with the ratification of the 17th Amendment in 1913, the Electoral College still stands as a monument to those eighteenth-century fears.

The Electoral College, in which each state has as many electors as it has Senators and Representatives,[7] was intended as a cushion or buffer against the 'turbulence' of the much-distrusted 'mob'. The theory was that the electorate in each state would vote for a slate of electors who would decide who was worthy to be President and Vice-President. To be successful a candidate must receive an absolute majority of the Electoral College votes cast. While the early development of parties and party slates committed to particular candidates soon thwarted the intentions of the Founding Fathers, by, in effect, turning presidential elections into direct elections, aspects of the system still play an important part in determining electoral strategy and still possess the potential to deny the Presidency to the candidate who receives the greatest number of popular votes.

A number of elements are involved in the use of the Electoral College system. There is, first, the unit rule which is operated, although not laid down in the constitution, whereby all the Electoral College votes in a state are given to the slate which secures a majority of the popular vote. There is no proportionate distribution of the votes. This has two repercussions. First, it militates against the emergence of strong third-party candidates for, while they may have widespread support across the country, unless they secure a majority in a state they will get no College votes. Secondly, under the unit rule it is possible for a candidate to receive a majority of the Electoral College votes with only a minority of the popular vote around the country.[8] Although this has not happened since 1888 it could easily have occurred in 1960 when John F. Kennedy was elected with a popular vote majority of only one-tenth of one per cent.

The possibility of denial of the electorate's wishes may also arise if the Electoral College fails to produce a winner. In such circumstances the House of Representatives is required to elect a President from among the leading three contenders, and the Senate a Vice-President from the leading two candidates for that post. What makes this particular procedure undesirable is the fact that in the House each state has one vote regardless of size of delegation. Apart from the obvious injustice this does the more populous states (for example, the two Dakotas having the same influence as New York and California) there is the possibility of the party with the most seats in the House being out-voted by the minority party, or of the candidate who received the fewest popular votes receiving a majority of House votes. When we add to this the fact that, should the House be deadlocked and unable to produce the majority necessary, the person chosen by the Senate to be Vice-President becomes acting President, we can see the dangers inherent in this archaic process. Fortunately there has been no need for recourse to the House of Representatives since 1824, although undoubtedly the strategy of third-party candidate George Wallace in 1968 was geared towards producing an Electoral College deadlock and consequently acquiring bargaining power in the inevitable negotiations which would take place in the House.

Proposals have been made for the abolition of the College and its replacement by a system of direct election. However, many Americans appear to regard the potential aberrations as a small price to pay for the continued emphasis that the College gives to the federal principle.

The Presidency, today, represents the focal point of the United States system of government. It is to the President that the people look when they seek leadership. It is around the election of a President that a brief semblance of unity and accord within the major political parties develops, and it is only a presidential election which can bring the voters to the polls in anything like respectable numbers (respectable, that is, by American standards). It is to the President that praise or blame are normally accorded for action or inaction, and when historians pass their judgements they usually do so in terms of presidential, not congressional, eras. Finally, it is the President who, to Americans and foreigners alike, symbolises or personifies the nation.

The President is, from the constitution, chief executive and, from the demands of modern society, chief legislator. As chief diplomat he has a peace-keeping role and, as Commander-in-Chief of the Armed Forces, a war-waging responsibility. As head of state he must speak for the nation; as a politician he is expected to promote the interests of his party. As head of government of the richest and probably most powerful nation in the world he has great potential for action; as part of a system of government in which considerable suspicion, even hostility may be generated between its separated branches, he is often circumscribed and subject to congressional policies which range from the statesmanlike to the picayune. Associated with the office of President, then, are contradictions and ambiguities which derive from both the political and constitutional aspects of the post.

While the British Prime Minister emerges, as we have already seen, after a progression through the hierarchical parliamentary party organisations which provide important training for future leaders, the path to the Presidency follows no such clear-cut lines. Party appears to dominate the presidential race, in that every President since 1856 has carried either the Democratic or Republican label,[9] but the backgrounds and training of those who represent the parties in the race differ widely. Their previous careers may have been tied closely to political or elective office or they may have been at best merely tangential to such roles. Thus claims to a presidential nomination may come from state governors, Senators, Vice-Presidents, Cabinet members or generals. All have provided at least one President this century, and yet none of these categories in itself provides a rounded background or training for the myriad responsibilities associated with the Presidency.

Of the various backgrounds, it might appear that the governorship of a state, particularly a large one, comes closest to providing relevant experience. The functions that governors have to perform and the problems they have to face supply, it is argued, a microcosmic training for the macrocosmic arena. This is only partially true, for while governors do have an executive role, dealing with a legislature and overseeing an administrative machine, many of their responsibilities are subject to the spread of Federal influence into state matters both in general terms — in its attempts to influence the state of the nation's economy — and in particular terms — in its pursuit of specific policy goals. Furthermore, a governorship provides no exposure to the massive external responsibilities of the Presidency which now occupy so much of a chief executive's time.

The Senate has proved a fruitful source of presidential candidates but again provides little training for the superior post. The six-year term does allow a Senator to see problems in national or even international terms (as opposed to the parochial) but the office involves no administrative responsibilities of the kind one would normally associate with the role of chief executive.

While more people have reached the Presidency from the Vice-Presidency than from any other single background, this experience of proximity to power has been no guarantee of ability or readiness for the premier role. Vice-presidential candidates have generally not been chosen for their potential as future Presidents but, rather, for their ticket-balancing qualities. If they do not have the Presidency thrust upon them by the death of the incumbent[10] they rarely seek the office of their own accord. During the course of this century only two Vice-Presidents have run for the highest office without first having succeeded to the Presidency, although Vice-President George Bush is actually seeking the Republican nomination for 1988. Vice-Presidents are, in large part, the forgotten men of American politics for, while they spend some time close to the centres of power, their acquaintance with the problems of state is largely a function of the roles that Presidents permit them to play. Most will have held some elective office before becoming Vice-President but, to the extent that they will generally have been put on the ticket to 'balance' it, it is a matter of accident rather than design if a Vice-President proves to have the qualities and experience that would be thought desirable in a President.

Finally, we should mention the two other backgrounds of Presidents this century. First there is the Cabinet. Two men have moved directly from Cabinet to Presidency — William Howard Taft, who had been Theodore Roosevelt's Secretary of War, and Herbert Hoover, Harding and Coolidge's Secretary of Commerce. Apart from Taft's election to a five-year term on the Superior Court in Hamilton County, Ohio, neither man had had experience as a politician in the world of hustings or had acquired the acumen essential for operating as such. Secondly, the army had been the lifetime career of Dwight D. Eisenhower. He was, of course, experienced in the art of military leadership, but such experience does not necessarily fit a person for the task of providing political leadership, for the two types are quite different. In simple terms, command is replaced by persuasion, and persuasion does not usually come easily to a mind schooled in a military tradition. Eisenhower's experience of negotiating with military and political leaders was no adequate preparation for the quite different style of leadership demanded for the White House. As Harry Truman said: 'He'll sit there and he'll say, "Do this! Do that!" And nothing will happen. Poor Ike — it won't be a bit like the Army'.[11]

Presidents have, thus, emerged from a multiplicity of backgrounds and the qualities demanded of them have not necessarily been those of long political apprenticeship or of proven vote-getting appeal. Indeed, even strong party attachment has not been regarded as a *sine qua non* of nomination. In 1919 Hoover was sought as a presidential candidate by both the major parties; in 1940 the Republican candidate, Wendell Willkie was an ex-Democrat; in 1948 Eisenhower was approached by the Democrats and Ronald Reagan, the successful Republican candidate in 1980, had been a Democrat in his earlier, acting days.

While there is no orderly progression to the White House, all modern Presidents, as we mentioned earlier, have carried the label of one or other of the major parties, but that label is, to use an American colloquialism, 'up for grabs'. Before the big increase in the number of states using direct primaries occurred in the 1960s and 70s, the role of party activists in smoke-filled convention halls was significant in determining who should receive the accolade. Today, candidates can make a direct appeal to the electorate and owe their success more to their own efforts than to those of any party clique. In many senses, the Presidency is a personal prize rather than a party gift and one commentator has been led to suggest that the manner in which American presidential candidates emerge represents 'one of the worst top-leadership recruitment systems in the democratic societies of the world'.[12]

The election of a person to the Presidency may ensure recognition of his role as leader of his party, but that role guarantees very little about the nature of the leadership that will ensue. Whereas a Prime Minister in the United Kingdom, with the support of party, is ideally placed for authoritative action, a President of the United States, often lacking the full-blooded support of his party in the legislature (and we must not forget that often his party will not be in a majority in Congress) is poorly placed to translate policies into working programmes. Congress, as an independent legislative body, with its own constituencies and its own life-span (which for many members of Congress and the Senate will be significantly longer than that of the President) does not readily acquiesce in presidential plans. The separation decreed by the constitution has not been bridged by party.

However, while the executive and legislative branches are strictly separate we must recognise the validity of Neustadt's observation that the system is one of 'separated institutions sharing power'.[13] The constitution itself provides the basis for the twentieth-century emergence of the President as legislative leader of the nation. Article II, section 3, requires the President to recommend to Congress 'such measures as he shall judge necessary and expedient'. Early Presidents were loth to enter the legislative arena, and wary of translating recommendations into specific legislative proposals, but early in the twentieth century Theodore Roosevelt started providing Congress with drafts of bills he wanted considered. The practice grew and in 1947 'the first comprehensive presidential programme of legislation was sent up to Congress by President Truman'.[14] Congress now expects the President to provide a detailed statement of his aims. Moreover, Congress has itself added to the presidential role through statutes such as the Budget and Accounting Act of 1921, which brought some order to hitherto chaotic budgetary processes, and provided the President with the authority to set out his objectives for the country and the means whereby he might hope to achieve them. Again, the 1946 Employment Act called for presidential policies to further the goals of full employment and stimulation of the economy.

While the President now does have obligations from the constitution and authority from Congress to offer leadership, there is no assurance that the legislature will accept the leadership or enact the proposals of the executive branch, and no guarantee that presidential goals will coincide with congressional goals. His authority may allow him to set the agenda but he does not have the power to control the debate. A President's reputation is established by the degree to which he can persuade people to follow his leads, for his powers to command are limited. The methods that he may employ to this end range from the public to the private, from open appeal to closed bargaining, and from the direct to the indirect.

The annual State of the Union message represents the most rounded public statement of presidential aspirations. It highlights his conceptions of the nation's needs and provides a backcloth for congressional operations. The message will be augmented during the year by other public statements urging the enactment (or defeat) of specific proposals. The general effect is to give forceful, nationwide publicity to the President's stand and thus, hopefully, to persuade Congress of the worth of the matter. In addition, the President may well make appeals to the general public in an effort to arouse public sentiment that will eventually be recognised by Congress. The near-universality of radio and television ownership makes this approach particularly suitable for the modern era. Franklin Roosevelt with his famous 'fireside chats' over the radio, was the first President to use the air waves to any significant degree: today, television is regularly used to exhort the nation and to pressure Congress.

The 'private' role of the President in securing congressional compliance involves a combination of gentle persuasion and political muscle; of reasoned argument and partisan appeal. Members of Congress may be invited to the White House for breakfast at which there may be soft reasoning or hard bargaining. Past presidential favours may be recalled or future disfavour hinted at. While the spread of civil service merit systems has decreased the patronage of the Presidency in terms of the number of jobs he can fill, the ever-growing role of the Federal government in society has increased its economic patronage. The promise of economic 'rewards' or the threat of economic 'sanctions' for a Congressman's district or a Senator's state can be potent weapons, for the redirection of Federal contracts or the phasing-in or out of Federal programmes may well be significant factors in the re-election chances of those involved.

As Meg Greenfield has written, it takes a 'combination of management, manipulation, inspiration, deceit, psychiatry and arm-wrestling to get things done when you are President', but to Presidents who have emerged as a result of 'going it alone' rather than from a process of co-operation with the power brokers of the party, such tactics do not come easily. One of the most telling indictments against President Carter was that he could not indulge in the 'blarney, bludgeon and boodle'[15] necessary to secure congressional co-operation. With the election more a personality contest than an ideological struggle, it would appear that the Presidency, to some at least, is seen as the goal itself rather than the means to goals.

But if a President's legislative power is limited, apart from the largely negative act of veto, to such influence or persuasion as he can bring to bear, his functions as Chief Diplomat and Commander-in-Chief provide him with scope for independent action which far exceeds what the Founding Fathers might reasonably have foreseen. Thus Jefferson, through the Louisiana purchase, almost doubled the size of the United States. Lincoln, in the Civil War, took actions as Commander-in-Chief which were an abridgement of civil rights. Wars were fought in Korea and Vietnam without the formal congressional declaration of war. Most recently, President Reagan, while exhorting America's allies not to trade with Iran, secretly approved the sale of arms to that country in the hope of securing the release of hostages, while some of his White House aides used the proceeds of that sale to provide weapons to aid the rebels in Nicaragua, contrary to congressional policy.

Even in these areas presidential actions may be curtailed by a Congress which has a different conception of the nation's best interest from that of the President. It may for instance refuse to vote the necessary funds for pursuing a particular policy, as when it cut off military aid to the Nicaraguan Contra rebels. Alternatively it may seek to curb presidential activities, as it did in the 1973 War Powers Act which apparently limits the President's authority to engage American troops in hostile situations without prior congressional approval.

The difficulties which face a President do not stop here. While a Prime Minister may have a Cabinet in which there are members not always eager to follow his or her lead and in which disputes may often occur, the fact of party and the realities of power usually combine to mute the differences and to provide the Prime Minister with the support needed for the successful promulgation of policy. The President does not have such a supportive body of party notables who can appeal to the Congress and secure for the White House the legislative support needed for the presidential programme. There does exist a Cabinet, made up of the heads of the Departments — Attorney-General, Secretaries of State, the Treasury, Defense, Interior, Agriculture, Commerce, Labor, Health and Human Services, Education, Housing and Urban Development, Transportation, Energy — but these people are not ranking members of the President's party and, of course, they are not part of the legislature. Indeed, many of them will not have held elective office in any sphere of politics. (President Nixon's first Cabinet was unusual in containing a majority of ex-governors.) They may, therefore, prove of little value to the President in pushing his programme through Congress. In fact, they may well develop sympathies out of keeping with presidential designs as they forge links with relevant committees and sub-committees in Congress or as they become 'captured by the traditional constituencies of their departments'.[16] Furthermore, the factors that encourage and nurture the development of collective responsibility in Britain have largely been absent in the United States. No party pressures induce a sense of a collectivity; no electoral demands impose an outward unity (apart, perhaps, from the need to ensure a first-term President's re-election if Cabinet posts are possibly to be retained). The American Cabinet resembles the British in little more than name. Created by the President it is not the President's creature (although he may dismiss members at any time) and it generally contributes little, as a body, to the enhancement of the presidential office, although some individual members, such as a Marshall, or a Dulles, or a Kissinger, have had a stature that has contributed significantly to the reputation of the White House.

But if the Cabinet does not provide the level of support and advice to the President that the British Cabinet gives to the Prime Minister, this does not mean that the President is lacking in advisers and supporters. Far from it, for even a cursory glance at the White House establishment will demonstrate the extent of the support services available. The Executive Office of the President, first established in 1939 to assist the President in his efforts to control a bureaucracy which some have described as the fourth branch of government, is today close to 2,000 strong. Its component parts have changed with changing administrations but central to its work are the White House staff, personal appointees of the President, usually long-time supporters, who are likely to be his closest advisers both for general strategy and for particular policy. Such is the influence of this inner coterie that to many the administration is no longer the President and his formal Cabinet, but the President and his informal advisers, and when they refer to a presidential team it is more likely to be to Nixon and his 'Prussian guards' of Haldeman and Ehrlichman, to Carter and Hamilton Jordan and Jody Powell, or to Reagan and Edwin

Meese (later to join the Cabinet as Attorney-General) James Baker and Michael Deaver, than to any of these Presidents and, with one or two outstanding exceptions, their Cabinet members. Such is the power of these assistants that they are even able, as more than one Cabinet member has complained, to deny access to the President.

In addition to the special assistance a President receives from his White House staff, there are a number of groups within the Executive Office which provide him with the means whereby he may influence policy. First and foremost there is the Office of Management and Budget, originally the Bureau of the Budget. The Bureau was created under the terms of the Budget and Accounting Act of 1921 and brought into the Executive Office from the Treasury in 1939. In a 1970 re-organisation, President Nixon effectively 'replaced a statutory agency (BOB) with an agency operating solely under the terms of executive orders',[17] thereby transferring to the Presidency 'functions that had been vested by law in the Budget Bureau or its Director'.[18] Control over the budgetary process is certainly one of the major bargaining tools in the hands of the President in his struggles with both Congress and the bureaucracy. Secondly, there is the Council of Economic Advisers, provided by the Employment Act of 1946, to keep a general eye on the economy. Comprising three economists, the Council produces annual reports which assist the President in making his policy recommendations to Congress. Thirdly, in 1947, the National Security Act, which also created the Central Intelligence Agency, created a National Security Council for the co-ordination of the nation's security policy. In addition, the Reagan Executive Office contained Councils for Wage and Price Stability, and Environmental Quality, offices for Science and Technology Policy, for the Special Representative for Trade Negotiations and for Policy and Development, and a Board for Intelligence Oversight.

The President is obviously not lacking in assistants or advisers but the Executive Office has grown to such an extent that it would appear that bureaucracy has been heaped upon bureaucracy and the new bureaucracy may well pursue objectives which are kept from the regular agencies or even the President himself. The 'Irangate' hearings of 1987, by a joint House–Senate committee, into the circumstances surrounding the sale of arms to Iran and the diversion of the subsequent profits to the Contra rebels were most revealing in this respect. George Shultz, the Secretary of State and a member of the National Security Council, testified that he had known nothing of either policy, which had been promulgated by NSC officials Admiral Poindexter and Colonel North, while the President asserted repeatedly that he had been unaware of the diversion of the funds to the Contras. (It should be recorded that many sceptical voices were raised insisting that the President must have known of what was happening.)

Presidents have taken to using *ad hoc* groups in their efforts to retain the reins of power within their grasp. President Reagan has had a legislative strategy group, for instance, which has been described as the 'forum within which the most important political decisions are made'.[19] Such groups, comprising personal advisers to the President, may prove valuable in one sense, but they also help to perpetuate the insulation of the President from the other actors in the political process. And as the Irangate hearings demonstrated, they are not proof against unauthorised, secret and even unconstitutional action by others in the bureaucratic rabbit warren.

Thus the contrasts between the two countries are considerable. While both nations suffer from the departmentalism which appears to be inevitably associated with the modern state and which makes the tasks of co-ordination difficult, Britain does possess an integrated leadership system with recognisable structures and lines of authority. Party and legislature provide the breeding ground for Prime Ministers and party the vehicle through which the Prime Minister can lead. In the United States such a system does not exist. Presidents emerge from a variety of backgrounds and party is a very weak tool in the President's leadership armoury. Presidents may be recognised as heads of state, as 'leaders of their people' in some metaphysical sense, but structures do not exist which permit them in any regular fashion to translate role into reality. Godfrey Hodgson has suggested that 'the modern Presidency has developed as a charismatic form of leadership in Weber's terms: one that depends on the followers' belief in the exceptional qualities of the leader',[20] but while these are qualities which may be recognised by the voters they rarely receive the same recognition from members of Congress, or bureaucrats, whose co-operation is necessary if effective leadership is to be forthcoming. 'Integrated' and 'isolated' are probably the terms which best characterise the respective positions of the Prime Minister and the President.

Interestingly, both institutions have been accused of arrogation of power. In Britain the term 'prime ministerial government' has acquired a certain currency, and the growth of media attention focused on the Prime Minister has given a kind of spurious authenticity to the charge. However, the constraints imposed by the need to retain the support of both prominent fellow party members and the bulk of the party's back-benchers, allied with the political realities associated with the desire to secure re-election, impose considerable limitations upon prime ministerial aggrandisement. There may have been a growth in prime ministerial influence and authority but this a long step from dictatorship.

In the United States, Arthur Schlesinger Jr has written of the 'Imperial Presidency' and others have taken up the theme, but the concept is limited and at times misleading. The areas in which a President may act in an 'imperial' fashion are largely limited to foreign affairs in which Congress has traditionally taken less interest, and in which the President, through his treaty-making responsibilities and his role as Commander-in-Chief, appears to have the constitutional authority to act on his own initiative. Schlesinger, in his book, cites examples of presidential imperialism from the earliest days of the Republic, but it was the onset of the nuclear age and the Cold War that brought the greatest acceptance of the special role of President in matters military and international. Thus, as we have already mentioned, in the two major conflicts in which America has been engaged since the Second World War, Korea and Vietnam, war was never declared by Congress. The Vietnam conflict did, in fact, occasion a backlash, with Congress seeking, through the War Powers Act, to curb Presidents who sought to engage American forces in hostilities without a congressional declaration of war. However, this is unlikely to prove a serious impediment to a determined President. Able to pursue military adventures abroad, and everywhere accompanied by the little black box which gives him the ability to unleash a nuclear holocaust at any time, the President has awesome power to destroy. This power is not, however, accompanied by a corresponding authority to create. To borrow the terms used by Burns in the title of his excellent biography of Franklin Roosevelt, abroad the President may be a lion, at home he needs to be a fox.

Those who live in the United Kingdom have, then, a fairly clear idea of where the powers of government are to be found. They rest with the Prime Minister in Cabinet for so long as the House of Commons (and the electorate) are prepared to provide the majority necessary for carrying on the business of the state. Those who live in the United States may think they recognise the seat of government in the Presidency, but so long as Congress has its own conceptions of what is best for the country and so long as political parties fail to provide the unifying element between executive and legislature which the Founding Fathers deliberately sought to exclude, government in the United States will remain diffused and often lacking in effective leadership.

Notes

1. De Smith, S.A. (1977) *Constitutional and Administrative Law*, 3rd edn, Penguin, p.145.
2. In addition to the exceptions noted in the chapter on the Legislatures, there have also been a few wartime exceptions to the general rule. See Hanson, A.H. and Walles, M., *Governing Britain, op. cit.* p.113.
3. De Smith, *op. cit.* p.168.
4. *Ibid.* p.163.
5. Hanson and Walles, *op.cit.* p.118.
6. *The Times,* 2 June 1968.
7. And in which, since the ratification of the 23rd Amendment in 1961, the District of Columbia, the nation's capital, has as many votes as the least populous state — at the moment three.
8. This is a possible outcome not unknown in Britain where, in both 1951 and February 1974, the party with the greatest number of popular votes failed to win a majority of seats in the House of Commons.
9. In fact, on only one occasion in this period — in 1912, when Theodore Roosevelt (an ex-Republican President) standing as the Progressive candidate, pushed the regular Republican candidate into third place — have the Democratic and Republican candidates failed to occupy the first two places in the voting.
10. Or, in one case, by the resignation of the President, Richard Nixon. (No President has yet been removed by impeachment.)

11. Quoted in Neustadt, R. (1960) *Presidential Power: The Politics of Leadership*, John Wiley.
12. Burns, J.M. (1984) *The Power to Lead*, Simon & Schuster, p. 43.
13. Neustadt, *op. cit.*
14. Hodgson, G. (1984) *All Things to All Men*, Penguin, p.116.
15. Burns, *op. cit.* p.32.
16. Hodgson, *op. cit.* p.101.
17. Woll, P. and Binstock, R. (1984) *America's Political System*, Random House, p. 375.
18. Fisher, L. (1975) *Presidential Spending Power*, Princeton University Press, p.49.
19. Hargrove, E.C. and Nelson, M. (1984) *Presidents, Politics and Policy*, Alfred A. Knopf, pp.184—5.
20. Hodgson, *op.cit.* p.110.

7

The bureaucracies

In writing of the means whereby the chief executives of the two countries may attempt effective leadership, and of the constraints which may surround them, references were made on a number of occasions to the bureaucracy. While the Cabinets and governments which contain the persons who stand at the head of the different departments of state were mentioned, nothing was explained about the vast bureaucratic machines which exist and their particular roles in their respective societies. We noted that the British Cabinet received no mention in an Act of Parliament until 1937, and the American Cabinet still remains unknown to the constitution, but neither fact has prevented the development of those institutions, albeit in quite different fashion, and beneath them the whole civil service apparatus which plays such a vital part in the governing of the two countries.

The early histories of the two civil services were similar in that they were characterised by jobbery and corruption. Nepotism and bribery were the principal means by which the largely inefficient services were staffed. Reform in both countries came during the nineteenth century. In Britain, Macaulay's aim to create an efficient and incorruptible service for India provided a spur for new thinking about the nature of the Home civil service, while in America, nearly half a century later, it took the assassination of a President, James Garfield, to stimulate a change of approach.

It was Lord Macaulay in the 1830s who set down the major criteria which were to prove the basis for the modern British civil

118

service — criteria which were based on the 'cult of the amateur'. As he wrote: 'we believe that men who have been engaged, up to 21 or 22, in studies which have no immediate connection with the business of any profession, and of which the effect is merely to open, to invigorate, and to enrich the mind, will generally be found in the business of every profession superior to men who have, at 18 or 19, devoted themselves to the special studies of their calling'. This approach was taken up by Charles Trevelyan and Stafford Northcote when, in 1853, they were asked to report on the future development of the civil service. They proposed, in their controversial and hard-hitting report, that civil servants should be chosen by competitive, written examination from the ranks of university graduates, with the emphasis placed on the 'amateur' principle. A clear distinction was also suggested between those who would be recruited for 'superior situations' (intellectuals) and those destined for a lower class of appointment (the 'mechanicals'). Although the Civil Service Commissioners were created in 1855 to conduct the examinations called for in the Trevelyan–Northcote report, it was not until 1870 that an Order in Council prescribed open, competitive examinations for entry to the service.

The modern civil service was thus established. Political patronage was largely done away with and 'the first great meritocracy', to use Anthony Sampson's term, was instituted. It was a strictly hierarchical system with, originally, a rigid distinction drawn between class 1 and class 2 civil servants. After 1920 this was replaced by a four-class division among administrative, executive, clerical and clerical assistant classes. At this time movement between civil service classes was rare. As government moved from the largely regulatory functions of the nineteenth century to involvement in all aspects of the economy during the twentieth, specialists were drawn into the service — engineers, scientists, economists, accountants. However, such was the ethos of the amateur, the trust put in classicists or historians to turn into first-class administrators, that the 'experts' were kept separate from the mainstream of the service. They were regarded, in many ways, as second-class citizens who could never aspire to major positions of responsibility.

As the twentieth century progressed, the rigid divisions between the main-line classes ultimately softened and promotion from one class to the next became not only possible but common. Indeed, by the late 1960s, more members of the administrative class came from lower classes than from direct entry through the open, competitive examination. Nevertheless, those who dominated the service, who rose above the rank of assistant secretary to become under-secretaries, deputy-secretaries and permanent secretaries, were drawn almost exclusively from the ranks of the direct entrants, the large majority of whom until the mid-1980s were graduates of Oxford and Cambridge.

But if some flexibility did creep into the service, this was not enough to quell the complaints of many critics who suggested that 'the structures and practices of the service have not kept up with the changing tasks'.[1] The Fulton Committee on the Civil Service, which reported in 1968, pointed to a number of respects in which it considered the service inadequate 'for the most efficient discharge of the present and prospective responsibilities of government'. In particular, it argued that it was still based too much on the philosophy of the amateur (or 'generalist') and that as a consequence members of the specialist classes were 'frequently given neither the full responsibilities and opportunities nor the corresponding authority they ought to have'. Furthermore, the committee argued, too few civil servants were skilled managers and personnel management and career planning were inadequate.

The committee's proposals for remedying these defects called for the creation of a Civil Service Department; the development of 'greater professionalism both among specialists . . . and administrators'; more specialisation in the recruitment of administrators, i.e. taking some account of the university courses pursued by applicants; the establishment of a Civil Service College to provide 'major training courses in administration and management'; more attention to career management to enable all civil servants to 'have the opportunity to progress as far and as fast as their talents and appropriate training can take them'. Finally, what was perhaps thought to be the most significant proposal was the recommendation that the old system of classes should be swept away and 'replaced by a single, unified grading structure covering all civil servants from top to bottom in the non-industrial part of the service'.[2]

Fulton came and went. Certain changes were instituted but those which survived were largely those of which the service approved. Thus, a proposal to increase the role of the service in advising the Prime Minister on senior appointments was quickly taken up. Other innovations were much slower to get off the ground and soon fell back again, either to extinction or to a pre-Fulton-style condition. The Civil Service Department, which had been given responsibilities for pay and recruitment as well as for promoting efficiency and professionalism, was abolished in 1981. The Civil Service College, established to provide training for civil servants in subjects such as public administration, economics and statistics, has never made the impression, with its half-yearly courses, that the French *Ecole Nationale d'Administration* has been able to make with its three-year training for top administrators. As for the unification of classes, the changes here have been more cosmetic than real. Oxbridge dominated the graduate intake until the early 1980s, although by 1986 only 47 per cent of the recruits to the administrative and higher executive posts were from Oxford or Cambridge. If anything, however, the system has become more élitist by the introduction of a 'fast' stream whereby the cream of a year's entrants are singled out for accelerated promotion. Arts graduates still predominate among the intake.

Apart from the spread of special advisers to ministers — introduced into a department on a temporary basis as the 'eyes and ears' of the minister — and the work done by the relatively new select committees of the House of Commons in throwing light on different aspects of civil service operations, the civil service today still demonstrates the same characteristics that it has displayed for most of the last hundred years. The social background of its members may have changed somewhat as society has become a little more fluid. More from the working and lower middle classes have been able to achieve the university education which is a pre-requisite for entry to the higher reaches of the service, but even they, having acquired the attributes and outlooks of the new social class they have entered, soon display the collegiate characteristics of the service they have chosen to join.

The service does, then, in many respects demonstrate the absorptive powers of a jelly-fish or, as Franklin Roosevelt put it when speaking of the Department of the Navy, of a feather bed: 'you punch it with your right and you punch it with your left until you are finally exhausted, and then you find the damn bed just as it was before you started punching'.[3] While the American bureaucracy may be as resistant to change as the British, its resistance springs from a quite different environment.

As mentioned earlier, until the late nineteenth century the United States civil service was characterised by the spoils system. When administrations changed, office-holders across the board changed. Political support was rewarded, opposition punished. Far from being, ostensibly, a politically neutral body, the bureaucracy was expected to be partisan. Of course such a spoils system carried with it considerable corruption, against which many inveighed, and much disappointment, in the persons of those who failed to receive an appointment. When, in 1881, one such disappointed office-seeker assassinated the President the stage was set for a major shake-up in the system. The Pendleton Act, following a call by President Arthur for legislation on the subject, came into effect on 16 January 1883. The Act set up a merit system under a three-person, bipartisan Civil Service Commission to be appointed by the President with the consent of the Senate. While the numbers to whom that Act applied accounted for only some 40 per cent of Federal employees in the early days, 80 per cent were covered by 1932 and this figure has now grown to around 85 per cent. The Commission, with its responsibilities for examining potential recruits, established examination boards around the country and acquired a staff of some eight to nine thousand. In 1978, the Civil Service Reform Act was passed 'to provide incentives and opportunities for managers to improve the efficiency and responsiveness of the Federal government',[4] and the Commission was reorganised into an Office of Personnel Management and a Merit System Protection Board.

The move towards greater de-politicisation of the service was carried further in 1939 with the Hatch Act. This Act was passed primarily to protect civil servants from threats or coercion from their superiors, but it also sought to impede civil servants from using their positions to influence or interfere with an election. While these motives were admirable, the Hatch Act is perhaps best remembered for section 9A (1) which states: 'It shall be unlawful for any person employed in any capacity by any agency of the Federal government ... to have membership in any political party or organisation which advocates the overthrow of our constitutional form of government ... '. Thus while on the one hand the Act was making it illegal to dismiss non-policy-making Federal officials for partisan reasons, it was denying employment to certain persons because of their political affiliations.

Whereas, to the extent that career civil servants in the United States are free from partisan pressures and do not themselves engage in active politics, they resemble British civil servants, we cannot overlook the fact that the top 15 per cent or so of appointments in the service are made outside the merit system: they change according to the will of the executive. The President appoints the secretaries, the under-secretaries, deputy-secretaries, commissioners and most bureau directors — the policy-making positions in the hierarchy — and thereby hopes to impose the authority of the White House upon the bureaucrats. This hope is, in many instances, forlorn.

It has long been received wisdom concerning the British system that civil servants dominate their political masters, that Weber was correct when he wrote that '... the trained permanent official is more likely to get his way in the long run than his nominal superior, the Cabinet minister, who is not a specialist'.[5] Certainly, when one puts into the equation the relatively short time that a minister is likely to stay in a particular post and add to that other responsibilities, as a Member of Parliament, as a representative of a constituency, and as a member of the government, one can appreciate the difficulties faced when dealing with a well-briefed civil servant. Richard Crossman has suggested that a 'minister needs eighteen months to get real control of his department',[6] and as many ministers do not serve much longer than this in one office the way is left open for civil servants, with their departmental views and loyalties, to promote their own policies or, perhaps more frequently, to obstruct the policies of their political masters.

One cannot, of course, draw a neat picture of the relationship between bureaucrat and minister. So much is dependent upon personality and circumstance. A determined minister, member of a government strongly committed to the enactment of certain policies, will generally, be able to overcome the most built-in conservatism. On the other hand, a more pliable minister, one simply pleased to have been given a portfolio and with no strong commitment of his or her own, may well prefer to avoid battle with officials and to rely upon the advice and suggestions which come from the department. Nevertheless, whichever the kind of minister, the influence of the officials, which derives from their control over the flow of information, their analyses and their choice of options to be forwarded to ministers, does help to establish parameters within which most decision making takes place.

In recent years there have been moves to redress the balance between civil servants and ministers, to give ministers a view into the departments which is not necessarily that of the permanent secretaries. Thus, after early experimentation in the 1960s, there was the widespread introduction of special advisers to ministers following the February 1974 election. These advisers were 'to help and provide political advice to ministers on their departmental activities' and to brief 'ministers for their governmental responsibilities on non-departmental questions, or on departmental questions involving political principles'.[7] It is important to note that these advisers are not mere 'experts' but are, rather, political advisers seeking to interpret and advise in the light of particular political viewpoints. As such they can prove a useful counterweight to the type of advice which may be proffered by officials. Even so, the assistance rendered a minister by these appointees is still limited and falls a long way short of that afforded a French minister by his or her *cabinet* of personal advisers.

Of course the bureaucratic complex in Britain does not just contain the departments of state staffed by civil servants. It extends much further to embrace a vast array of *ad hoc* agencies, often referred to, not terribly accurately, as 'quangos', an acronym for quasi-autonomous national government organisations.[8] Given the varying degrees of autonomy enjoyed by these agencies, and exemption from ministerial control and parliamentary accountability, it may be as well to think of them as non-departmental public bodies.

This sprawling edifice takes in a wide variety of functions, executive, commercial, promotional, regulatory and advisory. It ranges from the nationalised industries to the Research Councils, the Licensing Boards, the Commission for New Towns, and a horde of advisory committees. In 1979, Mr Philip Holland claimed that more than 3,000 such bodies existed and were responsible for the expenditure in one form or another of something approaching £6,000 million.

Opposition to this bureaucratic empire, which has grown in a haphazard fashion, following no clear organisational principles, has stemmed from a number of complaints concerning the lack of adequate responsibility to Parliament; the amount of patronage put into the hands of ministers (it was 'recently estimated that seventeen ministers have in their gift more than 8,400 paid and 25,000 unpaid appointments')[9] and the sizeable sums of money they disperse. Under the Conservative governments of Mrs Thatcher, a number of these bodies were abolished or reduced, but even so they represented only a very small part of the total, and there still exists a large group of agencies which does not fit easily into any neat organisational structure.

While at times it may appear that the bureaucracy has an unduly influential role on the British political scene, the independence of that role is almost as nothing compared with that of the bureaucracy in the United States. If, in Britain, considerable power has slipped from the grasp of ministers into the hands of civil servants, at least the constitutional position is relatively unchanged. Civil servants are responsible to ministers who are answerable to Parliament for what goes on in the departments: they do not have their own power bases and support which enable them to act independently of the executive and legislative branches. They are a long way from the autonomous bureaucracy which is such a feature of the American system of government.

We have noted above that the top positions in the American bureaucracy are held by people appointed by the President and it might be imagined that this would ensure that presidential control would be direct and complete, for he will only appoint those he believes to be in sympathy with his aims. The situation, in fact, is not as simple as this might imply. Political appointees supposed to give Presidents command capabilities too often 'go native', become part of the machine and act as spokesmen for the interests rather than as agents of the President. Presidents quickly discover that they can rarely command and that, as in their dealings with Congress, they must learn to persuade. And persuasion may often fail. As Sickels has written: 'even the strongest of chief executives can be blocked by alliances of bureaus, congressional committees and constituents'.[10] Or as a frustrated President Truman put it: 'I thought I was the President, but when it comes to these bureaucracies I can't make 'em do a damn thing.'[11]

The bureaucracy in the United States stands, not as a tool of the executive or even, as some would argue, as an arm of Congress, but as an active and largely independent participant in the political process, negotiating and bargaining with Congress, groups and Presidency alike. Each agency has its own clientele, its own power base, its own authority — and little of that authority derives from the Presidency. It is Congress which creates (or destroys) administrative agencies, as Presidents have found, often to their cost, when seeking to reorganise the bureaucracy contrary to congressional wishes. Even when Congress authorises the President to initiate reorganisation plans, any proposals he makes are subject to review by Congress.[12] It is Congress that defines agency power and appropriates agency funds. But even these apparently considerable powers are limited for, like Frankenstein, Congress often finds it cannot control the monster it has created. Once in being, agencies acquire a life of their own, supported by their clientele — both governmental and nongovernmental — which will defend them against those who threaten their powers or seek their abolition.

Coherent policy making in America, already hampered by the absence of disciplined political parties and by the separation of the legislative and executive branches, is further impeded, then, by the existence of some 2,000 Federal agencies with rule-making authority which are not directly amenable to presidential command or congressional directive. These agencies may, rather, pursue their own goals and defend their own interests without the development of any sense of a collectivity of purpose. Thus, the Federal Reserve Board may pursue policies which run counter to the wishes of the Administration; or a Secretary of the Treasury may publicly criticise the budget produced by the Bureau of the Budget (now the Office of Management and Budget); or, as Edwards cites, the day after a President announces his unalterable opposition to forced busing, the Justice Department may file suit to force busing for school integration.[13]

For those raised in the British tradition, where the formal, constitutional responsibility of bureaucrats through elected officials is readily recognisable, the American bureaucratic structure appears to be a negation of representative and responsible government. Peter Woll has argued that 'administrative agencies are forced to pay attention to political demands from many points in order to survive' and that 'this fact makes an important contribution to our system of administrative responsibility'. Further, he argues, the 'growth of bureaucracy is not a cause for alarm . . . as it enhances the meaning of constitutional democracy' and 'the bureaucracy is . . . in many respects more representative than Congress'.[14] Such a line of argument accords to 'representation' and 'responsibility' connotations which do not square very easily with more received notions of representative and responsible government. While one may readily accept that groups in society should have access to the decision-making processes of government — and in both countries this includes the bureaucracy — the degree of institutionalisation of groups within the bureaucratic system in the United States does not of itself make for more enhanced representative and responsible government. Representation of or reponsibility to certain groups does not necessarily entail government which is in accord with the wider desires or needs of the nation.

As bureaucrats are not elected and are not responsible either through the polls or through elected officials to the public at large, the argument that Woll makes could be said to reflect his views on the representative and responsible nature of the other parts of the American system of government. It certainly offers sharp contrast with Britain where officials may be very influential but where responsibility is ultimately shouldered by a government which may be held accountable to Commons or to electorate for its record in office. However, lest British readers should feel too complacent about their system, it should be noted that, while the formal organisational structure would suggest clearer lines of answerability in the UK than in the US, the actual picture is somewhat different. First, the committees of Congress, properly staffed and with a well-developed expertise, are much better equipped to oversee bureaucratic actions than are the relatively new and understaffed select committees of the House of Commons. Secondly, the absence of a Freedom of Information Act in Britain means that British governments can keep secret much that in the United States would be revealed by a vigilant press protected by 1st Amendment guarantees.

Notes

1. This and subsequent quotations in this paragraph are taken from *The Civil Service. Report of the Fulton Committee 1966—68*, Cmnd 3638.
2. All the above quotations in this paragraph are taken from the *Summary of the Main Findings of the Fulton Committee*, pp.104—5.
3. Quoted in Neustadt, R. E. (1960) *Presidential Power*, John Wiley, p.50.
4. President Jimmy Carter, quoted by Seidman, H. (1980) *Politics, Position and Power*, 3rd edn, OUP, p.98.
5. Quoted by Sickels, R.J. (1980) *The Presidency*, Prentice Hall, p.205.
6. Crossman, R. (1978) *The Diaries of a Cabinet Minister*, Hamilton, Vol.3, p.78.
7. Mitchell, J.E. (1978) 'Special Advisers: A Personal View', *Public Administration*, Vol. LV1, Spring 1978, pp.87—98.
8. The term, which originated in the United States, was originally taken to stand for quasi-autonomous non-governmental organisations, but as such bodies have been established by some form of governmental action — statute or adminstrative act — this original form would appear to be even more lacking in accuracy.
9. See Hanson and Walles, *op. cit.* pp.196—7.
10. Sickels, *op. cit.* p.217.
11. Quoted by Edwards, D.V. (1979) *The American Political Experience*, Prentice Hall, p.213.
12. And, of course, attempts to create new or abolish existing agencies are bound to run foul of some interest's concerns and to trespass upon some Congressman's hallowed turf.
13. Edwards, *op. cit.* p.214.
14. All the above quotations are taken from Woll, P. (1963) *American Bureaucracy*, Norton & Co.

8

Group activity

'Interest group', 'pressure group', 'the lobby', are all terms which
have been used to refer to those groups which operate within
and upon the political and governmental system. As none of these
terms exactly captures the full flavour of the operations of such
groups, I propose to use them interchangeably, thereby avoiding
(some might say 'ignoring') the semantic squabbles which have
often surrounded the subject.

Within any society a myriad of groups will exist to cater for the
interests, occupations or hobbies of its citizens. Most of the activities of these groups will not concern us here as they do not
impinge on the political sphere. Our study is of groups as they
seek to influence governmental activity, without themselves
assuming the reins of government. Groups are thereby
distinguished from political parties, which are concerned with
attaining office and the authority of the state which goes with
office. With this definition in mind, groups exist to fill the gaps
left by political parties. As citizens, we are given the opportunity
on a fairly regular basis to vote for representatives of political
parties which offer us a mixture of fairly specific policy commit-
ments and general panaceas that attempt to encompass the broad
range of the nation's concerns. But the programmes with which
we are presented are take-it or leave-it packages that do not permit
us to do more than opt for the bundle which most closely approxi-
mates our interests.

The parties claim then, in Robert Lane's words, to speak for the 'whole person', but this is, of course, in many ways a very limited representation. First, it would be remarkable if the broad party programmes coincided at all points with the interests and desires of all voters. Secondly, governments generally have the support of only a portion of the electorate and can claim only obliquely to represent the whole. Finally, the time that elapses between elections provides ample opportunity for electors and elected to drift apart or for new problems, not covered by election promises, to arise. Groups are needed in order that a society may have on-going opportunities for representation of its particular interests, in addition to its general, and that it may offer such representation to all regardless of the direction of their support in the election.

In Lane's ugly, but apposite term, groups provide the 'fractionated' person — the person (as we all are) of widely differentiated interests — with opportunities to be represented according to those particular interests. Thus a typical, married man with children and a mortgage may join a ratepayers' association to pressure his local authority over the level of local taxes or the services provided by those taxes. He may belong to a Parent–Teacher Association which makes representations to government both national and local about funding for schools in particular or education in general. He may belong to a trade union or to a professional association which may seek to persuade government towards a particular course of action. As a motorist he may join a motoring organisation which petitions government over fuel or road taxes or any other law affecting motorists. And the list can be extended far beyond the immediate interests which spring from family or occupational concerns. He may for example support capital punishment or oppose blood sports; seek unilateral nuclear disarmament or defend the right to carry guns; favour equal rights for blacks or oppose equal rights for women. Whatever the interest, an organisation will exist to promote or defend it and literally thousands of organisations do exist in both countries, although we must note that much of the activity of many of these groups is outside the political sphere and is directed not towards influencing governments but towards providing services for members. Thus motoring organisations like the AA or the AAA exist to provide services to members who break down or maps to those who are planning journeys: activities aimed at influencing government are ancillary to those service functions.

In this chapter we are concerned with groups when they are wearing their political hats, with the variety of types which exist and with the different tactics they employ.

While Peter Shipley has suggested that interest groups can be said to fall into a range of 12 categories,[1] we may find it easier to study and understand these organisations if we adopt a simple (hopefully not too simple) division between defensive or service groups and promotional or cause groups. The former, as the term implies, are concerned with defending the interests of and providing a service to their members, while the latter seek to promote a cause in which their members are interested. Among the defensive groups are to be found trade unions, both individually and in their umbrella organisations, the Trades Union Congress or the AFL—CIO (the American Federation of Labour—Congress of Industrial Organisations); business organisations like the Confederation of British Industry (CBI), the Institute of Directors, the United States Chamber of Commerce or the National Association of Manufacturers; professional associations like the British Medical Association or the American Medical Association; other organisations, such as the AA or the AAA referred to above, which combine service and defensive activities. Of the promotional or cause groups we might mention the League Against Cruel Sports or the National Council for Civil Liberties; the National Rifle Association or the Audubon Society; organisations to promote or abolish capital punishment or to prevent cruelty to animals or to children.

Membership, potential or actual, of the first type of group is usually easily recognisable in that it derives from a particular condition. Thus, membership of the BMA or the AMA is limited to the number of doctors within the country; of the AA or the AAA to the numbers who own powered vehicles; of a local PTA to the parents and teachers associated with a particular school or school district. Membership is then finite and defined by a communality of self-interest. Membership of the second type of group is far less easily defined or circumscribed. No one condition of life — education, training, occupation or ownership — provides the parameters of membership of, say, the Royal Society for the Protection of Birds or the Audubon Society. Unless they are potential killers, no self-interest motivates those who campaign for the abolition of capital punishment. Anyone may join the National Rifle Association. Some self-interest obviously motivates those who campaign for nuclear disarmament — the survival of the world — but their ranks are open to any who accept their arguments.

However, while the latter groups have the potential for much larger membership than the former, it is generally the defensive groups which attract the greater support. This is as we might expect, for an occupation may well carry with it an obligation or expectation of membership of the appropriate trade union or professional association, while companies or corporations may find it advantageous to be members of the Confederation of British Industry or the National Association of Manufacturers. Although ownership of a motor vehicle does not involve the same motivation for membership of a group as does a trade or an occupation, it does nevertheless put those owners into a particular category with impulses towards joining a motoring organisation. Promotional groups, on the other hand, do not have a ready-made clientele. They derive their membership from those who can be persuaded to overcome natural apathy or lethargy and to translate beliefs into action. We may all at times sit at home and express support for the good work being done by some group or another. How often do we go further and turn that fireside support into fee-paying membership?

In pursuit of their political ends, groups may approach governments at many points, employing a variety of tactics. The points and the tactics will vary according to a number of factors — the status of the group; the particular aim; the nature of the political system. Thus some groups with status in society — either from economic position or professional skills — and which may have something to offer to decision-makers are more likely to have access to positions of power than many promotional, single-interest groups which may often be regarded as annoying gadflies around the body politic. The availability of access (or lack of it) will then help to determine the tactics to be employed.

While recognising that much group activity is directed at governmental entities away from the centre, at the boroughs and districts, at the states and the counties, I shall for ease of exposition concentrate on an examination of activities directed at central government in the two countries. Both countries possess a number of institutions which have varying roles to play in the formulation, interpretation and application of policy. These bodies are the political parties, the legislature, the executive, the administration and the judiciary. If we look at each in turn as a target of group activity we should gain further insight into the inter-meshings of the systems of government.

Political parties in the United Kingdom campaign for election upon a programme which they promise to enact if they are returned to office, and some groups undoubtedly see parties as prime targets for their 'persuasive' activities. If a party adopts a group's policy and if it achieves power then the policy may be put into effect. But in those 'ifs' lies a potential problem, for if the policy becomes too identified with a particular party and that party does not win the election, the interplay of party politics may well doom it. Many groups therefore seek to avoid too close a party connection in order to appeal to governments of any political hue. This having been said, we have to recognise that in Britain there is a close and formalised link between trade unions and the Labour party. As we have seen elsewhere, the unions helped create the party, they provide the bulk of its membership through affiliation, the lion's share of its income, and now even have a major role to play in the election of its leader. It is hardly surprising then that unions seeking to have influence on the political scene should look first to the Labour party. But of course they can ill-afford to neglect totally other parties for Labour quite clearly does not hold a monopoly of power. The Conservative party, unlike Labour, does not have any system of affiliated membership, but many groups identify with it, providing financial and other assistance. Many large firms make donations to the party and also support organisations like the Economic League, Aims of Industry or the Institute of Directors which are undoubtedly oriented towards Conservative party philosophy. We should also note that just as trade unionists are represented in the ranks of Labour MPs so too are representatives of industry and commerce to be found on the Conservative benches. There is then some continuing linkage between the major economic interests and political parties which helps to determine the strategies which will be adopted.

While Parliament is the formal ratifying body for legislation, it has not proved to be much of a happy hunting ground for group activity generally. Operating, as they usually do, under the tight constraints imposed by party whips, MPs are rarely swayed by the importunings of groups if questions of a party political nature are involved. They may occasionally be persuaded to raise a question in the House, perhaps to pursue a point which is embarrassing to their leaders: rarely will they go to the extent of voting for the 'group' as opposed to the 'party' line.

A group has much more chance of success with the legislature if it is pursuing a matter which is not the subject of party political division. For instance, parties often seek to avoid taking a stance on delicate moral issues, claiming that they think it right to leave such questions to MPs' consciences, although a cynic might suggest that this is to avoid any possible loss of votes for the party which might be associated with a controversial stand. Thus, campaigns to abolish the death penalty or to permit abortions have been successful, while campaigns to reverse these decisions still continue. On these matters, if an MP can be persuaded, he can 'deliver his vote'. Although these occasions for independent, unwhipped action are rare, MPs are constantly bombarded by group literature and are often sought by groups as parliamentary 'consultants'. This activity is a reflection of an MP's usefulness not as a legislator but as a member of a party with access to decision-makers, and as an elected representative who may be able to push matters with a government department and thereby secure a favourable adjudication.

In recent years, the unelected chamber of the legislature, the House of Lords, has become the target of increased group activity. As peers are generally less ready to toe a party line automatically and are more susceptible to reasoned argument than the 'whipped' members of the elected House, they provide groups with further opportunities to pursue their goals.

It is, however, the administrative branch of government, not the legislative, which attracts most attention from groups in Britain. With the tentacles of the modern state reaching into every nook and cranny of people's lives — in social as well as economic spheres — the bureaucracy bears considerable responsibility, not only for the interpretation and administration of existing law but also for innovation through proposals made to its political masters. Most of the activity of defensive groups is therefore aimed at administrators in an effort to influence the manner in which laws are applied or to gain input into proposals for change. To this end, many groups or large companies will maintain offices or departments charged with sustaining on-going links with civil servants. Regular meetings will take place for an exchange of views, or of argument, or of information. Thus, for example, there is the special relationship which has long existed between the British Medical Association and the Department of Health and Social Security or the National Farmers' Union and the Department of Agriculture. And it should be noted that this two-way flow of information is of as much importance to the administrators as to the groups, for those involved directly in running an industry are probably privy to more information about how government policy is working than the civil service and, as Blondel wrote, 'if firms and other interests were to starve the Civil Service of information the administration of the country would come to a halt'.[2]

That the government recognises the value of such interchanges is demonstrated by the number of advisory committees that have been established or by the obligations put on ministers by statute to consult with interested bodies. Indeed, Harold Wilson highlighted the situation most succinctly when he stated in a speech in the House of Commons that it was the government's duty to consult with the CBI, the TUC and others.

There is, then, a vast 'anonymous empire', as Finer has called it, largely unknown to the general public, which, day in, day out, plays an informal but semi-institutionalised role in the system of government. Of course the relations between the various sides are not always harmonious for civil servants will be consulting with more than one group, and groups with different needs will be making demands upon the civil servants. When disharmony reaches a certain level, the cloak of anonymity may be lifted as disaffected groups seek other means of making their point or attaining their end. They may, for instance, hold a mass lobby of Parliament, in part to stir up MPs but more to secure publicity for their cause. They may hold marches or demonstrations in an attempt to win over public support. Public relations firms may be employed to launch an advertising campaign. Whatever the form of activity undertaken, the fact that it is public may usually be taken to mean that the normal processes of quiet consultation and negotiation have broken down.

The institutionalisation of contacts applies for the most part only to the defensive groups. Promotional or cause groups do not usually have such a cosy relationship with any part of government. They may on occasion be consulted by policy-makers, but their success will often depend on the strength of feeling they are able to generate in the country and the extent to which that feeling is transmitted back to MPs or, sometimes, governments. Thus publicity rather than anonymity tends to be their trademark. To preserve an area from development as an airport, to prevent a village becoming a nuclear-waste dumping ground, to fight for or against abortion or capital punishment or further development of nuclear power, all require publicity and the creation of a climate of opinion within the electorate. The recruitment of MPs to the cause will also be seen as a desirable end but there will always be the restriction mentioned earlier that MPs cannot be expected to deliver their votes in normal circumstances if their party has taken an opposite stand on the issue.

In the United States, the separation of powers, the weakness of the party system and the consequent absence of a dominant political authority able to impose its will, all combine to create conditions which seem at the same time to be more favourable to, and more difficult for, groups and their activities.

The most obvious difference between the British and American systems is to be found in the respective positions of Parliament and Congress within group strategies in the two countries. Members of Parliament, with their party allegiances, are, as we have noted, of limited value to most groups. Their hearts may be won but rarely their votes. Members of Congress and the Senate, on the other hand, with party ties of a different order, are considered prime targets for almost any group campaign. With party leaders unable to impose a whip or threaten significant sanctions, persuasion can be effective. Congressmen and Senators can deliver the vote if they so wish. In these conditions, it is not surprising that the halls of Congress swarm with the representatives of groups, and the avenues and streets of Washington with the offices of firms and associations committed to the business of persuasion. The presence of lobbyists at committee hearings on bills, ready to provide information and advice, bears testimony to the importance that groups attach to the activities of legislators, as do the welter of receptions held in and around Congress, hosted and funded by the National Association for this or the American Association for that. When one considers that in the area of trade alone there are more than 20,000 national and international trade associations — ranging from peak groups like the National Association of Manufacturers, representing some 13,000 corporations, or the United States Chamber of Commerce, representing 65,000 businesses, down to the interestingly named, although no doubt highly serious, groups like the National Association of Miscellaneous Ornamental and Architectural Products Contractors or the National Clay Pipe Institute — one can appreciate that Congress will be constantly subject to pressure from those seeking either to promote or to prevent change. And, of course, the pressures come not just from trade groups but, as in Britain, from across the whole spectrum of interests in the society.

Much of the work of lobbyists takes the form of gentle persuasion, through reasoned argument or appeals to self-interest, but at times it may also stray towards the dividing line between the acceptable and unacceptable where, for example, campaign contributions appear to be linked to a Congressman's ability to influence particular legislation. Occasionally harsh threats may enter the picture as when, for instance, the National Rifle Association, committed to retaining for Americans the right to bear arms as apparently guaranteed in the 2nd Amendment to the constitution, threatens to mount a massive campaign against the re-election of any member of Congress who supports attempts to impose tighter controls on gun ownership. (The NRA is so large and powerful that it does appear that on occasion it has successfully carried out such threats.)

As we have seen, British MPs are largely spared this level of pressure for they can usually take refuge in their party loyalty and commitment. Members of Congress, on the other hand, so much more their own persons, are forced to evaluate these importunings in terms of their own personal beliefs and their own electoral fortunes.

While the President does not have the legislative power of the British Prime Minister, he and his officials may still be fruitful targets of group activity. The President does, after all, play a major role in establishing priorities and setting the framework for political debate and action. Thus a President may be persuaded by groups such as Right to Life and New Right to take a public stand in opposition to abortion which may, in its turn, affect the way in which Congress approaches the subject. His opposition to proposals may occasion an ante-natal curb on some legislative activity in Congress or may be expressed in the form of a veto on proposals which have emerged from Congress. For groups with concerns in the international field, the President is an appropriate target for lobbying as he is often able to act in a way that may go unchecked by a Congress more immediately concerned with domestic matters. The power to appoint — to high positions in the federal bureaucracy or to the benches of the federal judicial system — also attracts lobbying activity for the views of those who administer or who interpret the law may have far-reaching consequences for those to whom the law applies.

As in Britain, a great deal of the time many groups spend on governmental activity will be directed towards the administrative agencies of government. What is often sought is not great change but slight adjustment, and it is usually the bureaucrats who are in the position to undertake such fine tuning. More than in Britain, however, American bureaux and agencies have considerable independence of other parts of the government. In the constant struggles they wage with Congress, President and other agencies they draw strength from the support of their client groups.

In the United States there is one more major channel open to a group seeking to change or obstruct change in the law: the courts of law. This is a channel largely denied to British groups, for the doctrine of the sovereignty of Parliament — that anything Parliament does is constitutional — puts strict limits on the power of the courts. They may declare, for instance, that ministers have acted *ultra vires* — beyond the powers bestowed by an Act — but they cannot declare that Parliament has acted beyond its powers or that any Act of Parliament is unconstitutional. The American courts of law, on the other hand, particularly in their ultimate embodiment, the Supreme Court, can and do declare acts of Congress or of President unconstitutional and can, as it were, through their judgments legislate for the country. This being so, it is only natural that groups have looked to the courts from time to time to achieve what they have been denied by the other branches of government. The end to segregation in the nation's schools is a good case in point. In 1954, in *Brown* v. *the Board of Education, Topeka, Kansas,* the Supreme Court ruled that the separate but equal doctrine, first enunciated in *Plessey* v. *Ferguson* in 1896, was unconstitutional, thus paving the way, albeit very slowly, for the integration of all public (state) schools. The case was essentially a test case brought by the NAACP, the National Association for the Advancement of Colored People.

Two sources of influence on government which we have not yet considered are those which are either government inspired or government generated. In the first, government takes steps to establish groups which will become conduits of information, both to itself and to industry. Thus a National Consumer Council was established by the British government in 1975 to represent consumer viewpoints. Across industry, a number of advisory groups have been established on which representatives of government and industry — employers and employees — meet for regular consultation and exchange of views concerning the industry.

Secondly, there is the existence of competing pressures within government, with agencies fighting agencies to preserve existing programmes or to promote new ones. This kind of pressure is quite common in the United States as agencies and their clients combine in a joint effort to achieve their ends. Perhaps the most obvious centre for such activity is the Department of Defense. As the 'primary employer, contractor, purchaser, owner and spender in the nation',[3] the Department is concerned both with attacks from other parts of government which may wish to reduce the amount of money spent on defence and with internecine struggles among its various parts. In these conflicts the DoD has considerable assistance from those parts of industry which benefit most from military contracts. The links between the Pentagon (Department of Defense) and military contractors are close as Edwards clearly established, pointing out that more than 2,000 high-ranking officers in the military went onto the payroll of the top 100 military contractors in 1969; that in 1976 another 1,044 officers followed the same course and that the same year 374 corporation executives were hired by the Pentagon. This 'military-industrial complex' which President Eisenhower (himself a former general) both named and warned against, undoubtedly exerts considerable pressure upon both Congress and Presidency in seeking to promote its interpretation of the country's needs. As Woll and Binstock have pointed out, the Department of Defense 'maintains a staff of over 150 officers to lobby the House and Senate Armed Services Committees and the Defence Appropriations sub-committees in the House and the Senate'. 'Virtually every major administrative agency has a "legislative liaison" office employing large numbers of civil servants whose sole task is to deal with Capitol Hill, protecting the agency's interests',[4] and it is apparent, therefore, that the institutionalisation of group pressures through this agency—client relationship has become an important factor in the American decision-making processes.

While the techniques employed by groups in both countries may be similar in many respects, there has been one growth area peculiar to the United States — the rise of political action committees (PACs). A concern with the manner in which corporate or union contributions to individual candidates might be construed as 'buying' the candidate led to the enactment of Federal campaign laws aimed at reducing that influence by limiting the size of direct contributions. The ingenuity that all new law seems to inspire soon managed to circumvent the law. The occasional PAC had already been in operation — for example the Committee on Political Education (COPE) of the AFL—CIO, which was founded in 1965 and which dispensed funds it raised voluntarily from union members to candidates it favoured — but as we saw when discussing campaign finance, following the enactment of the 1971 Federal Elections Campaign Act there was a vast increase in their numbers and by 1982 donations to such groups had grown to around $80 million. While limits are placed on the amount that a PAC can actually contribute to a candidate, there are no limits to the amounts that the PAC may itself spend in support of, or in opposition to, any candidate, and of course such support or opposition is related to the stands taken by candidates on issues of importance to the PACs.

Both the British and American systems of government derive their authority from an electoral decision which determines who shall control the reins of power for a particular period of time. But as we see with the rise of group activity, alongside the 'regular' system of representation, there has grown up what Professor Samuel Beer has described as a 'vast, untidy system of functional representation'.[5] This is not just a twentieth-century phenomenon: for instance, groups agitating for the abolition of slavery can be traced back to the eighteenth and early nineteenth centuries. However, as governments have taken on more responsibilities, or as society has perceived problems that can only be met by government action, so organised pressures on government have increased. While political parties do attempt to aggregate and perhaps refine the nation's problems as they see them, and to offer us, at election time, their own proposed solutions, they are necessarily weak vessels for representing us in all our facets. If representation is to have real meaning and is to be ongoing we need groups. That need, nevertheless, should not imply uncritical acceptance.

'The right to petition government for the redress of grievance' — the constitutional authority for group activity in the United States and the implied authority for such activity in the United Kingdom — does not imply equal rights so to petition, except in the sense that anyone may dine at the Ritz. And one of the major criticisms levelled at widespread functional representation is that some groups are much better placed than others to secure such representation. Thus farmers are much better represented in and by the Departments of Agriculture than are the consumers of farm products. Armaments manufacturers carry more clout than do peace movements. The poor, the homeless and the infirm are generally much less able to advance their own cause than are the well-off, the housed and the healthy.

Again, it is argued that oligarchic tendencies are to be found in groups: that the spokesmen for a group may be speaking not for the membership but for themselves. Such accusations carry a grain (sometimes perhaps a whole beach) of truth. That a relative handful of activists in an organisation should be able to perpetuate themselves in office is scarcely to be wondered at considering the size of many organisations and the difficulties faced by the rank and file who may wish to attend an annual general meeting perhaps hundreds (even thousands) of miles from home. And should those difficulties be overcome, it is still a formidable task to offer successful challenge to an entrenched leadership backed by the group's bureaucracy. We must also recognise that many members will have joined an organisation for the services it provides rather than for the political stances it might take, and so long as those services are provided considerable freedom of action may be left to the leadership to pursue its own policies. Even so, there will be the ultimate constraints imposed by a recognition that, should those policies be too out of line with members' aspirations, a revolt might succeed.

A number of points have been advanced in reply to these criticisms raised concerning group activity, but they do not apply equally to both countries. Defenders of group activity in Britain may argue that the very nature of the party system offers protection against the excesses of 'pressure' politics. As parties run for re-election on their record, any overt capitulation to special interests at the expense of other groups would, it is argued, provide political capital for opponents. In the United States, on the other hand, the absence of a coherent party record to be offered to the voters and the dependence of those seeking election on the support of group interests in their districts or states, provide an ideal climate for the nurturing and growth of group influence.

Furthermore, the whole process of governmental control of the legislative processes in Britain means that, generally speaking, groups will not have the opportunity to secure the enactment or defeat of legislation in the manner in which groups may secure their way in the United States Congress. Similarly, while the British civil service is very much the creature of the government and responsible, through the doctrine of ministerial responsibility, to Parliament, the American civil service presents a picture of competing fiefdoms over which the President often has difficulty in exercising his authority. The government agencies are then prime targets for group representatives. Indeed, far from this being a confrontational situation in which bureaucrat is ranged against lobbyist, it may well be a collaborative condition in which groups embrace agencies and congressional sub-committees to form 'iron triangles', often capable of standing firm against Congress or the President.

Of course in neither country, on any one issue, or in any one area of governmental activity, is it likely that only one group will be seeking to wield influence. Very few groups enjoy the luxury of having no countervailing group with which to contend. Societies to care for children, or the old or the infirm are generally free from such opposition but, as they are usually weak groups with little political muscle, this freedom does not bring with it much influence. Apart from these organisations it is normally possible to distinguish the competing groups within society, whether they be the large economic interests — TUC, CBI, AFL–CIO, NAM — or smaller cause groups fighting for or against legalised abortion or gun control. Even in those cosy situations to which we have already referred — for example, farming interests and the Departments of Agriculture — there are competing claims, for farmers are a heterogeneous group involved in many different agricultural activities. Thus the demands which arise from producing milk or beef or growing cereals or fruit may well come into conflict with each other. Governments and civil servants are then in the position of not just fending off, or yielding to, a particular interest but rather of acting as brokers among a wide range of competing interests.

If that brokerage role is to be performed effectively, all groups must have an opportunity to present an adequate case but, as suggested above, at times the resources available to the different groups are quite disparate: at other times the impulses towards organised representation are weak. In such circumstances governments have a responsibility to ensure that particular groups are heard. Public-interest groups may also offer protection and expression to the less-advantaged parts of society. Most famously, perhaps, Ralph Nader, having tilted at the windmill of General Motors and, unlike Don Quixote, having toppled it (over the question of safety in the ill-fated Edsel car) launched a range of groups representing the 'public interest'. Thus Public Citizen, the Centre for the Study of Responsive Law, the Health Research Group, the Tax Reform Research Group, Public Interest groups in states and universities across the nation, Congress Watch, all represent a broad-based concern with protecting citizens in general and consumers in particular. The work of such organisations — governmentally or privately inspired and sponsored — cannot, however, allay the suspicions that both systems operate to favour what Americans might call the 'fat cats' of the economy.

While concern over the role of organised groups in the governmental system has long been expressed in both countries, neither society has done much to impose legal constraints upon their activities. As free access to government is seen as one of the pillars of a representative system of government, anything which interferes with that access is seen as a challenge to constitutional rights. The most that has been done is an attempt to throw light on the activity, to render it a little less 'anonymous'. Thus, in the United States in 1946 the Federal Regulation of Lobbying Act was passed, calling for lobbyists to register their activities. However, the wording of the Act is such that many who are engaged in lobbying are able legally to avoid registration. In Britain, the House of Commons in 1975 established a Register of Members' Interests. While most MPs provide the relevant information, the disclosures do little to illuminate those activities directed neither at nor through Parliament.

When concluding the chapter on group activity in *Governing Britain*, I wrote '. . . like God, if groups did not exist they would have to be invented'.[6] While many are able to contemplate the idea of the universe without God, few I feel could imagine a society without groups at work within it. The opportunities which exist for expression of group views will naturally vary according to the nature of the political system. In societies such as those we are studying, freedom of association and of access to decision-makers may be considerable; in others circumscribed. But in all of them there will be a variety of interests not adequately represented through the formal machinery of government, and groups will be required to make demands, and supply information, whether it be in a dictatorship or a democracy.

The fact that groups exist and perform very necessary tasks does not, however, allay the disquiet that their activities arouse. The question has been asked, 'why should these semi-anonymous groups exert such influence?', but this, I suggest, is the wrong way of looking at the situation. Groups are successful largely to the extent that those who control the authority of the state allow them to be successful. Quite obviously, some groups, whether they be large financial organisations or unions in a major industry, will have considerable influence on governments and may at times appear to be the dominant voices in the decision-making process. But ultimate political authority in the state rests, in the UK and the USA, with the duly elected representatives and their officials. The success, or otherwise, of group activity depends in large part upon the ability of the duly constituted authorities to stand up to importunings and upon their ability to make rational decisions after adequate consideration of all relevant information. The ability to stand up to groups is dependent to a large degree upon the nature of the party system. If the parties, as the bodies electorally responsible to the nation for their record in office, are united in purpose they give both protection to their representatives and direction to their officials. In such a situation, then, groups are less of a threat and more of a valuable and necessary addition to representative and responsible government. If, on the other hand, the parties are not united and coherent in purpose, representatives and officials alike will stand unprotected against group pressure. Indeed, group contacts may well come to be seen as offering more political reward than party labels and group activity may become a substitute for party activity. The answer to those who worry about groups becoming too strong is not to weaken groups (which may be impossible) but to strengthen the hands of those in whom the reins of power officially rest.

To return to Lane's terms, society needs representation of both the whole and the fractionated person, but if the strong are not to flourish at the expense of the weak it is, in the final analysis, the whole person, as represented through the medium of responsible political parties, who should predominate.

Notes

1. Political; employers; industrial and professional organisations; trade unions; consumer groups and miscellaneous economic interests; international; social and women's organisations; health and medical; educational, scientific and cultural; religious and ethical; environmental; animal welfare. See Shipley, P. (1976) *The Guardian Directory of Pressure Groups and Representative Associations*, Wilton House Publications, p.24.
2. Blondel, J. (1963) *Voters, Parties and Leaders*, Pelican, p.225.
3. Edwards, D.V. (1979) *The American Political Experience*, Prentice Hall, quoting James Clotfelter at p.36.
4. Woll, P. and Binstock, R. (1984) *America's Political System*, 4th edn, Random House, p.244.
5. Beer, S. (1965) *Modern British Politics*, Faber, p. 337.
6. Hanson, A.H. and Walles, M. (1984) *Governing Britain*, 4th edn, Fontana, p.187.

9

Courts and politics

In all developed political systems there exists, alongside the legislature and the executive, a judiciary that will perform a number of functions which vary according to the nature of the state. In all it will generally have the adjudicative function we usually associate with courts of law: the determination of guilt or innocence in criminal cases or of rights or wrongs in civil suits. Some judicial systems will have the reputation (deserved or otherwise) of being mere impartial arbiters between citizen and citizen or citizen and government, largely free from involvement in the political arena. Others will be seen as explicit instruments of the regime for the perpetuation of a particular political dogma. Yet others will have creative as well as adjudicative functions and will stand alongside the other organs of government as major contributors to the rule-making processes.

The British and American systems, while having common antecedents in English jurisprudence and while displaying many common procedural patterns, have, in some respects, diverged in quite spectacular fashion and represent quite different conceptions of the appropriate role for judges in representative and responsible systems of government.

In both countries there is an ordered and elaborate system of courts for the upholding of law. These systems provide the arenas in which citizens may find themselves accused of a breach of the law and in which they are provided with an opportunity to defend themselves against the accusations. They are also the places in which civil actions may be pursued against government or citizen for the maintenance (or restoration) of a right which is threatened or has been denied. Whereas in Britain only one basic system exists,[1] in the United States, reflecting the federal nature of the country, two court systems operate — at the Federal and at the state and local level. (While, as we shall see, it is the Federal system, particularly the United States Supreme Court, which attracts most attention and is of most concern to us as we consider the courts in their political capacity, we should note that of the ten million or so cases that are heard each year throughout the United States fewer than two hundred thousand are before Federal courts.) Both the British and the American systems operate along adversarial lines with the contending sides represented in gladiatorial fashion by lawyers who seek, through their forensic skills, to persuade a jury and/or a judge of the merits of their case. And both provide opportunities to appeal from a lower court decision to a higher tribunal.

One distinction concerning those who practise law in the two countries may be made here. In the United States, a lawyer, like Gertrude Stein's rose, is a lawyer, is a lawyer. He, or she, may be engaged in all aspects of legal work, from a first interview with a client, to collection of facts and documents, to representation in the courts and, perhaps, ultimately to appeal before the Supreme Court. In Britain, on the other hand, the Stein typology does not apply. A lawyer is either a solicitor or a barrister. The former provides the initial contact point for a client and he it is who will perform most of the pre-trial, out-of-court functions. When a case goes to court the solicitor must retain a barrister to make the arguments before judge and jury. This division, which has a long history, is staunchly defended by barristers and bitterly resented by many solicitors as representing an upper-middle-class closed shop with little to commend it.

While the pinnacle of the British judicial system is to be found in the House of Lords, where the Judicial Committee, comprising the Lords of Appeal in Ordinary (the Law Lords), constitutes the final court of appeal for matters both criminal and civil, below the Lords the system is largely bifurcated with one branch dealing with criminal matters, the other with civil.

The starting point for criminal cases in Britain is to be found in the Magistrates' Courts, over which lay magistrates generally

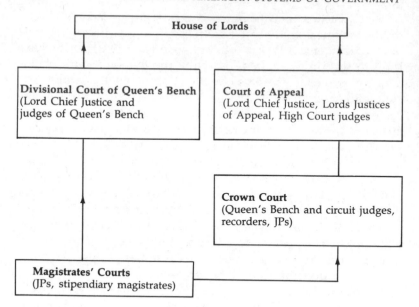

Figure 1 UK criminal jurisdiction

preside. Some 18,000 or so Justices of the Peace (JPs) serve on these courts — two or three usually sitting together — and dispense justice in a wide range of cases not considered sufficiently serious to warrant trial by judge and jury. Serious cases will also be brought before the magistrates to determine whether or not there is a case to be answered. If they decide there is, the cases will be sent to a Crown Court. These unpaid Justices, whose history may be traced back many centuries, represent the backbone of the application of criminal justice in the United Kingdom. Appeal from a decision in a Magistrates' Court may be made, as Figure 1 shows, either to a Crown Court or to the Divisional Court of Queen's Bench: to the former if on a question of fact and/or law, to the latter if on a question of fact. Appeals from decisions in more serious cases, which will have been dealt with in the Crown Courts, will be to the Court of Appeal where three judges will usually sit. Cases may only be appealed to the House of Lords if the Lords themselves or if the Court of Appeal approve.

On the civil side, cases will first be heard either in one of the

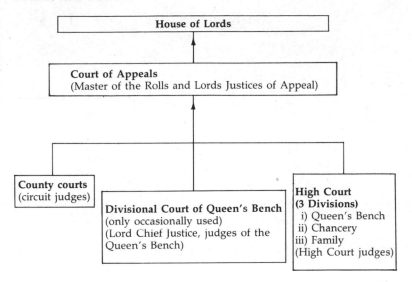

Figure 2   UK civil jurisdiction

county courts, before one of the more than 260 circuit judges, or in the High Court before one of the 70 or so High Court judges who sit, as Figure 2 shows, in one of three specialised divisions. When, for certain cases, the Divisional Court is used, two or three judges, usually including the Lord Chief Justice, will sit. Appeals will go to the Court of Appeals and will usually be heard by three judges. As with criminal cases, appeal may go to the House of Lords if the Appeal Court or the Lords themselves approve.

In the United States, for most citizens contact with the law and the courts will begin and end with their state's legal system. Most criminal and civil law, as we have noted elsewhere, is state law enacted by state legislatures, administered by state officials and adjudicated by state judges. As in Britain, there is a basic three-level hierarchy of courts performing the original and appellate functions. But while we can generalise about the structures and can produce a simple chart like Figure 3 to demonstrate the kind of relationships that exist, we cannot hope to give in a brief survey a comprehensive statement of all the types of court that exist or, indeed, even of the variety of names attached to those courts.

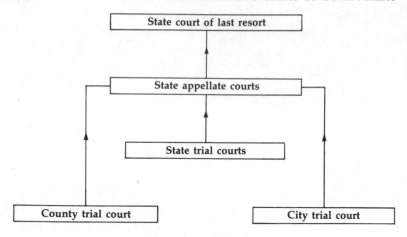

Figure 3　A generalised picture of the US state and local court structure

Each state has developed its own judicial branch and its own procedures and terminology (always bearing in mind that those procedures must not conflict with the Constitution of the United States). Thus the boxes, county or city trial court, may disguise the existence of courts of fairly limited jurisdiction and of varying formality, ranging from justices of the peace, sitting alone to deal with minor traffic offences, to small claims courts or juvenile courts. Furthermore, confusion can enter the picture if we assume, for instance, that terms mean the same in different states. Thus, in the California system the court of last resort is called the Supreme Court while in New York it is known as the Court of Appeals. On the other hand, the trial court of original jurisdiction in New York is known as the Supreme Court.

While the vast bulk of state cases will be finally resolved within the state system, a few, in which a Federal question is involved, may go to the Supreme Court of the United States for final resolution.

The Federal system of courts is authorised in Article 3 of the constitution which states that 'the judicial power of the United States shall be vested in one Supreme Court and in such inferior courts as the Congress may from time to time ordain and establish'. The original jurisdiction of the Supreme Court is strictly limited by the constitution to 'all cases affecting ambassadors, other public ministers and consuls, and those in which a state shall be a party'. In all other instances it acts as the final appellate court of the nation.

While Congress was not obliged to create a Federal system of courts, as Article 3 indicates — it could have ordained that Federal cases should be first heard in state courts — it very quickly created a judicial structure which in basic format resembled the state system with a court of first instance, the district court, an appeal court, the circuit court, and the final appellate court — called for by the constitution — the Supreme Court. There are now 89 district courts in the 50 states and one each in the District of Columbia and Puerto Rico, from which appeals may be made to one of the ten circuit courts of appeal or to the court of appeal for the District of Columbia.

Around this fairly simple, straightforward system there has grown up a somewhat more complicated system of courts which reflects the growing complexity of society. There are, then, four territorial courts for Puerto Rico, Guam, the US Virgin Islands and the Panama Canal Zone. There is a Customs Court for disputes over tariffs, a Court of Customs and Patent Appeals, and a Court of Claims for cases of claims for compensation against the United States. Tax courts and independent regulatory commissions which exercise judicial power also come within this ambit, as does the Court of Military Appeals. All, directly or indirectly, as Figure 4 demonstrates, may have their decisions appealed to the highest court in the land, the Supreme Court. While the individual states may establish separate courts to hear civil and criminal cases, at the Federal level no such distinction is made.

The procedural rights of those who fall foul of the law may differ somewhat between the two countries.

In Britain, the 'Judges' Rules' purportedly provide safeguards for a suspect when being questioned by the police, but as these 'rules' are guidelines rather than statute they do not have the force of law, and at times evidence obtained in ignorance of or in blatant breach of the 'rules' has been permitted in court. In 1977, the Criminal Law Act provided that a person in custody should have access to a solicitor with 'no more delay than is necessary', but there have been many complaints that the qualifying clause has often been interpreted 'generously' by the police when they have sought to continue questioning a suspect without the interference of a lawyer.

In the United States, all accused persons have rights which,

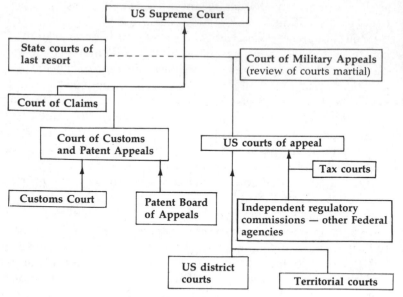

Figure 4   US Federal system

as any viewer of American television crime series of the last 20 years knows, must be read to them at the time of arrest. These rights, often read from a 'Miranda' card, derive from a Supreme Court ruling in *Miranda* v. *Arizona* (1966) which required that accused persons should be informed of their rights. In the words of the Court: 'Prior to any questioning, the person must be warned that he has a right to remain silent, that any statement he does make may be used in evidence against him, and that he has the right to the presence of an attorney, either retained or appointed.' Whereas in Britain disregard of the 'Judges' Rules' may at times, in effect, be condoned, in the United States any abridgement of an accused's rights will generally result in a case being dismissed, as will the introduction of evidence obtained in violation of a citizen's 4th Amendment rights 'to be secure in their persons, houses, papers and effects, against unreasonable searches and seizures'.

In matters of pre-trial procedure it would appear, then, that Americans possess greater safeguards against infringement of personal liberty than the British.[2] Nevertheless, once a case reaches the courts the citizens of both countries generally receive fair trials in which accused faces accuser before a judge — and a jury in all important cases — and has a right to a lawyer to help rebut the accusations or to make a plea in mitigation. Should a trial go against the accused, appeal may be made to a higher court, as it may in a civil case. The law that is applied in these courts is not secret or arbitrary but well known and administered according to established practices which generally follow the doctrine of *stare decisis* — precedent. In some instances however, in criminal cases, the sentences handed down appear to reflect the prejudices of the judge, while the highest courts of both countries have been prepared to depart from earlier judgments and to hand down decisions in keeping with their interpretation of the law according to contemporary mores or demands.

While it would be possible to pursue much further the operations of these courts in their application of the law, what most concerns us here is their interpretative role and the way it impinges upon the political processes. It is in this area that we see the greatest divergence between the roles of the courts in the two countries.

In the chapter on the Constitutions, we noted the development of the British constitution and the important role given to common or case law — the law as determined and applied by the courts. We have also noted how little authority was given to the courts by Article 3 of the American constitution. Had we, in 1800, been in a position to offer a forecast as to the relative developments of the courts within their own constitutional frameworks there is little doubt that all but the most far-sighted would have predicted a major, if perhaps diminishing, role for those in Britain and a largely peripheral place for those in America. The evidence that existed would certainly seem to support such a prediction. After all, the courts in Britain had generally provided the bulk of the law, with parliamentary statutes being relatively few, while in the United States the constitution appeared to share the law-making functions between Congress and President, with the Supreme Court apparently having little creative role to perform. Indeed, in the early years of the Republic the Court seemed to be held in low esteem and difficulties were experienced in getting people to accept appointment or, having accepted, to attend or even to remain as Justices.

Developments since 1800 demonstrate the dangers of crystal-ball gazing. The growth of the franchise in Britain, the emergence of nationally-organised political parties competing for the support of this expanded electorate through political manifestos, shifted the balance of the law-making functions of the nation firmly in the direction of the sovereign Parliament. And although as late as 1885 Dicey was still describing the British constitution as a 'judge-made constitution',[3] his assessment was more a reflection of his personal concerns and prejudices, which saw a constitution as being largely concerned with the liberties of the individual within the state, and with such things as freedom of expression and association, than an objective record of power relationships among the institutions of the state.

The British judiciary is now set within a framework of institutions which operate under the doctrine of the sovereignty of Parliament — the doctrine which denies to any person, or body of persons, the authority to question the constitutional validity of parliamentary actions. The judiciary thus operates under the laws and may not challenge or reverse any act properly promulgated by Parliament. Nevertheless, this restricted role does not render the courts totally impotent politically for while they may not challenge the law they do interpret it, and such interpretation, which governments may not have foreseen, will stand until such time as Parliament reverses it. Furthermore, the courts may challenge the application of the law, as agents of the government have discovered in recent years. Thus, on a number of occasions specific actions have been ruled void on the grounds of being *ultra vires* — beyond the powers authorised in the relevant act of Parliament. For example, in 1976 the courts ruled that the Secretary of Education did not have the authority to stop the Tameside Education Authority overturning a plan for comprehensive education and, the same year, that the Secretary of State for Trade could not act to deny a licence to Laker Airways. In 1981 it was the Greater London Council which was thwarted when the House of Lords upheld a decision by the Appeal Court in favour of the London borough of Bromley which had challenged the authority of the GLC to impose a supplementary rate to subsidise reduced fares on London Transport. In 1985 the GLC was on the winning side when the courts ruled that the attempts by Nicholas Ridley, Secretary of State for Transport, to overturn the GLC's ban on heavy lorries was illegal — one of three of Mr Ridley's decisions declared illegal that year. Indeed, the Thatcher governments have had more of their decisions 'found wanting' than any other previous government. It is important to note here, however, that while such decisions may — and should — embarrass a government or an individual minister or local authority, they in no way offer a check to the right of governments, through Parliament, to legislate on the matters involved and to extend their powers as they wish to meet the objections raised in court. It is action under the law, not the law itself, which is challenged. And herein lies a major difference between the British and American systems.

As we have indicated above, the United States constitution says little to suggest the role that would ultimately be exercised by the courts as a major participant in the political and constitutional development of the nation. No hint is given of the power, soon to be exercised, to declare acts of Congress or of the President unconstitutional, or of the far-reaching effects of judicial interpretation, although it is apparent from other sources that many of the Founding Fathers did envisage the Supreme Court as an arbiter within the system. But whatever the presumption, the constitution remained quiet on the matter: and yet the Republic was still in its infancy when the Court arrogated unto itself the power to declare void an act of Congress.

The case, *Marbury* v. *Madison* (1803), provides a classic example of an astute legal mind, in an awkward situation, not only avoiding a politically undesirable end but also adding to the authority of the Court over which he presided. Marbury had been appointed as a Commissioner of the Peace by President John Adams in the lame-duck days of his Presidency, but had not received his commission before the administration came to an end. He applied to the Supreme Court for a writ of *mandamus* to require the new Secretary of State, Madison, to deliver up the commission. The application originated in the Supreme Court under the terms of the 1789 Judiciary Act which apparently authorised such a procedure. Politics entered the picture because Chief Justice John Marshall, another Adams appointee, was a Federalist like Marbury while Madison was a Jeffersonian Republican. Marshall recognised that if the fledgling Court found for Marbury its decision would probably be ignored, its weaknesses revealed and its future development stunted. To find for Madison would, however, be repugnant. His answer to the dilemma was to state that Marbury was entitled to his commission but that the Supreme Court lacked the authority to hear the case. He argued that the constitution quite clearly spelled out the original jurisdiction of the Court and that the Congress, through the Judiciary Act, sought to extend that jurisdiction. There was clearly a conflict between two levels of law here and in such a conflict the superior law — the constitution — had to prevail. In one stroke Marshall had indicated his support for his fellow Federalist, had avoided finding for his political enemy, had rejected congressional attempts to add to the Court's responsibilities — in effect declaring part of an Act of Congress unconstitutional — and thereby had greatly enhanced the status of the Court for the future.

It was another half century before the Court again invalidated an act of Congress, but in the intervening years it acquired a status central to the whole system of government. In decisions which, for instance, gave broad construction to the 'elastic' clause of the constitution or expansive interpretation to the interstate commerce clause, the Court provided the constitutional framework within which the country developed and grew. The status that Marshall, in particular, was able to give the Court has stayed with it throughout the life of the Republic. Americans, a naturally litigious nation, have grown accustomed to turning to the courts to resolve matters which in other countries might well be left to politicians. The Court has not, of course, been beyond criticism for its decisions have inevitably from time to time hurt some or offended others. However, while the Supreme Court, as Hamilton pointed out, has the power of neither purse nor sword, its decisions have generally been accepted by the parties to a dispute, whether they be President, Congress or citizen.

The range and importance of the decisions involved and the place of the Court in controversies of a political/constitutional nature may be highlighted by noting some of the more significant disputes which have arisen.

The *Dred Scott* v. *Sandford* decision in 1857, in which the Court declared that a slave was property and had no rights, and in which the Missouri Compromise, separating slave areas from non-slave areas, was declared unconstitutional, caused an uproar in the North and did nothing to stop the slide of the nation into that bloody, internecine conflict, the Civil War. (While the Court cannot be blamed for the tensions that already existed between slave-owners and abolitionists, the ruling which opened up the territories once more to slavery undoubtedly helped exacerbate the antagonisms.) Later that century, by a strange reading of the 14th Amendment to the constitution, passed to assist newly-freed slaves, the Court, by declaring corporations to have the same constitutional rights as individuals, was able to curb governmental attempts to check the worst excesses of a rapidly expanding industrial state.

During the first term of President Franklin Roosevelt in the 1930s, a Court reflecting the conservatism of the affluent twenties consistently overturned programmes aimed at fighting the economic devastation of the great depression. So out of tune with the demands of the decade did the Court appear that the President was tempted into what became known as a court-packing plan. The attempt failed — such was the status of the Court in the nation's eyes — but it had a salutary effect upon later decisions, as the Justices recognised that they could not stand out too long against the decisions of the ballot box. In 1952, the Court ruled unconstitutional President Truman's seizure of the steel mills, undertaken, he claimed, in an attempt to avert a nationwide steel strike which would have weakened America's defence capabilities.

In the 1950s and 1960s, Earl Warren, as Chief Justice, led the Court into one of the most liberal periods in its history. Notable decisions of the era include *Brown* v. *the Board of Education of Topeka, Kansas*, which declared laws requiring segregation in schools to be unconstitutional. Such segregation had developed under the constitutional umbrella of the Court's decision of 1896 in *Plessey* v. *Ferguson* when it ruled that it was constitutional to segregate people according to colour on the railways so long as the separate facilities were equal in quality. By overturning this 'separate but equal' doctrine, in which the emphasis had always been on the 'separate' rather than on the 'equal', the Court launched the South into a long rearguard action to avoid compliance with the new constitutional requirement. When, later, the Court ruled that it was constitutional to bus children across school district lines to achieve racial equality denied by *de facto* housing segregation, many Northerners joined the protests against the Court's decision.When the Warren Court also launched its 'criminals' charter', referred to above, the cry went up 'Impeach Earl Warren' — the more intemperate posters read 'Hang Earl Warren' — and an abortive movement was launched to replace the existing court with a Constitutional Court of 50 members, one from each of the states.

These examples serve to hint at the vast range of Court involvement in American life and the potential for conflict involved. In the first half of the nineteenth century, Alexis de Tocqueville wrote, in *Democracy in America*, that 'hardly any question arises in the United States that is not resolved sooner or later into a judicial question'. This was a most telling observation, but even he can hardly have foreseen just how much that observation would apply to the Supreme Court throughout the life of the Republic, and how much criticism court decisions would from time to time evoke. Controversy is not to be wondered at for few of the judgments that courts hand down are mere 'exercises in constitutional exegesis'. Most are related to political or social questions that impinge directly upon different aspects of everyday life — may a Federal income tax be levied; may governments impose minimum working standards; may abortions be performed, contraceptives used, convicted murderers executed, races segregated, pornography banned? Apart from natural complaints of those who have lost before the courts, most criticism derives from two major sources which are perhaps two sides of the same coin. The first concerns the political or social consequences of a decision and can usually be ascribed to either the 'liberal' or the 'conservative' stance of the critic. The second appears to be concerned with a loftier, constitutional question — the encroachment of the judiciary into policy areas that, it is argued, rightly belong to the elective branches of government. This 'Imperial Judiciary' school would seem to be arguing at a somewhat higher level than the 'political' critics of the first strand. However, apart from a few dispassionate ivory-towered observers, most of those who advance this line of argument are to be found among the more conservative elements in society.

Court decisions, then, have political as well as judicial ramifications and the Supreme Court in particular is an integral part of the political process. The Court's potential as such has long been recognised. John Adams did not appoint John Marshall just for his brilliant legal mind but also for his political persuasion. Ever since that time, Presidents who, with senatorial approval, appoint the Federal bench have been concerned to get the 'right' person, i.e. one whose views closely reflect those of the President. The importance of this appointive function was shown by Ronald Reagan when, in his 1980 campaign for the Presidency, he promised to appoint conservative judges who would reverse the tendency to use the courts for social activism. It would appear that he has kept this pledge for his administration has demonstrated greater, more overt concern with the ideological stand of potential nominees to the Federal bench than previous administrations. By the time he completes his second term in office he will probably have appointed more than half of the 743 Federal judges in the country and have produced a major shift in the balance of the courts. In 1987, considerable controversy was aroused by the nomination of Circuit Judge Robert Bork to fill the Supreme Court seat made vacant by the resignation of Justice Lewis Powell. Such were the emotions aroused that liberal groups who opposed Bork's right-wing opinions pledged several million dollars to fight the nomination, while those who supported Bork raised similar large amounts. The nomination failed to secure senatorial confirmation. The political importance of the Court for the future trend of policy could not be better demonstrated.

As appointment is for life,[4] a President's influence on the political scene, through his court appointments, may well live on long after his presidential tenure has ended. President Reagan's 1986 elevation of Justice Rehnquist, a Nixon appointee of 1972, to the Chief Justiceship, is a good example of the long-term influence of a President through the courts. This having been said, we must enter one caveat here. As Justices *are* appointed for life, they are free to act as they see fit: in ways perhaps unanticipated by their appointing President. A number of Presidents have indeed been disappointed with some of their appointees, not least President Eisenhower with Chief Justice Earl Warren, a past Republican governor of California, who, as we have already noted, led the Court during one of its most liberal periods.

The British system eschews the open partisanship of appointment that characterises the American scene at the Federal level, or the election of judges that often takes place at state and local level. Nevertheless, many would argue that British judges are just as partisan as their American counterparts. Appointment to the bench in Britain is by the Lord Chancellor (for the highest posts after consultation with the Prime Minister). The Lord Chancellor, who presides over the House of Lords, is appointed by the Prime Minister and is a member of the government. While one might expect that those he appoints would to some extent reflect his (and his government's) political persuasion, the Lord Chancellor is limited in his choice to a fairly small group of practising barristers who generally come from similar upper- or upper-middle-class backgrounds, with political views to match their breeding. Thus even the advent of a Labour party to power does little to challenge the conservative (with both little and big 'c') bent of the bench.

In *The Politics of the Judiciary*, J.A.G. Griffiths is concerned to demonstrate the conservative nature of the bench and to highlight, quite rightly, a number of cases in which judicial discretion has been used to find in favour of the existing order and against those who challenge it. He also shows how certain basic freedoms are not always available to all in society. As he writes: 'minority groups, especially if they demonstrate or protest in ways which cause difficulty or embarrassment are not likely to find that the courts support their claims to free speech and free assembly'.[5] The book does not, however, move easily from description to prescription, and questions are raised but not answered (although to be fair it may be that there are no universally accepted answers).

The difficulties for Griffiths, and indeed for many others, may be perceived in his own words. Thus, at one point he writes, 'democracy requires that some group of persons acts as an arbiter not only between individuals but also between governmental power and the individual' and at another that 'the judiciary . . . is an essential part of the system of government and its functions may be described as underpinning the stability of that system and as protecting that system from attack by resisting attempts to change it' (p.213). But later he goes on to claim that 'judges are parasitic' because 'in both capitalist and communist society the judiciary has naturally served the prevailing political forces' (p.215). Thus, the judiciary is apparently needed as an essential part of government but is, at the same time, parasitic because it does not challenge prevailing forces. But we do need to ask, 'should the judges be the people to offer such a challenge?', or to put it in a more value-loaded way, 'should an appointed bench, electorally irresponsible, and removeable only after cumbersome processes rarely attempted, do more than uphold a state of affairs determined by the elected representatives of the people — by those to whom has been given the responsibility of government?'

While the question in its more 'loaded' form might seem to demand the answer 'No', life is not as simple as that and the 'No' must surely be followed by 'but'. After all, in societies which lay claim to be representative democracies, election to office does not confer unlimited powers. The representatives of the majority are expected to act within certain lines of procedure and with due respect for the rights of the minority. In the United States, the constitution and its amendments provide the guidelines and set out those rights. The courts have the task of adjudication if it is claimed that the boundaries have been breached or the rights denied. The non-elective judges can then be seen to be an integral part of the democratic processes. In Britain, in the absence of a written constitution or a bill of rights, the limitations upon government are much less apparent: the doctrine of the sovereignty of Parliament rendering, as we have seen, any Act of Parliament constitutional and thus beyond the review of the courts as to its legality. The courts are basically limited to a judgment as to whether or not an action under a law is permitted according to the terms of that law: there is no appeal to a higher law against which a government and its actions may be judged. Of course, with words open to more than one meaning or emphasis, the personal prejudices of judges in both societies will play an important part in the interpretation and application of the law. This having been said, we must recognise that in neither country does the judiciary have the last word. In both, procedures exist to legalise that which was declared illegal or to confer powers deemed not to exist. Thus, in Britain the simple passage of an Act of Parliament is sufficient to override any judicial decision, while on many issues in the United States an Act of Congress will be sufficient to deal with an adverse ruling. However, if the matter is of constitutional import it may need the difficult process of constitutional amendment to reverse a Supreme Court stand.

The proper place of the judiciary within the political and social framework is obviously different for different people, and these different perceptions are to be found not just between societies but also within them. In Britain, for instance, average citizens probably do not view the judicial system as part of the political apparatus of the state. For them, politicians sit in Westminster, judges in the Law Courts, performing different tasks. Even should they recognise, for instance, an abridgment of some fundamental right in a judicial decision — and in the absence of a codified bill of rights they may not perceive the loss — the linkage between the law and politics may still not be made. Others, of course, in the society do recognise the courts as political and wish to see them use their position to achieve certain political ends — those ends being determined by the political stance of the observer.

In America, on the other hand, few would fail to recognise the importance of judges, particularly the Supreme Court, within the political system. After all, its history is a history of political involvement. It has checked Presidents, Congress and state legislatures. The Supreme Court is the body which may ultimately offer a determination of a case in which civil rights or liberties are at stake. It has been applauded by some and denigrated by others for its 'imperialism' in the political arena. For most it is seen as 'guardian of the constitution', even though its judgments may be the determinant of what the constitution is on any particular point. Indeed, 'guardian' is a rather static word which does not capture the dynamic nature of the work of the Court. It not only interprets the constitution, it updates it, acting rather like an on-going constitutional convention which renders the eighteenth-century document relevant to succeeding generations. Through Court interpretations, major constitutional shifts have been made possible without the difficulties attendant upon the formal amendment process. Naturally, for those who see the difficulties of formal constitutional amendment as one of the strengths of the American system, such shifts, not by entrenched majorities of Congress and states but by a simple majority of what used to be known, until the arrival of a woman on the Court, as 'the nine old men' or 'the Brethren', represent a dangerous encroachment by one branch of government into the territory of others. For such critics, Hamilton's 'least dangerous branch' has become too powerful.

There are those who fear that, should the British adopt a written constitution, or at least a bill of rights, judicial aggrandisement of the type experienced in the United States would arrive in Britain. But such fears ignore the totally different political environments in the two countries. Indeed, the concentration of power in Britain, compared to its diffusion in America, probably makes it more desirable that some statement of the rights and privileges of the British be introduced. Such a statement could not act as the bulwark against the elective dictatorship about which Lord Hailsham has warned, for a bill of rights could not, in itself, diminish the sovereignty of Parliament. The power of the judges would, in the final analysis, be limited to demonstrating the withdrawal or loss of a right or privilege. While such a demonstration may be important it hardly implies an imperial judiciary.

Notes

1. The legal system in Scotland does differ in some respects from the system in the rest of the United Kingdom, but these differences need not concern us here.
2. Some Americans, far from rejoicing in this fact, prefer to castigate the Warren Court, under which many of the safeguards were spelled out, for having produced a 'criminals' charter' which 'handcuffs the police rather than the villains'.
3. Dicey, A.V. (1959) *Introduction to the Study of the Law of the Constitution*, 10th edn, Macmillan, p.196.
4. The constitutional provision for removal by impeachment has never been successfully invoked against a Supreme Court Justice.
5. Griffiths, J.A.G. (1977) *The Politics of the Judiciary*, Fontana, p.196.

10

Government beyond the centre

The British and American systems of government have been characterised respectively as unitary and federal. In the former, political power is constitutionally centred in Parliament and all other units of government in the state are subordinate to and derive their authority from the centre. Indeed, their very existence is dependent upon the sovereign Parliament. In the latter, the Federal government may now play a dominant role in most aspects of government activity but other units of government, the state governments, exist in their own right, with their continued existence guaranteed by the constitution.

Both systems of sub-national government have a long history — history which contributes to the present framework. In the United Kingdom, local government antedates the 'united' of the country's title. Its origins are to be found in the counties — the territorial price paid to earls in return for their allegiance to the monarch; in the boroughs, with their royal charters; and in the parishes, those units of ecclesiastical administration which were given secular responsibilities, through legislation, for local roads and the care of the indigent. For many centuries the primary tasks of county and borough concerned law and order, and the monarch's influence was vestigial, becoming evident only when he or she sought to strengthen the position of supporters in an area.

The growth and spread of these local institutions followed no tidy pattern, and geographic area and population size varied considerably from county to county, borough to borough, parish to parish. Nevertheless, while the country remained rural and its population largely static, these divergences did not matter unduly, although we should not overlook the fact that the varying degrees of wealth of the parishes, and of humanity of the Poor Law Guardians, did determine how well, or how badly, the nation's needy were treated. However, the growth of trade and industry from the eighteenth century onwards highlighted the shortcomings of existing institutions for dealing with the problems associated with greater mobility and a growing urban population. In response to these developments, a number of measures were introduced.

In the eighteenth century, turnpike trusts were created in an effort to improve the nation's major highways; improvement commissions were provided for the improvements within towns, and poor law unions were encouraged which could then build workhouses to provide work and accommodation for the poor. During the nineteenth century, the Poor Law Amendment Act (1834) established the Poor Law Commission to oversee the whole system of poor law relief and this represented 'the start of central control over the detailed administration of local services'.[1] Then, in 1848, growing concern over the nation's health produced the Public Health Act which established local Boards of Health, supervised by a Central Board of Health, for the provision of water supply and drainage. Twenty-four years later, 'the whole country was divided up into urban and rural sanitary districts . . . The urban authorities were boroughs, Improvement Commissioners and local Boards of Health: Poor Law Guardians became sanitary authorities for the parts of their union not included in the above.'[2]

The growth of educational facilities throughout the country had been sporadic, their existence largely dependent upon royal charters or voluntary agencies — usually the churches — but in 1870 the government required that all parishes should ensure that an adequate school existed within their area and six years later made school attendance compulsory.

The development of local government responsibilities and obligations was thus piecemeal and haphazard rather than part of a co-ordinated plan, and before the latter part of the nineteenth century little was done to rationalise the institutions themselves. Certainly, the Municipal Corporations Act of 1835 had attempted to bring order to the chaos (and sometimes corruption) of the boroughs, with new constitutions allowing for the election of councillors by the ratepayers and requiring the adoption of proper accounting procedures. But it was not until the Local Government Acts of 1888 and 1894 that a relatively coherent system of local government was established, based on the counties and the county boroughs — those boroughs with a population of 50,000 or more which possessed the same powers as the counties.[3] Beneath the counties were the second-tier authorities, the non-county boroughs and the urban and rural districts, and below these were third-tier authorities with very little authority — the parish councils. This was the basic structure which was to last until the implementation of the Local Government Act of 1972, a structure which, although it had created 62 county councils out of the 52 geographical counties, was 'the product of a combination of traditional, political and administrative factors [which] were never rationally delimited, in accordance with economic, demographic or functional criteria'.[4]

As the twentieth century progressed so the balance of responsibilities shifted. To the original concern with law and order and environmental health were added welfare, housing, education, planning and amenity functions, largely concentrated in the hands of the counties and county boroughs. On the other side of the coin, however, was the loss, usually to *ad hoc* bodies, of responsibility for gas, electricity and hospitals. Furthermore, as more demands were made upon local authorities by citizens seeking better standards, and by central governments concerned to improve uniformity of service among areas, local authorities, whose main source of revenue was the medieval tax known as the rate, came to be more dependent on central government grants.

The rate is a tax on property. Today, a valuation officer of the Board of Inland Revenue assigns a value to property related to its assumed rental value and local authorities tax that value at a level which will bring them the revenue they are seeking. Thus, in very general terms, if the total rateable value of a district is £10 million and the authority needs to raise £15 million, the rate will be set at £1.50 in the pound: i.e. a householder in a property with a rateable value of £500 will pay £750 in rates. Over the years, the income local authorities have derived from the rates has declined to about 33 per cent of their total revenue. The bulk of their income now derives from central government grants which take two basic forms. First, there are grants or subsidies for specific purposes such as the police, housing construction or rent rebates, and secondly there are block grants, not for particular purposes, but to supplement the rate income of authorities. Such grants, determined by the Secretary of State, are calculated according to formulae geared to producing a rough equality of resource among authorities in accordance with need and circumstance, i.e. taking into account such differences and demands as may arise from varying levels of population density, age groupings or geographic size.

While the rate is no longer the major source of revenue for local authorities, many still argue that such a local contribution to local financing is a valuable manifestation of local democracy, a last vestige of 'little brother' standing out against the encroachments of a centralising 'big sister'. However, the rate is undoubtedly an unfair tax for, like taxes on expenditure, it does not take into account 'ability to pay'. For example, a one-income family will pay the same rates as a neighbouring family living in a similar house but with several incomes. While the poorest in society may escape payment of rates, in part or in full, under rate rebate schemes, there is still an undesirable element of regressiveness about the tax. Further, while the arguments which speak in terms of local democracy and the link between the ratepayer and local government do have a certain appeal, a closer consideration of the existing situation reveals fundamental weaknesses. First, approximately 60 per cent of rateable income derives from businesses, not individual householders, and, therefore, a maximum of about 13 per cent (40 per cent of one-third) of the rate income is paid by householders. Secondly, as we have just mentioned above, many, because of economic status, pay little or nothing. Finally, many who live in rented accommodation are unaware of the fact that their rent includes an element towards the rates and therefore fail to relate their payment to the work of the local authority. In light of these facts, it would appear to make little sense to talk of the rates as 'providing a direct link

between what the local electorate demands in terms of local services and what it must pay for them'.[5]

That the rating system is far from perfect, either as an equitable
means of raising money or as a means of preserving local
democracy has long been recognised, but general agreement on
its replacement, or indeed on the appropriate role for local government, has been difficult to attain. In 1976 the Layfield Committee
argued for the introduction of a local income tax for the purpose
of enlarging the share of local taxation in total local revenue and
thereby sustaining local democracy.[6] However, an internal
departmental inquiry during the first Thatcher government
(which was pledged to reform the system) rejected the idea of
a local income tax, and it was not until the closing months of the
second Thatcher administration that a major change in local
government revenue-gathering was announced. Applicable
initially only to Scotland, its extension to the rest of the United
Kingdom is promised. Under the new scheme, the rate is replaced
by a poll tax called the 'community charge' to be paid by all adults,
rather than just householders, with the exception of the mentally
ill and elderly people living in homes and hospitals. Businesses
are to be made subject to a unified business rate to be levied
throughout the country and distributed to authorities according
to their adult population. While it spreads the financial burden
more widely across the community, the community charge is still
a regressive tax, taking no account of ability to pay. The poor and
students may be eligible for relief of 80 per cent of the charge,
but will still have to pay 20 per cent — where before they may
have paid nothing — in order that they may have, in the government's eyes, an incentive to take note of how their local authority operates.

The replacement of one inequitable tax by another has little to
commend it and a local income tax is surely the appropriate way
to combine fairness and local involvement. However, while the
source of finance for local authority activity is a major concern,
and while the major parties make appropriate statements which
seem to suggest a belief in the need for strong, healthy, local
democracy, developments over the last 20 years or so would seem
to suggest that no tinkering at the margin with the sources of
revenue is going to provide any significant check to the spread
of central government authority into areas traditionally considered
local.

By the 1960s, it was apparent that local authority units which had their origins in feudal times and which had only been 'tidied up' by the Victorians were not ideal for the provision of many services, whether they were centrally inspired or locally desired. Shifts in population from one area to another had produced a situation in which one county might have a population many times greater than another, and in which some districts were so small they could not effectively or efficiently perform the tasks demanded of them. As John Mackintosh wrote, citing an example of lilliputianism: '56 [Scottish burghs] have under 2,000 inhabitants and yet each constitutes a housing authority, several of which have an annual programme of one house'.[7] The 1972 Local Government Act which came into force on 1 April 1974 sought to provide an answer to these imperfections and also to create a balance 'between the claims of efficiency and the demands of representative democracy — the former generally calling for larger units of government which are, perforce, more remote from the electorate, while the latter, seeking to maintain some element of government relatively close to the people, calls for smaller units'.[8]

The new system established two basic levels of government, the county and the district, but also drew a distinction between the large conurbations where urban sprawl had long created problems whose resolution was hampered by the old boundaries, and non-metropolitan areas which represented a mix of urban and rural communities. In England and Wales, outside London,[9] six Metropolitan counties (Greater Manchester, Merseyside, South Yorkshire, West Yorkshire, West Midlands and Tyne and Wear) and 47 non-Metropolitan counties were established, as were 35 Metropolitan districts and 333 non-Metropolitan districts — the second-tier authorities. The counties were considered the most appropriate bodies for overall planning and co-ordination and were therefore given authority with regard to education, personal social services, libraries, planning, highways, housing (certain reserve powers, e.g. overspill), consumer protection, refuse disposal, museums and art galleries, parks and open spaces, playing fields and swimming baths, police and fire services.[10] The districts were given responsibility for services more closely related to local needs: planning (local); maintenance of unclassified roads; public transport (operation); housing and town development; building regulations; environmental health and services; refuse collection; museums and art galleries; parks and open spaces; playing fields and swimming baths; cemeteries and crematoria.

While the reforms of the 1970s did much to bring local government boundaries into line with twentieth-century conditions, the division of labour between county and district was, as indicated above, still confusing, and the changes were only achieved at a price — the greater remoteness of the institutions from the voter. But if the purpose of the 1972 Act was to rationalise and improve the efficiency of local government, subsequent actions by central government appear destined to transform the structure from a decision-making apparatus into an administrative rump operating more and more within the increasingly tight guidelines laid down in Westminster and Whitehall.

First, a number of acts during the 1970s undercut the authority and responsibility of local bodies. For example, the Housing Finance Act denied to the local authorities the right to determine the level of council house rents; the National Health Service Reorganisation Act replaced local authority health services by regional and area health authorities; the Water Act abolished local water undertakings in favour of regional water authorities. Secondly, while such steps did nothing for the morale of local government, an even greater threat to the manoeuvrability of local authorities came, during the 1980s, from Conservative government actions directed towards the twin goals of reducing inflation and of cutting back the role played by government, both national and local, in the life of the nation.

No government seeking to control or curtail government involvement in the economy could afford to ignore the fact that local authorities account for nearly a quarter of the nation's public expenditure and employ about three million people (virtually a tenth of the working population). Such large-scale expenditure could not be left unchecked if the Conservatives were to achieve their aims and during the 1980s there was massive intervention by the government in areas that had for long been in the competence of local authorities. In particular, the national government intervened to influence local authority expenditures. We have already noted that more than 50 per cent of local government income derives from the central government in grants of one kind or another and this power of the purse was a telling weapon in the government's armoury. Grants were withheld from authorities defined as over-spenders, and when some sought to raise supplementary rates to overcome this deficit such rates were made illegal. This was followed, in 1984, by the government taking powers to 'cap' the rate-levying powers of high-spending councils (i.e. to put a limit on the rate that could be raised). The following year 15 authorities were 'capped'.

Such use of financial muscle demonstrated quite clearly how subordinate local authorities are to the central government — to the extent that even the small amount of locally-raised finance is subject to central controls. But an even more significant, some would say sinister, display of governmental strength took place in 1986 when the Conservative government, dissatisfied with the way in which the Labour-dominated Greater London Council and six Metropolitan counties were conducting their affairs, abolished them and gave their functions largely to the boroughs and districts. The legislation providing for the abolition was hard fought, in both Commons and Lords, but a determined government — and the Conservative government was determined — can usually get its way. The Metropolitan county, created by one Conservative government, was thus destroyed by another.

While abolition of the GLC and the Metropolitan counties was the most visible of the attacks by the Thatcher government on what Mr Ridley, Secretary of State for the Environment, called 'municipal socialism', other actions in recent years have also demonstrated the power of the centre *vis-à-vis* the localities. Thus, in 1981, urban development corporations, whose chairmen and board members are appointed by the Secretary of State for the Environment, were established to deal with the problems of decay in the dockland areas of London and Merseyside, and in 1985 city action teams were set up to help in the rejuvenation of inner cities. Then, in 1987, Mrs Thatcher announced plans to establish other urban development corporations to which would be transferred, from the local authorities, the responsibility for reviving decaying, crime-ridden areas. The same year, the Conservative party election manifesto announced that a future Conservative government would require local authorities to put out to tender such services as refuse collection, street and building cleaning, vehicle maintenance, catering and ground maintenance. As 'privatisation' had played a major part in Conservative government strategy, both nationally and locally, such a commitment was, perhaps, not unexpected. However, the statement that individual schools would be able to opt out of local education authority control and, as independent charitable trusts, receive a direct grant from the Department of Education, was seen as another blow against the few significant remnants of local authority responsibility.

Gradually, then, units of local government which, in the past, have exercised a fair degree of local autonomy, even though their authority derived ultimately from Westminster, are becoming more like administrative arms of central governments which establish goals and priorities and demand acquiescence and implementation.

On the face of it, the situation in the United States is quite different, as the constitution guarantees to the states an independence never known to local authorities in Britain. Closer study will reveal, however, that the centralisation of government in the United Kingdom has a counterpart in the extension of Federal government influence into state and local matters.

The first governments of English-speaking peoples in North America developed, as we noted earlier, under the commercial charters granted by the monarch in Britain. While the exigencies of a frontier existence, far removed from London, required these colonial governments to exercise more power and authority than did local authorities in Britain, they were, nevertheless, still second-tier governments, subordinate and owing their existence to the central government in England. The American Revolution changed this picture entirely and 13 colonies became 13 independent states owing allegiance to no one and jealous of their hard-won autonomy. When the weaknesses of the Articles of Confederation became apparent, it was that jealousy which prescribed the terms for the creation of 'a more perfect union', the constitution.

At the formative stages then, developments in the two countries were in sharp contrast. In Britain, such authority as local units of government wielded they owed to the central government, whereas in the United States it was the local units, the states, which gave authority to the centre.

That small group of states which ratified the constitution and thereby created the United States has since grown to 50. During the century and a half following the Revolution, America expanded across the continent acquiring territory through purchase (the Louisiana purchase and that of Alaska representing the most spectacular real estate coups), through battle (with Indians or Mexicans), through annexation (Hawaii), or through simple and often peaceful settlement after a westward trek. As the nation expanded it did so on the principle of incorporating the new territories into the Union and ultimately according them statehood. In 1959, Alaska and Hawaii, the two non-contiguous territories, were admitted as the 49th and 50th states respectively.

All states are equal under the constitution and are guaranteed a republican form of government and territorial integrity. All but Nebraska, which is unicameral, have a bicameral legislature, and all are structurally similar to the national government in that they separate powers between legislative, executive and judicial branches. All have created a subordinate system of local government which in large part owes its existence and authority to the state government and which in a way, therefore, resembles the local government situation in the United Kingdom, although we must note that those sub-systems do vary, sometimes considerably, from state to state.

The 10th Amendment to the constitution declares that 'the powers not delegated to the United States by the Constitution, nor prohibited by it to the States, are reserved to the States respectively, or to the people' and this was taken by early Americans to imply the co-existence of two co-ordinate levels of government, each with its own clearly defined sphere. Even when it became apparent that the spheres were not clearly defined but, rather, overlapped and intertwined, the amendment was still looked to as the ultimate statement of the limits on the authority of the Federal government in relation to the states. But in reality, as the Supreme Court was to point out, the amendment merely stated a truism, 'that all is retained which has not yet been surrendered'.[11]

Furthermore, many were unaware of just how much had been surrendered, for lurking in Article I of the constitution, at the end of the list of the enumerated powers of Congress, was the so-called 'elastic clause' which gave Congress the authority 'to make all laws which shall be necessary and proper for carrying into execution the foregoing powers'. In 1819, Chief Justice John Marshall gave formal expression to what was involved here when he wrote: 'let the end be legitimate, let it be within the scope of the constitution, and all means which are appropriate, which are plainly adapted to that end, which are not prohibited, but consist with the letter and spirit of the constitution, are constitutional'.[12] This enunciation of the doctrine of implied powers arose during a case involving the attempt of the state of Maryland to tax a branch of the National Bank which had been opened within the state. The state had argued that the Federal government had no right to charter such a bank in the first place as no mention of this power was made in the constitution and secondly, that the state had the right to tax as this was a power reserved to the states. Marshall disposed of the first argument with the exposition of the doctrine quoted above, and of the second by arguing that 'the power to tax involves the power to destroy' and if the states had the power to destroy an agency of the national government 'the declaration that the constitution, and the laws made in pursuance thereof shall be the supreme law of the land is empty and unmeaning declamation'.[13]

In addition to the 'elastic clause', the constitution also contains the innocent-sounding interstate commerce clause: 'Congress shall have power . . . to regulate commerce . . . among the several states'. This was undoubtedly a much needed Federal power, since trade practices by the different states during the anarchic period under the Articles of Confederation had been a great hindrance to the development of commerce and industry. Indeed, it was concern to improve that situation which was one of the prime moving forces in securing the shift from the Articles to the constitution. This having been said, however, few could have foreseen how the clause would be interpreted at different times to advance or hinder (according to the predilections of Justices) Federal encroachment into areas thought to be the responsibility of states. The history of judicial interpretation of the clause merits a full-length book in itself. Suffice it here to note that interpretation has ranged from the very narrow, when 'commerce', for instance, was deemed not to include manufacture, thereby for a time preventing the Federal government from entering certain areas, to the most expansive so that today it would appear that virtually nothing in manufacture or commerce or any related activity, no matter how remote, can escape Federal regulation.

The interstate commerce clause and the 'elastic' clause have

provided the means whereby an expansionist Congress, backed
by a Supreme Court ready to interpret in expansionist fashion,
has been able to extend the area of Federal competence at the
expense of the states without the need to invoke the cumbersome
procedures of formal constitutional amendment. The growth has
been far from steady, its progress reflecting dominant political
values at different times, but it does appear to be inexorable,
despite the oft-expressed concern of some politicians, like President Ronald Reagan, at the spread of big government and big
bureaucracy. Their plans to return powers and responsibilities
to the states have achieved little and the dominant force in so
many areas remains the Federal government.

However, while the constitutional powers to which we have
just referred have been very significant factors in the shift of
responsibilities from state to Federal government, we must not
overlook that most important of tools in determining the ultimate
source of power within a state — the power of the purse (ignoring
here the power of the gun). The disbursement of money by the
Federal government, particularly in the twentieth century, has
been a major factor in the irrevocable enhancement of Federal
authority. Furthermore, the manner in which that money has
often been allocated directly to units of local government, by-
passing state authorities, has been a factor in the weakening of
state governments *vis-à-vis* their subordinate units.

Of course, before Congress can hand out money it needs to raise
it. Article I, section VIII of the constitution gives Congress the
'power to lay and collect taxes, duties, imposts and excises', the
last three to be applied uniformly throughout the United States
while 'direct taxes shall be apportioned among the several states
according to their respective numbers' (Article I, section II). This
apparent limitation on the ability of the Federal government to
lay taxes on incomes was largely circumvented for most of the
nineteenth century by Supreme Court rulings which 'proceeded
on the theory that the "direct tax" clauses should be confined
to land taxes and capitation taxes and should not be extended
to taxes which were not easily apportionable on the basis of
population'.[14] But in the tax cases of 1895 the Court changed its
stand, took a very narrow view of the constitutional wording, and
ruled that a tax on income from land was a 'direct' tax which had
therefore to be apportioned according to population. It also ruled

that incomes from state and municipal bonds were beyond the taxing capacity of the Federal government. As Corwin wrote, in one stroke 'most of the taxable wealth of the country [was put] out of the reach of the national government'. In 1913 the 16th Amendment to the constitution was ratified, giving Congress the 'power to lay taxes on incomes, from whatever source derived, without apportionment among the several states . . . '. Congress was now constitutionally equipped to meet the demands, both foreign and domestic, of the twentieth century.

Grants-in-aid have a history which long antedates the 16th Amendment for they can be traced back to as early as 1802. The earliest of these grants were of a general nature with money being given by the Federal government to the states for use at the states' discretion. Thus, in 1836 the Surplus Distribution Act gave surplus Federal funds from land sales to the states. However, the more general development of aid was in the form of specific or categorical grants for particular purposes. For instance, the Merrill Act of 1862 gave part of the public domain to the states for the support of higher education, while other programmes which received aid in the latter part of the nineteenth and early years of the twentieth centuries concerned agricultural experiment stations, state forestry and highways.[15]

While grants have a long history, it was not until the New Deal response to the depression of the 1930s that they really came into their own. During that period the Federal government greatly extended its authority in an effort to deal with the problems which individual states could not handle alone. A major economic recession could not be answered by piecemeal state programmes, and grants-in-aid became the principal means whereby the Federal government channelled help to the states through a variety of Federal programmes. Perhaps the most significant of these Acts was the 1935 Social Security Act which created a wide range of programmes providing assistance to the aged, the blind, dependent children, the unemployed. As Barfield has written, the Act 'provided a solid, enduring legal foundation for the Federal grant-in-aid system to reach into almost any area of domestic concern'.[16]

The New Deal may have been a 'take-off point' for grant-in-aid programmes but it was the 1960s and 1970s that witnessed the most dramatic increase in central dollar aid to state and local government. The 'Creative Federalism' of President Lyndon Johnson's 'Great Society', with its concern to find remedies for a wide range of society's ills — the problems of the inner city (urban decay and crime), of illiteracy, disease, racial discrimination — produced 240 categorical aid programmes which took the Federal government more and more into state and local matters. At times the Federal government went even further and some programmes, again as Barfield has written, 'by-passed state and local elected officials and established direct connections with local community groups and non-profit organisations or forced the creation of a new quasi-public structure (for instance Model Cities agencies) that operated beyond the effective control of state or local governments'.

Richard Nixon's 'New Federalism', with its revenue-sharing programme helped further weaken state authority at the same time as it sought to give to localities more responsibility for the money they spent. The thousands of local government units which were the recipients of financial assistance under the revenue-sharing acts were thereby freed, to some extent at least, from state control. Attempts have been made to check or even reverse this downgrading of state government. As McKay has written: 'devolving powers and responsibilities from the Federal to state governments was a constant theme in the 1981–1985 Reagan administration'[17] but moves to achieve these ends were largely checked by those entrenched interests which are to be found at all points in the grant 'chain'.

The Federal government has now taken on a vast array of responsibilities — totally or partially — for problems which were either historically left to the states or localities, or which are products of twentieth-century development, or for which no satisfactory answers could be found on a state-by-state basis. Thus Washington now plays a major role in providing funds to help the poor and disadvantaged, either through payments made directly to individuals, as with social security payments or veterans' benefits, or through categorical grants to states and cities for specific assistance programmes. Problems associated with the growth and decline of urban areas or of mass transit systems — two examples of twentieth-century problems — have attracted the attention of Federal politicians and planners, particularly as such problems have often been neglected by state governments. At times, problems which affect more than one state have evoked a state response as with, say, the Port Authority of New York, created in 1921 as a result of initiatives by the states of New York and New Jersey, and charged with developing the 'terminal, transportation and other facilities'[18] within the port district. At others, with pollution for instance, states have not had the political will or, sometimes, the financial resources to cure the evil and the Federal government has been obliged to act.

By the end of the 1970s 'there was almost no state or local activity — from library administration and art education to pothole repair and boating safety — that had not been penetrated by Federal dollars. The lines between national issues and sub-national issues were all but obliterated ... '.[19] Certainly the massed volumes of the Federal Register, listing all the Federal regulations issued in a year, stand as testimony to the extent of Federal involvement.

Given all this, an observer, viewing the American scene from Washington DC, could be forgiven for believing that American federalism is to all intents and purposes dead. Should he, however, manage to escape the marble corridors of the capital and spend some time in a variety of the states, he would discover that federalism is still alive, even though it is very different from the version created in the eighteenth century.

Much of the broad framework of law, both civil and criminal, within which Americans live is provided by state and local governments which thereby help determine the quality of the environment for their citizens. A few examples: it is the individual states which determine the age at which a resident may leave school; drive a car; drink alcohol; or marry. Crime, and punishment, are largely state matters. Thus, in a majority of states convicted murderers may be subject to the death penalty (by gas chamber, electric chair, hanging, shooting or lethal injection according to state) but in the remaining states face only a term of imprisonment. Or, again, in some states possession of marijuana for personal use may be treated as a misdemeanour, attracting only minimal penalty, while elsewhere it may be punishable by anything up to a 40-year prison sentence. Of course these laws and punishments must be consistent with the United States constitution as interpreted by the Supreme Court, and from time to time the Court has ruled that the states were in breach of the constitution. For instance, for a time capital punishment was suspended on the grounds that the laws providing for it were vague and imprecise. When they were re-written in precise fashion the punishment was upheld. States may no longer forbid abortions or the use of contraceptives. Laws with regard to censorship may fall foul of the 1st Amendment. Nevertheless, there does still remain a considerable body of law which is state not Federal law.

There are also those apparently small matters which are significant in determining the quality of life which will be enjoyed. These are largely dependent upon state and local decisions: for example, the state of the local roads; the provision (or not) of street lighting; the regularity of garbage collection; the supply of water; the disposal of sewage; the availability of libraries or of parks; of adequate police protection or of an efficient fire brigade service; the state of the public educational facilities. While Federal money and influence may have infiltrated into many of these areas, all are still largely the responsibility of the state or of its lesser units of government. All in all, then, despite the ubiquity of the McDonalds' hamburgers and Coca Cola, considerable diversity of lifestyle is apparent among the states

Diversity is also to be found in the manner in which the respective states raise the money to provide their services. While all Americans may be subject to a Federal tax on their incomes and to Federal taxes on alcohol and petrol (gasoline), their other liabilities to tax will depend upon the state and local jurisdiction within which they live. Sales and property taxes are the most common means of raising income in the states, but the rates at which they are levied will depend upon the state or the locality. Most states now have a state income tax although a few still resist its introduction. New York city offers a good example of the variety which may occur. Those who live or work there are subject not only to the Federal taxes and to state income tax and sales tax, but also to a city income tax and a city sales tax, as well as their normal property taxes. Even the resting place of the final authority for determining questions of tax will differ from state to state. In some, the elected officials, in the form of the state governor and state legislators, will make the decisions. In others, state constitutions demand that proposals for an increase in taxes be approved by the people in a referendum, or may provide opportunities for citizens to put a proposition to the electorate concerning a tax matter. The most famous — or infamous — use of the power of the proposition in recent years was Proposition 13 in California. This amendment to the state constitution, approved in 1978, cut property taxes and limited the authority of different units of local government — cities, counties, school districts — to raise taxes. It even diminished the authority of the state government by requiring a two-thirds vote in the legislature before state taxes could be raised.

Finally, we must remember that while their powers and responsibilities have been eroded slowly over the years, the states still provide the arenas within which many political battles occur and still help to set the tone of those conflicts. Many voters are still more concerned with questions that relate specifically to the district or the state, and the parties which are, as we have noted elsewhere, basically local not national in temperament or outlook, react accordingly. The integrity of the states as territorial units is reflected in their equal representation in the Senate and in the fact that the President is elected by electoral college votes which are distributed among the states according to the total number of Representatives and Senators they have in Congress. Presidential candidates, while seeking national office, are thus obliged to make parochial as well as national appeals. The states are, then, still central to the political process.

In conclusion, we see that in both the United Kingdom and the United States there has been a weakening of those units of government which lie beyond the centre. While many factors have contributed to the changes, the assumption by the central governments of responsibility for guiding and controlling the economy, whether in an attempt to defeat depression or to control inflation, has undoubtedly been a major force. The means whereby governments have sought to achieve those ends have been varied but central to them all has been the ultimate control of the purse through the progressive income tax.

In many respects, the shifts have been untidy and piecemeal, pragmatic responses to problems as they appeared or as they became uppermost in political consciousness. But at times, as one might expect, an overtly political dimension has entered the picture. Thus, in Britain the Conservative governments of Mrs Thatcher have 'privatised' or centralised in an effort, among other objectives, to weaken the 'hot-beds of socialism' supposedly to be found in some areas of local government. In the United States on the other hand, politicians of the Nixon or Reagan ilk have sought to reverse the trend towards the centre and to return to the states a greater responsibility for decision making. These efforts have largely failed, thanks to what David Stockman has called, despairingly, the 'Triumph of Politics'.[20]

America is still not as centralised as Britain, where even local elections have turned into microcosms of the national party battle, with local issues taking second place to political images. History, geography, constitutional arrangements will probably all conspire to preserve for Americans at least an outward shell of federalism behind which will survive some of those distinctive characteristics that contribute to the diversity that is the United States. In Britain, on the other hand, unless the nationalist parties of the Celtic fringes are able to secure some degree of independence from Westminster, it would seem that government will be more and more concentrated in the hands of the central government and that local authorities will become largely administrative appendages of a centralised decision-making and fund-raising apparatus.

Notes

1. Richards, P.G. (1973) *The Reformed Local Government System*, Allen & Unwin, p.16. This is a most useful volume for an introduction to the history and development of local government in Britain.
2. *Ibid.* p.18.
3. Four boroughs, for traditional or sentimental reasons, with populations less than 50,000 were also accorded county borough status.
4. Hanson and Walles, *op. cit.* p.252.
5. *The Future Shape of Local Government Finance*, Cmnd 4761, 1971, Appendix 3. Reproduced in Minogue, M. (ed.) (1977) *Documents on Contemporary British Government*, CUP, Vol.2, pp.267–78.
6. *Local Government Finance*, (The Layfield Report) Cmnd 6453. Reproduced in Minogue, *op.cit.* pp.284–98.
7. 'Devolution and Regionalism: The Scottish Case', *Public Law*, spring 1964, p.23.
8. Hanson and Walles, *op. cit.* p.266.
9. Local government in London has always been treated differently

from the rest of the country and, by the Local Government Act of 1963, the Greater London Council was established to provide co-ordinated planning for the conurbation. In Scotland, change came in 1975 with the establishment of seven top-tier authorities and 37 second-tier districts.

10. In the Metropolitan areas, education and personal and social services were given to the district not the county, but the county had the task of Passenger Transport Authority.

11. *US* v. *Darby*, 312 US 100, 1941.

12. *McCullough* v. *Maryland* 4 Wheat. 316.

13. *Ibid.*

14. Corwin, E.S. (1978) *The Constitution and What it Means Today*, Princeton, revised by Harold W. Chase and Craig R. Ducat, p.41. The cases cited are *Pollock* v. *Farmers Loan and Trust Co.*, 157 US 429 and 158 US 601. The next quotation is from the same work at p.41.

15. Barfield, C.E. (1981) *Rethinking Federalism*, AEI.

16. *Ibid.* p.12 and next quotation p.16.

17. McKay, D. (1985) 'Theory and Practice in Public Policy', *Political Studies*, XXXIII 1985, pp.181–202.

18. Sayre, W.S. and Kaufman, H. (1960) *Governing New York City*, Norton & Co.

19. Barfield, *op.cit.* p.17.

20. Stockman, D.A. (1985) *The Triumph of Politics*, Harper & Row. Apart from the very interesting highlights this book throws on decision-making processes, it is a rather frightening tale of how a young, impassioned naive, armed with a spurious theory, could so impress those with no theories at all that he became Director of the Office of Management and Budget at the tender age of 34.

Bibliography

This selection does not in any way attempt to be comprehensive but seeks rather to draw to your attention a number of books, in addition to those already noted in the text, which may broaden your understanding of and deepen your insight into the two systems of government. It is, of course, important for students of government and politics to keep abreast of contemporary developments through a regular reading of journals and the quality newspapers.

Societies

Annual Statistical Abstracts of the United States, US Department of Commerce, Bureau of the Census.
Britain: An Official Handbook (annually) HMSO London.
Goldthorpe, J. (1980) *Social Mobility and Class Structure in Britain*, Clarendon Press.
Hartz, L. (1955) *The Liberal Tradition in America*, Harcourt, Brace and World.
Lipset, S.M. (1964) *The First New Nation*, Heinemann.
Social Trends (annually) HMSO.
Zentner, P. (1982) *Social Democracy in Britain*, John Martin.

Constitutions

Corwin, E.S. (1978) *The Constitution and What it Means Today* (Revised by Harold W. Chase and Craig R. Ducat) Princeton University Press.
Johnson, N. (1980) *In Search of the Constitution*, Methuen.
Norton, P. (1982) *The Constitution in Flux*, Martin Robertson.

Representation

Butler, D. *et al.* (1951 to date) *The British General Election Series*, Macmillan.
Heath, A., Jowell, R. and Curtice, J. (1985) *How Britain Votes*, Pergamon Press.
Jacobsen G.C. (1980) *Money in Congressional Elections*, Yale University Press.

McGinnis, J. (1969) *The Selling of the President 1968*, Trident Press.
Maisel, L.S. (1987) *Parties and Elections in America*, Random House.
Maisel, L.S. and Cooper, J. (eds) (1981) *Congressional Elections*, Sage.
Malbin, M.J. (1984) *Money and Politics in the United States*, American Enterprise Institute.
Nie, N.H. *et al.* (1979) *The Changing American Voter*, Harvard University Press.
Polsby, N.W. and Wildavsky, A. (1980) *Presidential Elections*, 5th edn, Charles Scribner & Sons.
Pomper, G. (1975) *Voters' Choice*, Harper & Row.
Pomper, G. *et al.* (1985) *The Election of 1984*, Chatham House.
Pomper, G. and Lederman, S. (1980) *Elections in America*, Longman.
Pulzer, P.G.J. (1975) *Political Representation and Elections in Britain*, 3rd edn, Allen & Unwin.
Wayne, S.J. (1980) *The Road to the White House*, Macmillan.
White, T. (1961) *The Making of the President 1960*, Atheneum. (And subsequent volumes to 1972.)

Legislatures

Arnold, R.D. (1979) *Congress and the Bureaucracy*, Yale University Press.
Bradshaw, K. and Pring, D. (1973) *Parliament and Congress*, Quartet.
Dodd, L.C. and Oppenheimer, B.I. (1981) *Congress Reconsidered* Congressional Quarterly Press.
Fisher, L. (1985) *Constitutional Conflicts between Congress and the President*, Princeton University Press.
How Congress Works (1983), Congressional Quarterly Press.
Judge, D. (ed.) (1983) *The Politics of Parliamentary Reform*, Heinemann.
Mann, T.E. and Ornstein, N.J.(eds) (1981) *The New Congress*, AEI.
Mayhew, D. (1974) *Congress: The Electoral Connection*, Yale University Press.
Norton, P. (ed.) (1985) *Parliament in the 1980s*, Blackwell.
Norton, P. (1981) *The Commons in Perspective*, Martin Robertson.
Sundquist, J.L. (1981) *The Decline and Resurgence of Congress*, Brookings.
Walkland, S.A. (ed.) (1979) *The House of Commons in the Twentieth Century*, OUP.
Walkland, S.A. and Ryle, M. (eds) (1981) *The Commons Today*, Fontana.

Parties

Ball, A.R. (1987) *British Political Parties*, 2nd edn, Macmillan.
Beer, S.H. (1982) *Modern British Politics*, 3rd edn, Faber.
Bogdanor, V. (ed.) (1983) *Liberal Party Politics*, OUP.
Bogdanor, V. (1983) *The People and the Party System*, CUP.

Bogdanor, V. (1983) *Multi-Party Politics and the Constitution*, CUP.
Bradley, I. (1981) *Breaking the Mould*, Martin Robertson.
Broder, D.S. (1972) *The Party's Over*, Harper & Row.
Burns, J.M. (1963) *The Deadlock of Democracy*, Prentice Hall.
Chambers, W.N. and Dean Burnham, W. (eds) *The American Party Systems*, OUP.
Drucker, H. *et al.* (eds) (1987) *Developments in British Politics*, Macmillan.
Ewing, K. (1987) *The Funding of Political Parties in Britain*, CUP.
Finer, S.E. (1980) *The Changing British Party System*, AEI.
Finer, S.E. (ed.) (1975) *Adversary Politics and Electoral Reform*, Wigram.
Gamble, A.M. and Walkland, S.A. (1984) *The British Party System and Economic Policy 1945–1983*, Clarendon Press.
Ingle, S. (1987) *The British Party System*, Blackwell.
Kavanagh, D. (ed.) (1982) *The Politics of the Labour Party*, Allen & Unwin.
Keefe, W.J. (1984) *Parties, Politics and Public Policy in America*, 4th edn, Holt, Rinehart & Winston.
Key, V.O. (1964) *Politics, Parties and Pressure Groups in America*, 5th edn, Thomas Y. Cromwell.
Kogan, D. and M. (1982) *The Battle for the Labour Party*, Fontana.
Layton-Henry, Z. (ed.) (1980) *Conservative Party Politics*, Macmillan.
Ladd, E.C. Jr and Hadley, C.D. (1975) *Transformations of the American Party System*, 2nd edn, Norton.
Sorauf, F.J. (1980) *Party Politics in America*, 4th edn, Little, Brown.
Wattenberg, M.P. (1984) *The Decline of American Political Parties 1952–1980*, Harvard University Press.
Young, A. (1983) *The Re-selection of Parliamentary Candidates*, Heinemann.

The Executives

Bowles, N. (1987) *The White House and Capitol Hill*, Clarendon Press.
Blake, Lord (1975) *The Office of Prime Minister*, OUP.
Burns, J.M. (1984) *The Power to Lead*, Simon & Schuster.
Corwin, E.S. (1984) *The President: Office and Powers*, University of London Press.
Hargrove, E.C. and Nelson, M. (1984) *Presidents, Politics and Policy*, Alfred A. Knopf.
Heclo H.L. and Salamon, L. (eds) (1981) *The Illusion of Presidential Government*, Westview Press.
Herman, V. and Alt, J. (eds) (1977) *Cabinet Studies: A Reader*, Macmillan.
King, A. (ed.) (1985) *The British Prime Minister*, 2nd edn, Macmillan.
Mackintosh, J.P. (1977) *The British Cabinet*, 3rd edn, Stevens.
Neustadt, R. (1980) *Presidential Power*, John Wiley.
Schlesinger, A.M. Jr (1984) *The Imperial Presidency*, Houghton Mifflin.
Walker, P.G. (1972) *The Cabinet*, rev. edn, Fontana.
Wilson, H. (1977) *The Governance of Britain*, Sphere Books.

Bureaucracy

Barnett, J. (1982) *Inside the Treasury*, André Deutsch.
Crowther-Hunt, Lord and Kellner, P. (1977) *The Civil Servants*, Macdonald-Futura.
Garrett, J. (1980) *Managing the Civil Service*, Heinemann.
Heclo, H. (1976) *A Government of Strangers*, Brookings.
Heclo, H. and Wildavsky, A. (1981) *The Private Government of Public Money*, 2nd edn, Macmillan.
Seidman, H. (1980) *Politics, Position and Power*, 3rd edn, OUP.

Groups

Berry, J.M. (1977) *Lobbying for the People*, Princeton University Press.
Berry, J.M. (1984) *The Interest Group Society*, Little, Brown.
Deakins, J. (1966) *The Lobbyists*, Public Affairs Press.
Grant, W. and Marsh, D. (1977) *The Confederation of British Industries*, Hodder & Stoughton.
Kimber, R. and Richardson, J. (1974) *Pressure Groups in Britain*, Dent.
Lowi, T.J. (1979) *The End of Liberalism*, 2nd edn, Norton & Co.
McConnell, G. (1967) *Private Power and American Democracy*, Alfred A. Knopf.
Ornstein, N.J. and Elder, S. (1978) *Interest Groups, Lobbying and Policy-Making*, Congressional Quarterly Press.
Richardson, J.J. and Jordan, A.G. (1979) *Governing Under Pressure*, Martin Robertson.
Sabato, L. (1981) *The Rise of Political Consultants*, Basic Books.
Wilson, G. (1981) *Interest Groups in the United States*, Clarendon Press.

Courts

Abraham, H.J. (1980) *The Judicial Process*, OUP.
Bickel, A. (1962) *The Least Dangerous Branch*, Bobbs-Merrill.
Blasi, V. (ed.) (1983) *The Burger Court*, Yale University Press.
Hartley, T.C. and Griffith J.A.G. (1981) *Government and Law*, 2nd edn, Weidenfeld & Nicolson.
Morrison, F.L. (1973) *Courts and the Political Process in England*, Sage.
Scarman, L. (1974) *English Law — The New Dimension*, Stevens.
Wade, H.W.R. (1980) *Constitutional Fundamentals*, Stevens.
Witt, E. (ed.) (1979) *Congressional Quarterly Guide to the United States Supreme Court*, Congressional Quarterly Press.
Woodward, B. and Armstrong, S. (1979) *The Brethren*, Simon & Schuster.

Government Beyond the Centre

Alexander, A. (1982) *The Politics of Local Government in the United Kingdom*, Longman.

Byrne, T. (1985) *Local Government in Britain*, 3rd edn, Pelican.

Elcock, H.J. (1982) *Local Government*, Methuen.

Hogwood, B. and Keating, M. (eds) (1982) *Regional Government in England*, OUP.

Lowi, T. and Stone, A. (eds) (1978) *Nationalising Government*, Sage.

Morehouse, S. (1981) *State Politics, Parties and Policy*, Holt, Rinehart & Winston.

Reagan, M. and Sanzone, J. (1981) *The New Federalism*, OUP.

Sharkansky, I. (1977) *The Maligned States*, 2nd edn, McGraw Hill.

Wright, D.S. (1982) *Understanding Intergovernmental Relations*, 2nd edn, Duxbury.

Appendix

The Constitution of the United States of America

We the People of the United States, in Order to form a more perfect Union, establish Justice, insure domestic Tranquility, provide for the common defence, promote the general Welfare, and secure the Blessings of Liberty to ourselves and our Posterity, do ordain and establish this Constitution for the United States of America.

Article 1

Section 1. All legislative Powers herein granted shall be vested in a Congress of the United States, which shall consist of a Senate and House of Representatives.

Section 2. The House of Representatives shall be composed of Members chosen every second Year by the People of the several States, and the Electors in each State shall have the Qualifications requisite for Electors of the most numerous Branch of the State Legislature.

No Person shall be a Representative who shall not have attained to the age of twenty five Years, and been seven Years a Citizen of the United States, and who shall not, when elected, be an Inhabitant of that State in which he shall be chosen.

Representatives and direct Taxes shall be apportioned among the several States which may be included within this Union, according to their respective Numbers, which shall be determined by adding to the whole Number of free Persons, including those bound to Service for a Term of Years, and excluding Indians not taxed, *three fifths of all other persons.*[1] The actual Enumeration shall be made within three Years after the first Meeting of the Congress of the United States, and within every subsequent Term of ten Years, in such Manner as they shall by Law direct. The Number of Representatives shall not exceed one for every thirty Thousand, but each State shall have at Least one Representative: and until such enumeration shall be made, the State of New Hampshire shall be entitled to chuse three, Massachusetts eight, Rhode-Island and Providence Plantations one,

---

[1] Italics indicate passages altered by subsequent amendments. This was revised by the Sixteenth (apportionment of taxes) and Fourteenth (determination of persons) Amendments.

188

Connecticut five, New-York six, New Jersey four, Pennsylvania eight, Delaware one, Maryland six, Virginia ten, North Carolina five, South Carolina five, and Georgia three.

When vacancies happen in the Representation from any State, the Executive Authority thereof shall issue Writs of Election to fill such Vacancies.

The House of Representatives shall chuse their Speaker and other Officers; and shall have the sole Power of Impeachment.

Section 3. The Senate of the United States shall be composed of two Senators from each State, *chosen by the Legislature thereof,*[2] for six Years; and each Senator shall have one Vote.

Immediately after they shall be assembled in Consequence of the first Election, they shall be divided as equally as may be into three Classes. The Seats of the Senators of the first Class shall be vacated at the Expiration of the second Year, of the Second Class at the Expiration of the fourth Year, and of the third Class at the Expiration of the sixth Year, so that one third may be chosen every second year; *and if Vacancies happen by Resignation, or otherwise, during the Recess of the Legislature of any State, the Executive thereof may make temporary Appointments until the next Meeting of the Legislature, which shall then fill such Vacancies.*[3]

No Person shall be a Senator who shall not have attained to the Age of thirty Years, and been nine Years a Citizen of the United States, and who shall not, when elected, be an Inhabitant of the State for which he shall be chosen.

The Vice President of the United States shall be President of the Senate, but shall have no Vote, unless they be equally divided.

The Senate shall chuse their other Officers, and also a President pro tempore, in the Absence of the Vice President, or when he shall exercise the Office of President of the United States.

The Senate shall have the sole Power to try all Impeachments. When sitting for that Purpose, they shall be on Oath or Affirmation. When the President of the United States is tried, the Chief Justice shall preside: And no Person shall be convicted without the Concurrence of two thirds of the Members present.

Judgment in Cases of Impeachment shall not extend further than to removal from Office, and disqualification to hold and enjoy any Office of honor, Trust or Profit under the United States; but the Party convicted shall nevertheless be liable and subject to Indictment, Trial, Judgment and Punishment, according to Law.

Section 4. The Times, Places and Manner of holding Elections for Senators and Representatives, shall be prescribed in each State by the Legislature thereof; but the Congress may at any time by Law make or alter such Regulations, except as to the Places of chusing Senators.

The Congress shall assemble at least once in every Year, and such

[2] Revised by Seventeenth Amendment.

[3] Revised by Seventeenth Amendment.

Meeting shall be *on the first Monday in December,*[4] unless they shall by Law appoint a different Day.

Section 5.   Each House shall be the Judge of the Elections, Returns and Qualifications of its own Members, and a Majority of each shall constitute a Quorum to do Business; but a smaller Number may adjourn from day to day, and may be authorized to compel the Attendance of absent Members, in such Manner, and under such Penalties as each House may provide.

Each House may determine the Rules of its Proceedings, punish its Members for disorderly Behavior, and, with the Concurrence of two thirds, expel a Member.

Each House shall keep a Journal of its Proceedings, and from time to time publish the same, excepting such parts as may in their Judgment require Secrecy; and the Yeas and Nays of the Members of either House on any question shall, at the Desire of one fifth of those Present, be entered on the Journal.

Neither House, during the Session of Congress, shall, without the Consent of the other, adjourn for more than three days, nor to any other Place than that in which the two Houses shall be sitting.

Section 6.   The Senators and Representatives shall receive a Compensation for their Services, to be ascertained by Law, and paid out of the Treasury of the United States. They shall in all Cases, except Treason, Felony and Breach of the Peace, be privileged from Arrest during their Attendance at the Session of their respective Houses, and in going to and returning from the same, and for any Speech or Debate in either House, they shall not be questioned in any other Place.

No Senator or Representative shall, during the Time for which he was elected, be appointed to any civil Office under the Authority of the United States, which shall have been created, or the Emoluments whereof shall have been encreased during such time; and no Person holding any Office under the United States, shall be a Member of either House during his Continuance in Office.

Section 7.   All Bills for raising Revenue shall originate in the House of Representatives; but the Senate may propose or concur with Amendments as on other Bills.

Every Bill which shall have passed the House of Representatives and the Senate, shall, before it become a Law, be presented to the President of the United States; if he approve he shall sign it, but if not he shall return it, with his Objections to that House in which it shall have originated, who shall enter the Objections at large on their Journal, and proceed to reconsider it. If after such Reconsideration two thirds of that House shall agree to pass the Bill, it shall be sent, together with the Objections, to the other House, by which it shall likewise be reconsidered, and if approved by two thirds of that House, it shall become a Law. But in all such Cases the Votes of both Houses shall be determined by Yeas and Nays, and the Names of the Persons voting for and against the Bill

[4] Revised by Twentieth Amendment.

shall be entered on the Journal of each House respectively. If any Bill shall not be returned by the President within ten Days (Sundays excepted) after it shall have been presented to him, the Same shall be a Law, in like Manner as if he had signed it, unless the Congress by their Adjournment prevent its Return, in which Case it shall not be a Law.

Every Order, Resolution, or Vote to which the Concurrence of the Senate and House of Representatives may be necessary (except on a question of Adjournment) shall be presented to the President of the United States; and before the Same shall take Effect, shall be approved by him, or being disapproved by him, shall be repassed by two thirds of the Senate and House of Representatives, according to the Rules and Limitations prescribed in the Case of a Bill.

Section 8. The Congress shall have Power To lay and collect Taxes, Duties, Imposts and Excises, to pay the Debts and provide for the common Defence and general Welfare of the United States; but all Duties, Imposts and Excises shall be uniform throughout the United States;

To borrow Money on the credit of the United States;

To regulate Commerce with foreign Nations, and among the several States, and with the Indian Tribes;

To establish an uniform Rule of Naturalization, and uniform Laws on the subject of Bankruptcies throughout the United States;

To coin Money, regulate the Value thereof, and of foreign Coin, and fix the Standard of Weights and Measures;

To provide for the Punishment of counterfeiting the Securities and current Coin of the United States;

To establish Post Offices and post Roads;

To promote the Progress of Science and useful Arts, by securing for limited Times to Authors and Inventors the exclusive Right to their respective Writings and Discoveries;

To constitute Tribunals inferior to the Supreme Court;

To define and punish piracies and Felonies committed on the high Seas, and Offences against the Law of Nations;

To declare War, grant Letters of Marque and Reprisal, and make Rules concerning Captures on Land and Water;

To raise and support Armies, but no Appropriation of Money to that Use shall be for a longer Term than two Years;

To provide and maintain a Navy;

To make Rules for the Government and Regulation of the land and naval Forces;

To provide for calling forth the Militia to execute the Laws of the Union, suppress Insurrections and repel Invasions;

To provide for organizing, arming, and disciplining, the Militia, and for governing such Part of them as may be employed in the Service of the United States, reserving to the States respectively, the Appointment of the Officers, and the Authority of training the Militia according to the discipline prescribed by Congress;

To exercise exclusive Legislation in all Cases whatsoever, over such District (not exceeding ten Miles square) as may, by Cession of particular

States, and the Acceptance of Congress, become the Seat of the Government of the United States, and to exercise like Authority over all Places purchased by the Consent of the Legislature of the State in which the Same shall be, for the Erection of Forts, Magazines, Arsenals, dock-Yards, and other needful Buildings; — And

To make all Laws which shall be necessary and proper for carrying into Execution the foregoing Powers, and all other Powers vested by this Constitution in the Government of the United States, or in any Department or Officer thereof.

Section 9. The Migration or Importation of such Persons as any of the States now existing shall think proper to admit, shall not be prohibited by the Congress prior to the Year one thousand eight hundred and eight, but a Tax or duty may be imposed on such Importation, not exceeding ten dollars for each Person.

The Privilege of the Writ of Habeas Corpus shall not be suspended, unless when in Cases of Rebellion or Invasion the public Safety may require it.

No Bill of Attainder or ex post facto Law shall be passed.

No Capitation, or other direct, Tax shall be laid, unless in Proportion to the Census or Enumeration herein before directed to be taken.[5]

No Tax or Duty shall be laid on Articles exported from any State.

No Preference shall be given by any Regulation of Commerce or Revenue to the Ports of one State over those of another; nor shall Vessels bound to, or from, one State, be obliged to enter, clear, or pay Duties in another.

No Money shall be drawn from the Treasury, but in Consequence of Appropriations made by Law; and a regular Statement and Account of the Receipts and Expenditures of all public Money shall be published from time to time.

No title of Nobility shall be granted by the United States: And no Person holding any Office of Profit or Trust under them, shall, without the Consent of the Congress, accept of any present, Emolument, Office, or Title, of any kind whatever, from any King, Prince, or foreign State.

Section 10. No State shall enter into any Treaty, Alliance, or Confederation; grant Letters of Marque and Reprisal; coin Money; emit Bills of Credit; make any Thing but gold and silver Coin a Tender in Payment of Debts; pass any Bill of Attainder, ex post facto Law, or Law impairing the Obligation of Contracts, or Grant any Title of Nobility.

No State shall, without the Consent of the Congress, lay any Imposts or Duties on Imports or Exports, except what may be absolutely necessary for executing its inspection Laws: and the net Produce of all Duties and Imposts, laid by any State on Imports or Exports, shall be for the Use of the Treasury of the United States; and all such Laws shall be subject to the Revision and Controul of the Congress.

No State shall, without the Consent of Congress, lay any Duty of Tonnage, keep Troops, or Ships of War in time of Peace, enter into any

[5] Revised by Sixteenth Amendment.

Agreement or Compact with another State, or with a foreign Power, or engage in War, unless actually invaded, or in such imminent Danger as will not admit of delay.

Article II

Section 1. The executive Power shall be vested in a President of the United States of America. *He shall hold his Office during the Term of four Years,*[6] and, together with the Vice President, chosen for the same Term be elected as follows:

Each State shall appoint, in such Manner as the Legislature thereof may direct, a Number of Electors, equal to the whole Number of Senators and Representatives to which the State may be entitled in the Congress but no Senator or Representative, or Person holding an Office of Trust or Profit under the United States, shall be appointed an Elector.

The Electors shall meet in their respective States, and vote by Ballot for two Persons, of whom one at least shall not be an Inhabitant of the same State with themselves. And they shall make a List of all the Persons voted for, and of the Number of Votes for each; which List they shall sign and certify, and transmit sealed to the Seat of the Government of the United States, directed to the President of the Senate. The President of the Senate shall, in the Presence of the Senate and House of Representatives, open all the Certificates, and the Votes shall then be counted. The Person having the greatest Number of Votes shall be the President, if such Number be a Majority of the whole Number of Electors appointed; and if there be more than one who have such Majority, and have an equal Number of Votes, then the House of Representatives shall immediately chuse by Ballot one of them for President; and if no Person have a Majority, then from the five highest on the List the said House shall in like Manner chuse the President. But in chusing the President, the Votes shall be taken by States, the Representation from each State having one Vote. A quorum for this purpose shall consist of a Member or Members from two thirds of the States, and a Majority of all the States shall be necessary to a Choice. In every Case, after the Choice of the President, the Person having the greatest Number of Votes of the Electors shall be the Vice President. But if there should remain two or more who have equal Votes, the Senate shall chuse from them by Ballot the Vice President.[7]

The Congress may determine the Time of chusing the Electors, and the Day on which they shall give their Votes; which Day shall be the same throughout the United States.

No Person except a natural born Citizen, or a Citizen of the United States, at the time of the Adoption of this Constitution, shall be eligible to the Office of President; neither shall any Person be eligible to that Office who shall not have attained to the Age of thirty five Years, and been fourteen Years a Resident within the United States.

---

[6] See Twenty-second Amendment.
[7] Superseded by Twelfth Amendment.

In case of the Removal of the President from Office, or of his Death, Resigna-
tion, or Inability to discharge the Powers and Duties of the said Office, the Same
shall devolve on the Vice President, and the Congress may by Law provide for
the Case of Removal, Death, Resignation or Inability, both of the President and
Vice President, declaring what Officer shall then act as President, and such Officer
shall act accordingly, until the Disability be removed, or a President shall be
elected.[8]

The President shall, at stated Times, receive for his Services, a Compensation which shall neither be encreased nor diminished during the Period
for which he shall have been elected, and he shall not receive within
that Period any other Emolument from the United States, or any of them.

Before he enter on the Execution of his Office, he shall take the following Oath or Affirmation. — "I do solemnly swear (or affirm) that I will
faithfully execute the Office of President of the United States, and will
to the best of my Ability, preserve, protect and defend the Constitution
of the United States."

Section 2.   The President shall be Commander in Chief of the Army
and Navy of the United States, and of the Militia of the several States,
when called into the actual service of the United States; he may require
the Opinion, in writing, of the principal Officer in each of the executive
Departments, upon any Subject relating to the Duties of their respective Offices, and he shall have Power to grant Reprieves and Pardons
for Offences against the United States, except in Cases of Impeachment.

He shall have Power, by and with the Advice and Consent of the
Senate, to make Treaties, provided two thirds of the Senators present
concur; and he shall nominate, and by and with the Advice and Consent of the Senate, shall appoint Ambassadors, and other public Ministers
and Consuls, Judges of the supreme Court, and all other Officers of the
United States, whose Appointments are not herein otherwise provided
for, and which shall be established by Law: but the Congress may by
Law vest the Appointment of such inferior Officers, as they think proper,
in the President alone, in the Courts of Law, or in the Heads of
Departments.

The President shall have Power to fill up all Vacancies that may happen
during the Recess of the Senate, by granting Commissions which shall
expire at the End of their next Session.

Section 3.   He shall from time to time give to the Congress Information
of the State of the Union, and recommend to their Consideration such
Measures as he shall judge necessary and expedient; he may, on extra-
ordinary Occasions, convene both Houses, or either of them, and in Case
of Disagreement between them, with Respect to the Time of Adjournment, he may adjourn them to such Time as he shall think proper; he
shall receive Ambassadors and other public Ministers, he shall take Care

[8] Revised by Twenty-fifth Amendment.

that the Laws be faithfully executed, and shall Commission all the Officers of the United States.

Section 4. The President, Vice President and all civil Officers of the United States, shall be removed from Office on Impeachment for, and Conviction of Treason, Bribery, or other high Crimes and Misdemeanors.

Article III

Section 1. The judicial Power of the United States, shall be vested in one supreme Court and in such inferior Courts as the Congress may from time to time ordain and establish. The Judges, both of the supreme and inferior Courts, shall hold their Offices during good Behavior, and shall, at stated Times, receive for their Services, a Compensation, which shall not be diminished during their Continuance in Office.

Section 2. The judicial Power shall extend to all Cases, in Law and Equity, arising under this Constitution, the Laws of the United States, and Treaties made, or which shall be made, under their Authority; — to all Cases affecting Ambassadors, other public Ministers and Consuls; — to all Cases of admiralty and maritime Jurisdiction; — to Controversies to which the United States shall be a Party; — to Controversies between two or more States; — *between a State and Citizens of another State[9]; —* between Citizens of different States; — between Citizens of the same State claiming Lands under Grants of different States, *and between a State or the Citizens thereof, and foreign States, Citizens, or Subjects.[9]*

In all cases affecting Ambassadors, other public Ministers and Consuls, and those in which a State shall be Party, the supreme Court shall have original Jurisdiction. In all the other Cases before mentioned, the supreme Court shall have appellate Jurisdiction, both as to Law and Fact, with such Exceptions, and under such Regulations as the Congress shall make.

The Trial of all Crimes, except in Cases of Impeachment, shall be by Jury; and such Trial shall be held in the State where the said Crimes shall have been committed; but when not committed within any State, the Trial shall be at such Place or Places as the Congress may by Law have directed.

Section 3. Treason against the United States, shall consist only in levying War against them, or in adhering to their Enemies, giving them Aid and Comfort. No Person shall be convicted of Treason unless on the Testimony of two Witnesses to the same overt Act, or on Confession in open Court.

The Congress shall have Power to declare the Punishment of Treason, but no Attainder of Treason shall work Corruption of Blood, or Forfeiture except during the Life of the Person attainted.

---

[9] Revised by Eleventh Amendment.

Article IV

Section 1. Full Faith and Credit shall be given in each State to the public Acts, Records, and judicial Proceedings of every other State. And the Congress may by general Laws prescribe the Manner in which such Acts, Records, and Proceedings shall be proved, and the Effect thereof.

Section 2. The Citizens of each State shall be entitled to all Privileges and Immunities of Citizens in the several States.

A Person charged in any State with Treason, Felony, or other Crime, who shall flee from Justice, and be found in another State, shall on Demand of the executive Authority of the State from which he fled, be delivered up, to be removed to the State having Jurisdiction of the Crime.

No person held to Service or Labour in one State, under the Laws thereof, escaping into another, shall, in Consequence of any Law or Regulation therein, be discharged from such Service or Labour, but shall be delivered up on Claim of the Party to whom such Service or Labour may be due.[10]

Section 3. New States may be admitted by the Congress into this Union; but no new State shall be formed or erected within the Jurisdiction of any other State; nor any State be formed by the Junction of two or more States, or Parts of States, without the Consent of the Legislatures of the States concerned as well as of the Congress.

The Congress shall have Power to dispose of and make all needful Rules and Regulations respecting the Territory or other Property belonging to the United States; and nothing in this Constitution shall be so construed as to Prejudice any claims of the United States, or of any particular State.

Section 4. The United States shall guarantee to every state in this Union a Republican Form of Government, and shall protect each of them against Invasion; and on Application of the Legislature, or of the Executive (when the Legislature cannot be convened) against domestic Violence.

Article V

The Congress, whenever two thirds of both Houses shall deem it necessary, shall propose Amendments to this Constitution, or, on the Application of the Legislatures of two thirds of the several States, shall call a Convention for proposing Amendments, which, in either Case, shall be valid to all Intents and Purposes, as Part of this Constitution, when ratified by the Legislatures of three fourths of the several States, or by Conventions in three fourths thereof, as the one or the other Mode of Ratification may be proposed by the Congress; Provided that no Amendment which may be made prior to the Year one thousand eight hundred and eight shall in any Manner affect the first and fourth Clauses in the Ninth Section of the first Article; and that no State, without its Consent, shall be deprived of its equal Suffrage in the Senate.

---

[10] Superseded by Thirteenth Amendment.

Article VI

All Debts contracted and Engagements entered into, before the Adoption of this Constitution, shall be as valid against the United States under this Constitution, as under the Confederation.[11]

This Constitution, and the Laws of the United States which shall be made in Pursuance thereof; and all Treaties made, or which shall be made, under the Authority of the United States, shall be the supreme Law of the Land; and the Judges in every State shall be bound thereby, any Thing in the Constitution or Laws of any State to the Contrary notwithstanding.

The Senators and Representatives before mentioned, and the Members of the several State Legislatures, and all executive and judicial Officers, both of the United States and of the several States, shall be bound by Oath or Affirmation, to support this Constitution; but no religious Test shall ever be required as a Qualification to any Office or public Trust under the Unites States.

Article VII

The Ratification of the Conventions of nine States, shall be sufficient for the Establishment of this Constitution between the States so ratifying the Same.

Done in Convention by the Unanimous Consent of the States present the Seventeenth Day of September in the Year of our Lord one thousand seven hundred and eighty seven and of the Independence of the United States of America the twelfth. In witness whereof We have hereunto subscribed our Names.

. . .

ARTICLES IN ADDITION TO, AND AMENDMENT OF, THE CONSTITUTION OF THE UNITED STATES OF AMERICA, PROPOSED BY CONGRESS, AND RATIFIED BY THE SEVERAL STATES, PURSUANT TO THE FIFTH ARTICLE OF THE ORIGINAL CONSTITUTION. (Ratification of the first ten amendments was completed 15 December, 1791.)

Amendment I

Congress shall make no law respecting an establishment of religion, or prohibiting the free exercise thereof; or abridging the freedom of speech, or of the press; or the right of the people peaceably to assemble, and to petition the Government for a redress of grievances.

[11] See Fourteenth Amendment, Section 4.

Amendment II

A well regulated Militia, being necessary to the security of a free State, the right of the people to keep and bear Arms, shall not be infringed.

Amendment III

No Soldier shall, in time of peace be quartered in any house, without the consent of the Owner, nor in time of war, but in a manner to be prescribed by law.

Amendment IV

The right of the people to be secure in their persons, houses, papers, and effects, against unreasonable searches and seizures, shall not be violated, and no Warrants shall issue, but upon probable cause, supported by Oath or affirmation, and particularly describing the place to be searched, and the persons or things to be seized.

Amendment V

No person shall be held to answer for a capital, or other infamous crime, unless on a presentment or indictment of a Grand Jury, except in cases arising in the land or naval forces, or in the Militia, when in actual service in time of War or public danger; nor shall any person be subject for the same offence to be twice put in jeopardy of life or limb; nor shall be compelled in any criminal case to be a witness against himself, nor be deprived of life, liberty, or property, without due process of law; nor shall private property be taken for public use, without just compensation.

Amendment VI

In all criminal prosecutions, the accused shall enjoy the right to a speedy and public trial, by an impartial jury of the State and district wherein the crime shall have been committed, which district shall have been previously ascertained by law, and to be informed of the nature and cause of the accusation; to be confronted with the witnesses against him; to have compulsory process for obtaining witnesses in his favor, and to have the Assistance of Counsel for his defence.

Amendment VII

In Suits at common law, where the value in controversy shall exceed twenty dollars, the right of trial by jury shall be preserved, and no fact tried by a jury, shall be otherwise reexamined in any Court of the United States, than according to the rules of the common law.

Amendment VIII

Excessive bail shall not be required, nor excessive fines imposed, nor cruel and unusual punishments inflicted.

Amendment IX

The enumeration in the Constitution, of certain rights, shall not be construed to deny or disparage others retained by the people.

Amendment X

The powers not delegated to the United States by the Constitution, nor prohibited by it to the States, are reserved to the States respectively, or to the people.

Amendment XI (8 January 1798)

The Judicial power of the United States shall not be construed to extend to any suit in law or equity, commenced or prosecuted against one of the United States by Citizens of another State, or by Citizens or Subjects of any Foreign State.

Amendment XII (25 September 1804)

The Electors shall meet in their respective states and vote by ballot for President and Vice President, one of whom, at least, shall not be an inhabitant of the same state with themselves; they shall name in their ballots the person voted for as President, and in distinct ballots the person voted for as Vice President, and they shall make distinct lists of all persons voted for as President and of all persons voted for as Vice President, and of the number of votes for each, which lists they shall sign and certify, and transmit sealed to the seat of the government of the United States, directed to the President of the Senate; — The President of the Senate shall, in the presence of Senate and House of Representatives, open all the certificates and the votes shall then be counted; — The person having the greatest number of votes for President, shall be the President, if such number be a majority of the whole number of Electors appointed; and if no person have such majority, then from the persons having the highest numbers not exceeding three on the list of those voted for as President, the House of Representatives shall choose immediately, by ballot, the

President. But in choosing the President, the votes shall be taken by states, the representation from each state having one vote; a quorum for this purpose shall consist of a member or members from two-thirds of the states, and a majority of all the states shall be necessary to a choice. And if the House of Representatives shall not choose a President whenever the right of choice shall devolve upon them, *before the fourth day of March next following*,[12] then the Vice President shall act as President, as in the case of the death or other constitutional disability of the President. — The person having the greatest number of votes as Vice President shall be the Vice President, if such number be a majority of the whole number of Electors appointed, and if no person have a majority, then from the two highest numbers on the list, the Senate shall choose the Vice President; a quorum for the purpose shall consist of two-thirds of the whole number of Senators, and a majority of the whole number shall be necessary to a choice. But no person constitutionally ineligible to the office of President shall be eligible to that of Vice President of the United States.

Amendment XIII (18 December 1865)

Section 1. Neither slavery nor involuntary servitude, except as a punishment for crime whereof the party shall have been duly convicted, shall exist within the United States, or any place subject to their jurisdiction.

Section 2. Congress shall have the power to enforce this article by appropriate legislation.

Amendment XIV (28 July 1869)

Section 1. All persons born or naturalized in the United States, and subject to the jurisdiction thereof, are citizens of the United States and of the State wherein they reside. No State shall make or enforce any law which shall abridge the privileges or immunities of citizens of the United States; nor shall any State deprive any person of life, liberty, or property, without due process of law; nor deny to any person within its jurisdiction the equal protection of the laws.

Section 2. Representatives shall be apportioned among the several States according to their respective numbers, counting the whole number of persons in each State, excluding Indians not taxed. But when the right to vote at any election for the choice of electors for President and Vice President of the United States, Representatives in Congress, the Executive and Judicial officers of a State, or the members of the Legislature thereof,

---

[12] Revised by the Twentieth Amendment.

is denied to any of the male inhabitants of such State, being twenty-one years of age, and citizens of the United States, or in any way abridged, except for participation in rebellion, or other crime, the basis of representation therein shall be reduced in the proportion which the number of such male citizens shall bear to the whole number of male citizens twenty-one years of age in such State.

Section 3. No person shall be a Senator or Representative in Congress, or elector of President and Vice President, or hold any office, civil or military, under the United States, or under any State, who, having previously taken an oath, as a member of Congress, or as an officer of the United States, or as a member of any State legislature, or as an executive or judicial officer of any State, to support the Constitution of the United States, shall have engaged in insurrection or rebellion against the same, or given aid or comfort to the enemies thereof. But Congress may by a vote of two thirds of each House, remove such disability.

Section 4. The validity of the public debt of the United States, authorized by law, including debts incurred for payment of pensions and bounties for services in suppressing insurrection or rebellion, shall not be questioned. But neither the United States nor any State shall assume or pay any debt or obligation incurred in aid of insurrection or rebellion against the United States, or any claim for the loss or emancipation of any slave; but all such debts, obligations, and claims shall be held illegal and void.

Section 5. The Congress shall have power to enforce, by appropriate legislation, the provisions of this article.

Amendment XV (30 March 1870)

Section 1. The right of citizens of the United States to vote shall not be denied or abridged by the United States or by any State on account of race, color, or previous conditions of servitude.

Section 2. The Congress shall have power to enforce this article by appropriate legislation.

Amendment XVI (25 February 1913)

The Congress shall have power to lay and collect taxes on incomes, from whatever source derived, without apportionment among the several States, and without regard to any census or enumeration.

Amendment XVII (31 May 1913)

The Senate of the United States shall be composed of two Senators from each State, elected by the people thereof, for six years; and each Senator shall have one vote. The electors in each State shall have the qualifications requisite for electors of the most numerous branch of the State legislatures.

When vacancies happen in the representation of any State in the Senate, the executive authority of such State shall issue writs of election to fill such vacancies: *Provided,* That the legislature of any State may empower the executive thereof to make temporary appointments until the people fill the vacancies by election as the legislature may direct.

This amendment shall not be so construed as to affect the election or term of any Senator chosen before it becomes valid as part of the Constitution.

Amendment XVIII (29 January 1919)

Section 1. After one year from the ratification of this article the manufacture, sale, or transportation of intoxicating liquors within, the importation thereof into, or the exportation thereof from the United States and all territory subject to the jurisdiction thereof for beverage purposes is hereby prohibited.

Section 2. The Congress and the several States shall have concurrent power to enforce this article by appropriate legislation.

Section 3. This article shall be inoperative unless it shall have been ratified as an amendment to the Constitution by the legislatures of the several States, as provided in the Constitution within seven years from the date of the submission hereof to the States by the Congress.[13]

Amendment XIX (26 August 1920)

The right of citizens of the United States to vote shall not be denied or abridged by the United States or by any State on account of sex.

Congress shall have power to enforce this article by appropriate legislation.

Amendment XX (6 February 1933)

Section 1.   The terms of the President and Vice President shall end at noon on the 20th day of January, and the terms of Senators and Representatives at noon on the 3rd day of January, of the years in which such terms would have ended if this article had not been ratified; and the terms of their successors shall then begin.

Section 2.   The Congress shall assemble at least once in every year, and such meeting shall begin at noon on the 3rd day of January, unless they shall by law appoint a different day.

[13] Repealed by the Twenty-first Amendment.

Section 3. If, at the time fixed for the beginning of the term of the President, the President elect shall have died, the Vice President elect shall become President. If a President shall not have been chosen before the time fixed for the beginning of his term, or if the President elect shall have failed to qualify, then the Vice President elect shall act as President until a President shall have qualified; and the Congress may by law provide for the case wherein neither a President elect nor a Vice President elect shall have qualified, declaring who shall then act as President, or the manner in which one who is to act shall be selected, and such person shall act accordingly until a President or Vice President shall have qualified.

Section 4. The Congress may by law provide for the case of the death of any of the persons from whom the House of Representatives may choose a President whenever the right of choice shall have devolved upon them, and for the case of the death of any of the persons from whom the Senate may choose a Vice President whenever the right of choice shall have devolved upon them.

Section 5. Sections 1 and 2 shall take effect on the 15th day of October following the ratification of this article.

Section 6. This article shall be inoperative unless it shall have been ratified as an amendment to the Constitution by the legislatures of three-fourths of the several States within seven years from the date of its submission.

Amendment XXI (5 December 1933)

Section 1. The eighteenth article of amendment to the Constitution of the United States is hereby repealed.

Section 2. The transportation or importation into any State, Territory, or possession of the United States for delivery or use therein of intoxicating liquors, in violation of the laws thereof, is hereby prohibited.

Section 3. This article shall be inoperative unless it shall have been ratified as an amendment to the Constitution by conventions in the several States, as provided in the Constitution, within seven years from the date of the submission hereof to the States by the Congress.

Amendment XXII (26 February 1951)

Section 1. No person shall be elected to the office of the President more than twice, and no person who has held the office of President, or acted as President, for more than two years of a term to which some other person was elected President shall be elected to the office of president more than once. But this Article shall not apply to any person holding the office of President when this Article was proposed by the Congress, and shall not prevent any person who may be holding the office of President, or acting as President, during the term within which this Article becomes operative from holding the office of President or acting as President during the remainder of such term.

Section 2. This Article shall be inoperative unless it shall have been ratified as an amendment to the Constitution by the legislatures of three-fourths of the several States within seven years from the date of its submission to the States by the Congress.

Amendment XXIII (29 March 1961)

Section 1. The District constituting the seat of Government of the United States shall appoint in such manner as the Congress may direct:

A number of electors of President and Vice President equal to the whole number of Senators and Representatives in Congress to which the District would be entitled if it were a State, but in no event more than the least populous State; they shall be in addition to those appointed by the States, but they shall be considered, for the purposes of the election of President and Vice President, to be electors appointed by a State; and they shall meet in the District and perform such duties as provided by the twelfth article of amendment.

Section 2. The Congress shall have power to enforce this article by appropriate legislation.

Amendment XXIV (23 January 1964)

Section 1. The right of citizens of the United States to vote in any primary or other election for President or Vice President, for electors for President or Vice President, or for Senator or Representative in Congress, shall not be denied or abridged by the United States or any state by reason of failure to pay any poll tax or other tax.

Section 2. The Congress shall have the power to enforce this article by appropriate legislation.

Amendment XXV (10 February 1967)

Section 1. In case of the removal of the President from office or of his death or resignation, the Vice President shall become President.

Section 2. Whenever there is a vacancy in the office of the Vice President, the President shall nominate a Vice President who shall take office upon confirmation by a majority vote of both Houses of Congress.

Section 3. Whenever the President transmits to the President pro tempore of the Senate and the Speaker of the House of Representatives his written declaration that he is unable to discharge the powers and duties of his office, and until he transmits to them a written declaration to the contrary, such powers and duties shall be discharged by the Vice President as Acting President.

Section 4. Whenever the Vice President and a majority of either the principal officers of the executive departments or of such other body as Congress may by law provide, transmit to the President pro tempore of the Senate and the Speaker of the House of Representatives their written declaration that the President is unable to discharge the powers and duties of his office, the Vice President shall immediately assume the powers and duties of the office as Acting President.

Thereafter, when the President transmits to the President pro tempore of the Senate and the Speaker of the House of Representatives his written declaration that no inability exists, he shall resume the powers and duties of his office unless the Vice President and a majority of either the principal officers of the executive departments or of such other body as Congress may by law provide, transmit within four days to the President pro tempore of the Senate and the Speaker of the House of Representatives their written declaration that the President is unable to discharge the powers and duties of his office. Thereupon Congress shall decide the issue, assembling within forty-eight hours for that purpose if not in session. If the Congress, within twenty-one days after receipt of the latter written declaration or, if Congress is not in session, within twenty-one days after Congress is required to assemble, determines by two-thirds vote of both Houses that the President is unable to discharge the powers and duties of his office, the Vice President shall continue to discharge the same as Acting President; otherwise, the President shall resume the powers and duties of his office.

Amendment XXVI (30 June 1971)

Section 1. The right of citizens of the United States, who are eighteen years of age or older, to vote shall not be denied or abridged by the United States or any state on account of age.

Section 2. The Congress shall have the power to enforce this article by appropriate legislation.

Index